Business-To-Business Marketing and Promotion

Business-To-Business Marketing and Promotion

A Practical Guide to Promoting Goods and Services in Business Markets

Martyn P Davis

BSc (Econ), F CAM, FIPR, F Inst M, Dip F Ed.

Business Books

Copyright © Martyn P. Davis

First published in Great Britain by
Business Books Limited
An imprint of Century Hutchinson Limited
62–65 Chandos Place, London WC2N 4NW

Century Hutchinson Australia (Pty) Limited
89–91 Albion Street, Surry Hills,
New South Wales 2010, Australia

Century Hutchinson New Zealand Limited
PO Box 40–086, 32–34 View Road, Glenfield,
Auckland 10, New Zealand

Century Hutchinson South Africa (Pty) Limited
PO Box 337, Bergvlei 2012, South Africa

British Library Cataloguing in Publication Data

Davis, Martyn P.
  Business-to-business marketing and promotions
  1. Business firms. Marketing
  I. Title
  658.8

ISBN: 0–09–173708–7
ISBN: 0–09–173713–3 pbk

Printed and bound in Great Britain by
Mackays of Chatham PLC, Chatham, Kent

Business-To-Business Marketing and Promotion

Contents

Preface xiii
Acknowledgments xv

Part 1   **THE WORLD OF MARKETING COMMUNICATIONS**

What marketing communications is, and the difference between consumer and business-to-business applications.

Chapter   1   **Marketing Communications in Perspective**   3
Marketing communications media: an overview – Existing media – Created media

2   **Business-to-Business – An Overview**   11
The firm – The product or service – Business versus consumer markets – Target market motivation – Industrial versus consumer marketing policy

---

Part 2   **THE ORGANIZATION OF MARKETING COMMUNICATIONS**   17

The organizations involved, and how they can best co-operate in achieving effective business-to-business marketing communications.

Chapter   3   **The Role of the Supplier Organization**   19
Marketing planning – New developments – Positioning – People – Purchasing patterns – The changing structure of the Marketing Communications department – Relevant organizations

4   **The Role of External Services**   31
The advantages of external services – The drawbacks of external services – Selecting external services – Service organization procedure – Professional and other organizations

CONTENTS

    5 **The Role of the Media Owners**   47
The financial circle – The media owner's structure – Editorial – Production – Circulation – Subscriptions and controlled circulation – Promotion – Research – Marketing and merchandising – The Advertisement Department

Part 3   **THE TOOLS OF MARKETING COMMUNICATIONS**   61

The main types of marketing communications media and their component categories, their inter-relationship, and the criteria by which they can be evaluated.

Part 3A   **MARKETING COMMUNICATIONS MEDIA**   63

Chapter   6 **The Range of Media, and Criteria for Comparison**   65
Media evaluation (criteria for comparison) – Promotional units – Cost and value for money – Overall media comparison

Part 3B   **EXISTING MEDIA – THE ADVERTISING ROUTE**   81

Chapter   7 **Advertising – An Overview, and General Databases**   83
The advantages of advertising – The drawbacks of advertising – The range of advertising media – General information sources

    8 **Press Media**   97
Magazines – Research data – Further research data – General magazines research – Newspapers – Free newspaper research data – The press medium overall

    9 **Specialist Readership Surveys**   111

CONTENTS

	10	**Exhibitions**	127

Types of exhibition – Other forms of demonstration – Exhibition audience research – Further information sources

	11	**Direct Mail**	133

The advantages of direct mail – The disadvantages of direct mail – Direct and database marketing – Sources of information

	12	**Outdoor Advertising**	141

Poster sizes – The advantages of poster advertising – The drawbacks of poster advertising – Buying poster advertising – Poster research

	13	**Television**	145

Terrestrial broadcasting – TV research – Satellite transmissions – Satellite/cable audience research – Cable television – Cable audience research – Non-broadcast sources – New Government proposals - The consequences of increased programme provision

	14	**Radio**	159

The structure of independent local radio – Radio audience research – Other radio advertising

	15	**Cinema**	163

Overview – Further information – Miscellaneous advertising media

Part 3C		**EXISTING MEDIA – THE EDITORIAL ROUTE**	167

Chapter	16	**Public Relations**	169

Public Relations 'publics' – Public Relations Media – Issue of news material – Top ten errors – PR's golden rules – Other Public Relations activities – Public relations organizations

CONTENTS

| | 17 | **Public Relations Reference Sources**
Services – Monitoring | 177 |

| **Part 3D** | | **CREATED MEDIA** | **183** |

| *Chapter* | 18 | **The Range of Created Media**
Planning created media – The range of created media – Further information on sponsorship | 185 |

| **Part 4** | | **EFFECTIVE MARKETING COMMUNICATIONS** | **199** |

The planning stages involved when the organizations described in Part 2 use the marketing communications media described in Part 3

Chapter	19	**Research and Investigation** The organization – The product or service – The target market – Marketing policy – Previous promotion – Constraints – Competition – Marketing communications media – Background – The importance of research – The next step – Relevant organizations	201
	20	**Setting Specific Campaign Objectives** Analysis of specific objectives – The next step	215
	21	**Purchasing Patterns** How purchasing decisions are made – The next step	231
	22	**Budgeting** The rewards of promotional expenditure – The need for a budget – Long-term planning – The next step	237
	23	**Preparation of Campaign Proposals – The Message** The attention factor – Message content – Some creative approaches – Business-to-business applications – Business-to-business messages – Message presentation – Constraints – Continuity – Other media – The next step	249

CONTENTS

24 **Preparation of Campaign Proposals – The Media** 263
Media in context – The media brief – Message/media interaction – Media allocations – Market weighting – Detailed planning – Resolving the inevitable conflict – The shotgun principle – Media planning stages – The next step

25 **Approval of Promotional Proposals** 273
Internal aspects – External aspects – Promotional aspects – The next step

26 **Execution of Promotional Proposals** 279
Implementation of proposals – Improving the proposals – Flexible execution – Other changes – Further routine administration – The next step

27 **Follow Through** 285
The next step

28 **Evaluation of Results** 287
Checking back – Allowing for other influences – Looking ahead – Direct response – Indirect response – Future action – The next step

Institute of Public Relations Recommended Practice Papers
Appendices 1 *The News Release* 295
2 *Photographs Accompanying News Releases* 297
3 *Press kits* 299

Index 300

Preface

There are innumerable books on marketing and promotion, so why another one? Quite simply, there is a surprising gap in the market: this book differs from others in three significant respects:

- It concentrates on business rather than on consumer markets, and analyses industrial buying behaviour in detail;
- It covers the full range of marketing communications media – advertising, merchandising, public relations, sales promotion, created media and the sales staff themselves;
- It examines how these media can help companies achieve business-to-business objectives, since business-to-business marketing differs markedly from consumer marketing. Business-to-business marketing, and the promotional planning process, are both examined in detail.

Business-to-business marketing was, until recently, known as 'industrial marketing' and, as such, covered the selling of machine tools and the like to manufacturing industry. The term industrial is too restrictive, however: 'business-to-business' is more accurate, and this book therefore covers both products and services, marketed to a range of organisations far wider than manufacturing industry alone. For reasons of simplicity, however, the term 'industrial' may be used interchangeably with 'business-to-business' or the shorter 'business' marketing.

Throughout this book certain general terms are used, again for simplicity – 'products' should be taken to encompass services, while 'purchasers' may mean private or public companies, or local or national government. Other general terms are used when referring to marketing communications. 'Message' covers illustrations (still or moving) as well as words, while words could be spoken just as much as printed, and could be delivered through editorial or advertising columns, or created media such as an organisation's own printed material or house journals. The term 'media' is used to encompass the full range of marketing communications media and activities, while 'promotion' covers the complete marketing communications process, embracing both messages and media. Unless specifically stated, terms should be interpreted as broadly as possible.

This book is a logical development of – but differs markedly from – my *The Effective Use of Advertising Media*. Anyone who has read that book will recognise my 'building blocks' approach, which recommends that business-to-business marketing communications, like consumer advertising, should be tackled as a logical process of analysis, setting objectives as a result of that analysis, and then planning how best to achieve those objectives.

PREFACE

They will equally recognise that, for this process to be tackled effectively, it is essential to analyse the inter-relationships of the organisations involved – the companies wishing to promote their goods and services, the promotional media available to them, and the external services on which they can call for assistance. They will also recognise some advertising content – except that this has been updated in the light of new developments, and the emphasis is on business-to-business media.

Although I have built on this earlier approach, there the similarities end, other than two points of common principle. To produce a comprehensive volume incorporating all the facts and figures needed for effective promotional planning would be an impossible, unnecessary and pointless task. Impossible in that any volume incorporating all these facts and figures would be vast beyond proportion; unnecessary in that the information is readily available elsewhere in the sources listed in this book, and pointless in that, should any statistics be included, they would soon be out-of-date. This book therefore concentrates on principles, and statistics are conspicuous by their absence.

The second point of common principle is that where specific posts are mentioned, jobs are described in terms of their being held by men: this is again for reasons of simplicity, rather than any male chauvinism or discrimination.

Martyn P. Davis

Acknowledgments

I wish to express my sincere thanks to many individuals and organizations for the co-operation and encouragement I received when writing this book:

To David Osborn, Kevin O'Sullivan, Margaret Sealey, and Graham Williams for their helpful comments and suggestions.

To Anne Stacey, and Peter Thomson-Smith for so carefully checking the proofs.

To the Institute of Public Relations, for permission to reproduce their Recommended Practice Papers.

To the following organizations for their co-operation in providing information of great value: Advance, The Advertising Association, Association of Business Advertising Agencies, Association of British Market Research Companies, Association for Business Sponsorship of the Arts, Association of Free Newspapers, Association of Independent Radio Contractors, Association of Media Independents, Audit Bureau of Circulations, Benn's Direct Marketing Services Directory, Benn's Media Directory, Blue Book of British Broadcasting, British Business Press, British Direct Marketing Association, British List Brokers Association, British Rate & Data, British Satellite Broadcasting, British Tourist Authority, Broadcast Marketing Services, Broadcasters' Audience Research Board, Broad Street Associates Public Relations, Cable Authority, CACI Inc., Centre for Construction Market Information, Channel Four Television, Chartered Institute of Marketing, Cinema Advertising Association, Cinema & Video Industry Audience Research Committee, Codex Partnership, Conferences & Exhibitions Diary, Department of Trade & Industry, Direct Mail Producers Association, Direct Mail Sales Bureau, Direct Mail Services Standards Board, Editors Media Directories, Exhibitions Bulletin, Exhibitions & Conferences Factfinder, Exhibition Industry Federation, Hollis Press & Public Relations Annual, Incorporated Society of British Advertisers, Independent Broadcasting Authority, Independent Television Association, Industrial Data, Industrial Marketing Research Association, Institute of Directors, Institute of Practitioners in Advertising, Institute of Public Relations, Joint Industry Committee for Cable Audience Research, Joint Industry Committee of Medical Advertisers for Readership Surveys, Joint Industry Committee for National Readership Surveys, Joint Industry Committee for Poster Audience Research, Joint Industry Committee for Radio Audience Research, London Transport Advertising, Magazine Page Exposure Consortium, Marketing and Promotion Association, Market Research Society, Mass Observation (UK), Media Expenditure Analysis Ltd, Media Monitoring Services, Media Register, MediaTel, Morgan-Grampian, MORI, NOP Market Research, Pan

ACKNOWLEDGEMENTS

European Television Audience Research, Periodical Publishers Association, PIMS London, PNA, Poster Audit Bureau, Poster Marketing, Post Office (Direct Marketing Section), Produce Studies, PR Planner-UK, PR-Tel, Public Relations Consultants Association, Radio Marketing Bureau, Research Services, Target Group Index, Sky Channel, Sports Sponsorship Advisory Service, Super Channel, Taylor Nelson, Telex Monitors, Travel & Tourism Research, TV-AM, Universal News Services, Verified Free Distribution, and Willings Press Guide.

The author readily acknowledges his debt to those whose brains he has picked, with or without their knowledge.

Martyn P. Davis

PART 1

The World of Marketing Communications

1. Marketing Communications in Perspective.
2. Business-to-Business – an Overview.

CHAPTER ONE

Marketing Communications in Perspective

The Chartered Institute of Marketing gives the following definition:

'Marketing is the management process responsible for identifying, anticipating and satisfying customer requirements profitably.'

The marketing concept has revolutionised production and selling. At one time, a firm would manufacture a product, the Sales Manager sold it, and the Advertising Manager devised a suitable campaign. Later still, public relations activities were added to the promotional mix. This joint effort was to sell merchandise already in production. Salesmen perhaps passed back comments they received or, more recently, there may have been some research to define the market and learn purchasers' reactions to the product. Then, on the basis of this limited information, the company (and its agency or consultancy) planned the advertising and public relations campaigns. In essence, however, all activity was aimed at selling a product already manufactured: in short, the product came first and was followed by selling and promotion.

This brief description over-simplifies the process, but illustrates how the modern concept of marketing has reversed this approach. Rather than manufacture a product and then hope to sell it, marketing now attempts to locate a need and define in advance the potential purchasers' ideal product. Research ascertains the form, price and quantity that will best suit the market. Only then does marketing assess how best to produce, distribute and promote the product itself. Thus, long before production facilities exist, and while the concept is still at development stage, marketing plans the complete manufacturing and selling operation, and considers production levels, distribution, trade discounts and sales staff structure, and the degree of emphasis to be placed on promotion and personal selling.

Today, most marketing plans extend further: they look to the future and attempt to predict a product's life cycle (introduction, growth, maturity and decline) and also include research & development activity to improve existing products, as well as providing new ones for the company to market in future.

Marketing unites many activities. None are new: the only new concept is linking them under the common heading of marketing. The marketing executive must have a full appreciation of the respective roles of advertising, branding, distribution, margins, market research, merchandising, packaging, price, personal selling, production, public relations and sales promotion in successfully producing and selling the company's lines, and in planning future business development. Sales and promotion departments have always been complementary, but the marketing concept has led to these 'separate' activities being united under a single Marketing Director, who controls a number of executives responsible for various marketing activities or for individual products in the range. Being 'market-orientated' does not simply mean having a marketing department: it means the whole organization is conscious that the all-important factor is not what the company wishes to sell but what customers want to buy. The two are not necessarily the same and, as consumers have freedom of choice, company profitability must be balanced by corresponding customer satisfaction.

MARKETING COMMUNICATIONS IN PERSPECTIVE

Before examining marketing communications, consider the products or services to be promoted. Promotion will not sell poor products: if it does, buyers soon recognize the poor quality, there will be no repeat purchases and the harm done goes beyond the gains from the initial sales. Promotion should therefore never be used to sell 'mistakes'. Why should potential purchasers buy inferior products, just because they have been promoted? This point is stressed because manufacturers do sometimes try to clear dead stocks through promotional campaigns, and then blame marketing communications when no sales result. Surplus stocks can be featured from time to time, at reduced prices, but these are special cases. For promotion to be effective, it must offer potential purchasers a benefit, such as a new or improved product, or advantageous prices. Thus a first essential for effective marketing communications is a good product or service.

The second essential is that these products must be promoted to the right people. This is perhaps obvious, but there is no point in telling people about goods of no use to them, however much of a bargain is offered. So careful consideration of the market is another essential. Also, if potential purchasers are unaware of the merchandise they will not buy it, hence effective marketing communications means telling the right people about the right products.

With the right products and the right people to inform, a third essential is the right means of conveying information to them. No one medium is best – they all reach different markets by different means, so it is vital to select promotional media that reach target markets and deliver marketing communications messages most effectively.

A fourth essential is to get the right promotional message. If an organization produces the right goods, knows who prospective customers are and has the means to contact them, successful promotion must then attract their attention and convey the product's benefits. Hence great care must be paid to the wording and layout of advertisements, news releases or printed material, and the selection of supporting illustrations or photographs.

Fifth, but of equal importance, is timing. Promotions that occur too early or too late, before customers are in a position to think about buying or after the purchase has been made, are wasteful.

Finally, goods must be readily available when potential purchasers wish to buy. Any weakness in distribution could result in the campaign merely increasing *competitors'* sales, for prospective purchasers may buy from a rival supplier.

In short, for marketing communications to be effective, careful planning must ensure that several factors are right:

- *Right products* – which people would buy if they knew about them
- *Right people* – to whom the products are of interest
- *Right media* – which reach these people effectively
- *Right message* – which conveys the product's benefits
- *Right time* – when potential customers are likely to buy
- *Right distribution* – when the goods are available, or agents ready to respond

and

- *Right budget* – when the right amount is spent on promotion

This discussion of *rights* oversimplifies matters, but does make clear that any marketing communications campaign must be carefully planned. Promotion is not a separate operation unconnected with other marketing activities: all must be co-ordinated. With careful planning, marketing communications expenditure is controlled and spent to maximum advantage, and bring results which more than pay for the promotional campaign. Part 4 describes how this planned promotion can best be achieved.

MARKETING COMMUNICATIONS MEDIA – AN OVERVIEW

There are numerous ways to communicate with target markets, examined in the chapters following. Before so doing, however, it is important to differentiate between them, and examine their inter-relationship. A starting point is to review marketing communications activities at their most basic level.

EXISTING MEDIA

There is a wide variety of media available to communicate with target markets, through both advertising and editorial columns.

THE ADVERTISING ROUTE

The Advertising Standards Authority defines this as:

> 'The use of paid-for media space or time as a means of persuading people to take a particular course of action, or to reach a point of view.'

An essential element of this definition is 'paid-for media' – there is a contractual agreement with a media-owner who undertakes to transmit a promotional message for a given sum of money. He has a legal obligation to transmit the advertising message, and the advertiser has a legal obligation to pay him for so doing. Which advertising media to use, and what the advertising message should be, are examined later.

THE EDITORIAL ROUTE

PR practice is defined by the Institute of Public Relations as:

> 'The planned and sustained effort to establish and maintain goodwill and mutual understanding between an organization and its public.'

Any organization launching a new product or service should consider the editorial as well as advertising columns of appropriate media. The new product is NEWS and, as such, could be of interest to the editors of various publications wishing to keep their readers up-to-date with new developments.

It would be very wrong, however, to think of public relations as free write-ups. They are NOT free in the sense that, although no payments are made to media-owners as they are for advertising space, it costs a great deal in terms of staff time and effort (as well as money) to distribute information to the various media. It would be equally incorrect to think of public relations as restricted to write-ups – the new product or service could be of interest to television or radio, and there are many other public relations activities to be examined later.

CREATED MEDIA

If existing media do not fully meet an organization's needs, through either their editorial or advertising columns, the Promotion Manager may have to create his own. These special needs often arise from merchandising and sales promotion objectives.

MERCHANDISING AND SALES PROMOTION

Having stimulated potential purchasers, it is essential to be ready to meet market response. What a waste of effort if potential customers, on contacting distributors or agents, find that they know nothing about the new product! So effective marketing includes communicating with distributors just as much as with potential purchasers.

Key figures in contacting distributors are sales representatives, who must be considered a communications medium just as much as a means of selling products. Their communications role is as important as their selling function – accordingly, for effective marketing communications, the sales force must be kept fully informed.

Bearing in mind at least three target groups for marketing communications messages – potential purchasers, distributors or agents, and the sales force – it is important to consider merchandising and sales promotion just as much as advertising and public relations.

Sales promotion is defined in *The British Code of Sales Promotion Practice* as:

> 'Those marketing techniques which are used, usually on a temporary basis, to make goods and services more attractive to the consumer by providing some additional benefits in cash or kind.'

The code also applies to sales and trade incentive promotions, to editorial promotional offers, and to some aspects of sponsorship.

I am happy to accept the code, but find it unsatisfactory to group these techniques under the single heading of 'sales promotion' since this does not distinguish between two very different directions for marketing communications activities, ie sales promotion and merchandising, discussed below. In consequence, I offer my own alternative definition:

> 'Activities which pull people towards products or which push products towards people.'

(In support of this definition, I cite a renowned marketing authority from Lewis Carroll's *Through The Looking Glass – and what Alice Found There*.

> 'When I say a word,' Humpty Dumpty said in a rather scornful tone, 'it means just what I choose it to mean – neither more nor less.')

SALES PROMOTION

To encourage potential purchasers to consider its products, a firm might undertake sales promotion activities such as a free product trial, or the offer of an informative booklet. There is a host of sales promotion incentives, discussed later, which can serve as useful devices for pulling potential purchasers towards products.

MERCHANDISING

When prospective customers respond to the sales promotion stimulus, the organization must be geared to take full advantage of potential demand. Accordingly, the company may undertake merchandising activities aimed at distributors or agents, to encourage them to push its products towards potential purchasers. Dealer conferences, financial incentives, mailings and competitions for best performance can all serve to stimulate the distribution network. These and other forms of merchandising are considered later.

SALES FORCE ACTIVITY

The vital link with distributors or agents, or indeed with customers direct, are sales representatives, so merchandising activities should extend to these staff; they then push products towards agents, who in turn will push them towards ultimate purchasers. Many of the same merchandising activities apply, but this time aimed at the sales force rather than distributors – sales conferences, properly organized, can effectively introduce representatives to new lines, inform them about product literature or other sales aids, give details of promotional campaigns that will support their selling efforts, brief them about sales targets and financial or merchandising incentives for those who perform well, and generally build their confidence and enthusiasm to push products when making contact with agents and distributors, or direct with ultimate purchasers.

SUMMARY

The marketing communications media so far considered in outline are thus:

Through existing media:

- The advertising route – paid-for specific communication

- The editorial route – public relations activity, to achieve mutual understanding through news columns

Through created media:

- Merchandising – to push products
- Sales Promotion – to pull customers

These are not, however, watertight compartments – to 'establish and maintain goodwill and mutual understanding between an organization and its public', the organization may well book advertising space to convey public relations information. Advertising might equally be the means of announcing sales promotion incentives. Response to these offers may in turn serve a merchandising function, by providing sales leads for representatives. All these activities will influence mutual understanding. Furthermore, if existing media do not fully meet the organization's marketing communications needs, it may be necessary to create other media not yet mentioned: printed material, training and sales aids, seminars, videos and many others discussed later.

PROMOTION

Rather than worry about definitions, or where one activity ends and another begins, the important thing is to consider *all* means of communicating with prospective purchasers – the full range of media must be evaluated, and equally must be planned in such a way that the separate activities integrate to maximum effect. Within this book, the overall term 'promotion' is used to encompass the full range of marketing communications activities. Promotion differs from publicity in that the latter is something an organization *receives* rather than does. Should an organization receive bad publicity, positive promotion will be called for to counter the harm done.

OTHER MARKETING COMMUNICATIONS MEDIA

It is important to consider these marketing communications media in context. Those involved in marketing planning often categorize their activities under the heading of The Four P's – Product, Price, Place and Promotion.

This review has so far considered only promotion, but the other three P's have equally important marketing communications roles.

The product (or service) itself delivers a marketing communications message through its name, design, presentation and packaging.

Price also has marketing communications implications – lower price does not necessarily result in increased sales. Prospective purchasers often equate price with quality, and may suspect that low prices mean cheap and unreliable merchandise rather than price-advantageous products.

Place too has marketing communications overtones – consider products widely available through any outlet which wishes to sell them irrespective of facilities and expertise, and – by way of contrast – merchandise available only direct from the manufacturer or appointed distributors, carefully selected for their ability to provide expert advice and effective after-sales service.

OTHER MESSAGE SOURCES

Marketing communications should also be considered in terms of message sources, and how existing and potential customers receive information about an organization and its products. Needless to say, promotional campaigns should be planned in such a way that they encompass all the target market's message sources.

Before examining these and other promotional activities in detail, the next chapter reviews how business-to-business campaigns differ from those mounted for consumer products and services.

CHAPTER TWO

Business-to-Business – an Overview

Before getting down to detail, a further stage remains – to consider how business-to-business promotion differs from that undertaken for consumer goods and services.

Promotional planning for any product or service – consumer or industrial – must be based on thorough knowledge of the firm and its products, the target market, marketing policy, and other aspects discussed later. The Promotion Manager can then (in-house or by calling on external services) devise a suitable marketing communications programme and, in due course, evaluate its results. Each element differs, however, between consumer and business-to-business campaigns.

THE FIRM

Most consumer manufacturers are well aware of the vital importance of effective communication with their markets. Those responsible for business promotion, however, often find their problem is internal rather than external, since company management is 'production-orientated'. The Board's sole concern is product performance and manufacturing efficiency: little attention is given to the vital need to inform potential purchasers about these products, and 'publicity' is a secondary activity synonymous with advertising which, in turn, is equated with dreaming up snappy slogans and pretty pictures. Everybody thinks they are an expert at two jobs – their own, and advertising! There is thus a major internal problem of convincing management that marketing communications is an important activity, to be tackled in a practical manner. This problem may be compounded if management's previous experience is of advertising agencies or public relations consultancies which, in their proposals, revealed they were not, alas, really competent in the specialist field of business communications.

THE PRODUCT OR SERVICE

An organization may manufacture a product or provide a service. What is not immediately apparent for business-to-business promotion is that, rather than think of 'product OR service', it is usually more correct to consider marketing communications in terms of 'product AND/or service'. Business marketing has a far higher service component than most consumer goods – either a service as such, or a product so technical that potential purchasers cannot buy it as they might pick a packet off the shelf; they are unable to purchase without the benefit of technical advice. 'Service' may encompass 'turnkey' operations whereby the organization provides and maintains the necessary plant for its client's staff to operate, as well as 'facilities management' where it both provides and operates this equipment. Under such circumstances marketing communications is more than relatively simple product announcements.

PACKAGING

With consumer merchandise, packaging serves multiple purposes – it acts as an attention device at point-of-sale and thus serves a display function; it often has an educational role in giving instructions for use; it protects the product and sometimes also serves as a store or dispenser.

Industrial packaging has a more practical role, since products are rarely purchased on impulse. Product protection is always vital, but it is wrong to consider the display element as having no role in industrial packaging – it can be vital in giving the correct impression of a product's quality and reliability; it can also undertake the practical function of telling buyers how to use the product, and it can perhaps inform them of other items in the range.

PRICE

Much consumer promotion is on a straightforward price basis. With business marketing, however, it is difficult to promote on a price basis projects which may be worth hundreds or thousands of pounds or more. In many business operations there is indeed no set price to promote, as quotations are submitted after analysis of each prospective purchaser's individual needs. Business pricing could equally include leasing or contract hire. In cases of major contracts extending over several years and various countries, the simple concept of 'price' no longer applies: there is instead high level financial negotiation, with hard bargaining over currencies and cash flow, payment terms and interest levels, and even financial guarantees or incentives and penalties for early or late delivery.

PRODUCT DEMAND

Business products differ markedly from consumer merchandise in that the latter is purchased for direct use, whilst many industrial products depend on what enconomists term 'derived demand'. For an organization manufacturing widgets for washing machines, demand for its widgets depends on the demand for washing machines. If a firm supplies components rather than making an end product, derived demand means that the market size depends on factors beyond its control. Manufacturers of consumer products, on the other hand, often devote considerable effort to increasing overall market size, rather than competing with rivals for a larger share of a static market.

BUSINESS *VS* CONSUMER MARKETS

Consumer product manufacturers are accustomed to classifying their target markets in demographic terms such as age, sex, and socio-economic groupings, or by other criteria such as interests, activities and hobbies. Those concerned with business marketing and promotion, however, classify their markets differently, in terms of industrial classifications and occupational groupings. An organization may well, for example, define its target group as accountants.

Target market definition can be taken to more sophisticated stages since 'accountants' may be too sweeping a term and, for effective marketing communications, promotional messages are targeted more precisely – to accountants holding board-level posts within a clearly defined list of industries. These facts are far more relevant than the age or sex of those who receive the marketing communications messages.

Manufacturers of consumer products also have business-to-business campaigns. In this respect their market is the retail trade and they define their targets equally precisely in terms of departmental stores, self-service chains or other types of retail outlet, and wholesalers. And what they market is not simply the 'pick it off the shelf' product they sell to ultimate consumers, but a complex package of product ranges and prices, discounts and incentives, backed by promotional campaigns which convince retailers that the consumer *will* pick the promoted products off the shelf, thus giving opportunity for profit if they stock and display them.

Having defined market segments, it is vital to establish their size and the order of priority for promotional planning. Another difference between consumer and business campaigns becomes apparent, in that business communication is with a smaller number of potential buyers. This smaller number, which may be concentrated in a limited number of locations, reach their buying decisions in a different way to purchasers of consumer products. They are often better informed, more discriminating, and have a different search process; these differences lead to promotional campaigns very different from those mounted for consumer products.

TARGET MARKET MOTIVATION

When analysing their potential purchasers' decision-process, those concerned with industrial products set about promotional planning in a very different way. Most consumer manufacturers need to communicate their promotional messages to single individuals, whilst some might be concerned with husband/wife decisions, and an even smaller number consider the entire family involved in the decision-process. In business marketing, however, collective decisions are the rule rather than the exception. There is more often than not a purchasing committee, formal or informal. A later chapter examines this 'Decision Making Unit' in detail.

Industrial purchasing decisions differ in motivation as well as structure – most are made on a rational basis rather than for the emotional reasons which apply to many consumer goods. Never forget, however, that those purchasing business products are still human beings, and nobody was ever bored into buying anything! Much business promotion fails to recognize this, and accordingly does not achieve its purpose.

Another difference between industrial and consumer purchases lies in what is best described as 'industrial inertia'. If a toothpaste manufacturer wishes you to switch to his brand, your 'investment' is relatively low – perhaps a half-used tube of toothpaste. Depending on your degree of brand loyalty, he has a relatively simple task in persuading you to try his product. For industrial products, however, there can be numerous hurdles to overcome – users of rival products may have stocks of spare parts; a service arrangement with the present supplier; established financial arrangements; and staff (from management through to actual operators and unions) are accustomed to the present situation. In some cases, this inertia may be so strong that promotional policy necessarily concentrates on locating new prospects.

These factors also often mean a considerable time lag before business purchasing decisions are made, and this has direct implications for the timing of promotional activities.

INDUSTRIAL *VS* CONSUMER MARKETING POLICY

Most business suppliers sell direct to actual users, or perhaps operate through distributors or agents. Contrast this with the many consumer manufacturers who mount business-to-business campaigns to retail outlets, but have no direct contact with actual users of their products. In some cases, lack of contact goes even further – they sell direct only to larger retailers, and rely on wholesalers to service smaller outlets whose orders are insufficiently large to merit a sales call. They are thus even further removed from direct consumer contact.

Another difference between consumer and industrial marketing lies in the role of the sales force. The technical nature of many business products means the service element is vital, since without it potential purchasers are incapable of reaching a buying decision.

For many consumer goods, emphasis lies on selecting staff with sales potential and then developing their ability in this respect; product knowledge is relatively simple and thus receives minor emphasis in the organization's training programme. This 'sales plus technical' approach may suffice with some industrial products but, in an increasing number of cases, the emphasis is on 'technical plus sales'. Expert product knowledge is so important that it calls for the selection of staff with technical qualifications and experience, and then the training of these experts to become salesmen. This training programme involves giving a thorough understanding of the promotional campaign the organization is mounting in support of their efforts.

A final difference between the marketing of consumer and business products lies in the concepts of 'push' and 'pull'. With new consumer products, it is possible to adopt a pull approach: the retailer receives a minimal amount for each unit sold, but massive consumer promotion is used to 'pull' merchandise through the distribution chain. Retailers often stock new merchandise in the belief they will sell large amounts in response to the demand heavy consumer advertising will generate, and in this way make substantial profits. With a push campaign, on the other hand, a minimal amount is spent on consumer promotion but, as the retailer receives a substantial mark-up for each unit he sells, merchandise is 'pushed' towards consumers who, when they enter the shop to make a customary purchase, have their attention drawn to the new product – the retailer hoping to make two sales instead of one and, in this way, make more profit.

With business operations, it is rarely possible to adopt a pull approach, and marketing policies tend towards the push end of the scale. Having said this, promotion still has a vital pull role to play in encouraging sales staff, distributors and agents.

INDUSTRIAL *VS* CONSUMER MARKETING COMMUNICATIONS CAMPAIGNS

This area is discussed in detail later – and indeed is the subject of this book! This chapter, however, makes a swift review of how promotion differs between consumer and industrial products or services.

For one thing, promotion budgets for industrial products are usually smaller, if only because media costs are lower. Secondly, different media are used – rather than TV or national newspapers and magazines, much promotional effort is directed through specialist periodicals. Direct mail, exhibitions and other selective media also receive greater emphasis. Public relations, too, differs – rather than issue news releases in the hope of brief editorial comment, PR often takes the form of specially written feature articles. Advertising and public relations messages both place greater emphasis on rational argument rather than emotional appeal.

Another way in which business promotion differs lies in its planning and execution. With consumer goods, the manufacturer's role is often the relatively passive one of briefing an advertising agency or public relations consultancy, checking their proposals before giving approval, and then letting them mount the campaign on his behalf. With business campaigns, however, much of the work – both planning and execution – is often undertaken in-house, rather than through external services.

INDUSTRIAL VS CONSUMER CAMPAIGNS – AN OVERALL VIEW

The underlying principles for both consumer and industrial campaigns are the same – research and investigations, identification of target markets and analysis of their purchasing decision process, setting specific promotional objectives, preparation of proposals to achieve these objectives, followed by mounting the campaign and evaluating its results. The practical application of these common principles is, however, very different – markets are defined differently, and very different messages are delivered through very different media.

A final – and cheerful – note on which to end this swift review is that, although the application of these principles may be difficult, it is often easier for business organizations to evaluate the results. They are in contact with potential purchasers, either direct through their sales representatives or through distributors or agents, and thus have more feedback regarding the outcome of their promotional efforts. Business marketers who complain of how difficult it is to mount industrial campaigns should spare a thought for consumer colleagues who have no direct contact with potential purchasers: they sell to wholesalers or retailers who then sell to the ultimate purchasers. To find out who the ultimate purchasers are, or how effective their marketing communications programme has been, they must mount massive market research operations. Indeed, in some cases their market research expenditure may exceed a total business promotion budget. Consumer companies may be most envious of business firms' enviable position of having a customer feedback they can evaluate direct.

Needless to say, this promotional effort must be built on a sound marketing base, and planning must follow on from clear marketing objectives. This is no one-way process, however, since marketing policy should reflect the vital importance of promotion in '. . . satisfying customer requirements profitably'.

PART 2

The Organization of Marketing Communications

3. The Role of the Supplier Organization.

4. The Role of External Services.

5. The Role of the Media Owners.

CHAPTER THREE

The Role of the Supplier Organization

The Promotion Manager's tasks that, whether undertaken in-house or in association with external services, make for effective marketing communications, comprise:

- *Research and investigation* – gathering the company, product and market data essential for effective planning;
- *Promotional strategy* – deciding the campaign objective, which directly affects both media selection and the promotional messages to be delivered;
- *Budgeting* – fixing the promotional budget, so the company spends the right amount on achieving the chosen objective;
- *Preparation of promotional proposals* – planning a marketing communications campaign to achieve the determined objective;
- *Approval of proposals* – checking, prior to executing the campaign, that the proposals are likely to be successful;
- *Execution of proposals* – putting the plan into effect;
- *Follow through* – ensuring that the company is geared up to cope with response generated by the promotional campaign;
- *Evaluation of results* – checking that the company received value for money, and seeing what lessons can be learned for the future.

This process is a closed loop, and evaluation of this year's results should provide additional information on which to base next year's planning. All these tasks are examined in Part 4. This chapter, however, reviews the role of the Marketing Communications Manager, and how he can best tackle it. First it is necessary to examine the marketing process itself and new developments in business marketing, on which promotional planning must be based.

MARKETING PLANNING

Chapter one quoted the Chartered Institute of Marketing's definition:

'Marketing is the management process responsible for identifying, anticipating and satisfying customer requirements profitably.'

The following review of conventional marketing is brief, in the knowledge that numerous books cover the subject, and on the assumption that most readers already understand the marketing concept. Those not fully conversant with the process will, hopefully, find this outline sufficient. Those already experienced in conventional marketing are welcome to take a crash revision course, or alternatively skip the next few sections and jump to the *New Developments* heading on page 21.

THE ORGANIZATION OF MARKETING COMMUNICATIONS

Marketing planning encompasses two inter-related areas:
- *Assessing external forces*
- *Deciding the marketing mix*

EXTERNAL FORCES

These comprise those variables over which the company has no direct control but which, through marketing mix decisions (see below), it attempts to influence. These include:

- *General conditions* – political, economic, sociological and technological;
- *Potential purchasers* – those who might buy the product or service;
- *Distribution* – the channels through which the product could be distributed;
- *Competition* – rival manufacturers, competing for the same market. Also, indirect competition from other products or services, the purchase of which might take precedence;
- *Constraints* – the legal restraints or voluntary codes which restrict promotional activities.

The necessary research and investigation into these extermal forces is discussed in detail in Chapter 19.

THE MARKETING MIX

After analysis of *S*trengths and *W*eaknesses, and the *O*pportunities and *T*hreats facing an organization (known in marketing terminology as a *SWOT* analysis), the firm then decides upon its 'marketing mix' – the variables over which there is direct control, i.e. the four P's of Product, Price, Place and Promotion, which encompass the following decisions:

- *Product planning* – the exact nature of the product(s) to manufacture, or service(s) to supply;
- *Pricing policy* – the price structure at which to supply this product or service;
- *Branding* – this is more than simply selecting a name and (as signified by its 'Wild West' origins) concerns the indelible identification of a product. In business marketing, the company itself is often the 'brand';
- *Packaging* – to ensure the product arrives in perfect condition, and presents a favourable image for the organization;
- *Market segment(s)* – which particular groups, selected from the total market, should be the target for marketing effort. Possible target segments must be evaluated by various criteria:
  - *Identity:* in terms of distinctive needs, demographic or other traits;
  - *Responsiveness:* evidence of positive reaction;
  - *Potential:* large enough to be profitable;
  - *Accessibility:* can be reached economically;
  - *Stability:* replaces itself, or preferably grows in size;
- *Distribution channels* – to make the product or service readily available to the selected market segments;
- *Personal selling* – sales force structure and organization;
- *Promotion* – how best to promote the product or service (to which this book is devoted);

- *Servicing* – the service element to be provided. Should the organization provide a service rather than manufacture a product (this is of course the first item above).

THE MARKETING PLAN

The marketing plan is a formal document prepared (usually annually) for the purpose of establishing goals for the company's marketing, and determining the strategy and programme of action needed to reach those goals. The plan quantifies objectives, places them on a time scale, allocates responsibilities, and estimates the expenditure required and expected profit. This data is then used during subsequent execution and evaluation to see if marketing is proceeding to plan.

Marketing planning also encompasses other activities:

- *Market research* – to ensure decisions are soundly based;
- *Product testing* – to ensure any proposed product truly meets market needs;
- *Product life cycle* – marketing should attempt to predict the new product's life cycle (introduction, growth, maturity and decline) and monitor where present products are on the cycle;
- *New product development* – marketing plans should seek to improve existing products and develop new ones, to ensure that the organization has a suitable 'portfolio' for the future.

Many authorities suggest that marketing planning is more important than the plan itself, because it disciplines loose thinking into rigorous analysis, reveals any gaps in information, and ensures that there is consultation between key people. A joint planning process assists in resolving possible differences of opinion and getting all concerned to agree and work to a common objective.

NEW DEVELOPMENTS

Conventional marketing has concentrated on the traditional four P's of Product, Price, Place and Promotion. New developments suggest that business marketing demands at least three new P's:
- *Positioning*
- *People*
- *Purchasing patterns*

Chapter 2 established the traditional differences between business and consumer marketing. To mount effective promotional campaigns, it is essential to understand how marketing planning is affected by the three new P's, since these directly influence both media and messages.

FROM THE INSIDE, LOOK OUT

Before analysing these new P's, remember that your organization is the target market for suppliers of other products and services.

Analysis of your own firm, its buying practices and structure, and how it obtains the information necessary to reach sound purchasing decisions, can provide a valuable insight into how decisions are made by other organisations. This in turn can be of immense practical value when planning your own promotional programme.

POSITIONING

This concept, taken from consumer advertising is:

> The presentation of a product so that consumers distinguish it from competitors in terms of satisfying an unfilled need.

As industrial marketing becomes more competitive, it is increasingly important to consider the company's position – from the standpoint of its customers – in relation to consumer choice and the competition faced from rival suppliers.

Tactical marketing planning should be preceded by strategic planning, setting down broad objectives, policies and allocation of resources over a period of at least five to ten years.

What does the market seek in the kind of company the organization wishes to be? Having defined its target image and positioning, the organization must then devote its marketing efforts to tailoring the company and its products to meet that image in reality.

PEOPLE

This second new marketing 'P' acknowledges that industrial planning differs in its person-to-person interactive elements, which are of key importance. Viewed in this way, business marketing is not solely concerned with manipulating the traditional four P's, but more with developing a critical network of relationships. Furthermore, these are long-term relationships demanding on-going interaction – contrast this with relatively straightforward repeat purchases of consumer merchandise. These different relational aspects directly affect marketing planning.

EXTERNAL PEOPLE

The executives who comprise the target market merit analysis from various standpoints:

- *Target people.* Chapter 2 established that industrial markets are defined differently. The point made here is that the way these target groups are organized and operate within their firms has direct implications for promotional planning, discussed below.

- *Committee people.* Also already established is that industrial purchases are made on a committee basis, either formal or informal. The organization members participating in the buying function are neither purely concerned with economics, nor are their motives purely rational (or irrational): they are human beings whose decisions are influenced by many factors. Various models of this decision-making unit are examined in Chapter 21. The nature of the decision process clearly influences selection of targets for marketing communications messages, and their content.

- *Partnership people.* With consumer marketing, ultimate customers have no direct contact with manufacturers' internal departments. Many business products, on the other hand, are produced and consumed in an interactive relationship between the purchaser and the supplier firm. The potential purchaser's ability to brief suppliers on his technical and other requirements is as important as their ability to design and produce the product he wants. When a potential purchaser is not fully experienced, marketing communications may necessarily take the form of client education.

- *Division people.* Much depends on the management structure of the firm to which the organization hopes to sell, since it may function in distinct operating divisions. Sometimes these are autonomous and, as such, amount to different target markets each calling for individual marketing campaigns. These functional units, in multi-national corporations, may operate in different countries. Some large national companies, on the other hand, divide internally into individual profit centres. A key matter for promotional planning is therefore to ascertain if campaigns should be targeted to these operational units, or alternatively to some internal service section. If the latter, on what basis does this central purchasing unit meet the needs of *its* clients? Are they restricted to obtaining supplies through the internal channel, or can they buy from external sources if they so wish? The answers to these questions influence the content and direction of promotional messages.

- *Cross-company people.* Many high-level businessmen hold non-executive directorships in several companies. Their opinion of an organization's efficiency in servicing one such company can directly influence the likelihood of getting a contract from another.

  The same principle applies when scientific, technical or other staff serve on industry-wide working parties or research groups.

- *Ex-market people.* For some industrial purchases, the real decision is not what to buy or which supplier to buy from, but whether or not the project itself is to proceed. This in turn may be determined by government views about the project's effects on a country's economy and employment levels. Until the decision to proceed is taken, the relevant purchasing organization has no authority to buy and there is thus little hope of securing an order. The scheme must be authorised before a sale can be made and, under such circumstances, marketing communications may be concerned with convincing governments of the benefits their country will receive from the project.

INTERNAL PEOPLE

In-company staff demand equally careful analysis, since they comprise a very expensive resource and, in many respects, *are* the company:

- *Service people* this reference simply recognises a point already established: an organization may provide a service rather than manufacture a product. The service element has major implications which apply equally to many technical products. These implications are discussed here.

- *Two-business people*. To operate successfully in business marketing, staff must be experts in customers' businesses as well as their own. Unless they fully understand their customers' problems, and can communicate with them in their own language, there is little prospect of securing an order.

- *Team people*. If the concept of decision-making teams is extended within the selling organization, it is clear that in industrial marketing there are selling teams just as much as there are committee buyers. Business marketing involves teams from both sides, since the Sales Department could be just one of the many sections from which various employees may be in contact with different individuals in several departments within the buying organization. Service staff are of prime importance, whether providing pre-sales service (product information, costings, specifications, etc) or post-sales service (such as repairs and maintenance, training of operators, advice on operation etc). This calls for promotional planning which encompasses staff training to prepare these personnel for vital external contacts.

- *Division people*. Just as potential purchasers break their activities into separate profit-centre operations, so do supplier organizations. All too often, alas, this leads to a fragmented marketing effort. At worst, conflicting promotional activities are counter-productive, weakening each other's effectiveness. Alternatively, the various campaigns are merely self-contained, and fail to capitalise on the synergistic approach whereby careful co-ordination of separate promotional efforts actually increases their individual effectiveness and thus that of the overall campaign.

- *Partnership people*. Just as a product is produced in an interactive relationship with customers, so there are equally important interactive relationships with suppliers or sub-contractors. Their ability to supply satisfactorily depends on the organization's participative approach. This in turn directly affects the ability to meet customers' requirements efficiently.

- *Company people*. In extreme cases, where management is production oriented, the marketing problem is an internal one of convincing the board that marketing is a vital activity calling for expenditure of time and effort (as well as money). Hopefully, such cases will be few!

Even when management is more enlightened, there is still a vital need for internal marketing. At its simplest level, this involves keeping sales staff informed about promotional activities and providing them with copies of advertisements and media schedules, reprints of editorial coverage, and an outline of the promotional campaign which they can then use as effective sales tools when making contact with potential customers.

Frequently, however, internal marketing is far more complex – particularly when there are multiple contacts between numerous individuals in different sections of the selling organization and their counterparts in the corresponding sections of potential purchasing organizations. When an organization operates in autonomous divisions, there is an even greater need for internal marketing –

the concept of 'message sources' points out that target markets receive promotional messages from several such divisions. Internal marketing, on the lines of project management, should ensure that each division is aware of the activities of the others, and that their joint efforts are co-ordinated to maximum effect.

PERMANENT PEOPLE

It is important to recognize that these contacts between and within internal and external people are continuing relationships. Once a purchaser has established a relationship with a supplier, the purchasing company becomes dependent upon that supplier, and the purchased products are expected to contribute dependably to the purchaser's performance over long periods of time. Under such circumstances, the original decision is likely to be made in a cautious and thorough manner. There is therefore a need for two distinct but inter-related and continous promotional campaigns – one aimed at target markets, and another at the organization's own staff.

PURCHASING PATTERNS

This third new marketing 'P' recognizes that business purchases differ in numerous ways from purchases of consumer products or services. Various analytical models of buyer behaviour which facilitate marketing analysis are examined in Chapter 21.

With complex purchasing patterns involving multi-facet operations within both buyer and seller organizations, and multiple contacts between different sub-sections of both, there is a clear need for these relationships to be co-ordinated to maximum effect. This is increasingly achieved through database marketing, whereby information from internal and external sources is integrated. This new development is discussed in more detail in Chapter 11.

THE CHANGING STRUCTURE OF THE MARKETING COMMUNICATIONS DEPARTMENT

Promotional activities are no longer considered in isolation: marketing communications now plays an important part in influencing overall company policy rather than merely reflecting it. Many promotional staff now operate at director level, and the vital contribution of marketing communications is thus formally recognized.

Other changes relate to the range of work. In some organizations a single executive is responsible for the full range of advertising, marketing, market research, merchandising, public relations and sales promotion. In other firms, these activities are divided among several individuals, each the head of a separate department, the title of which changes accordingly.

Whatever the structure, it is essential that all activities interlock: unless advertising ties in with public relations, merchandising and sales promotion in aiming to achieve identical marketing objectives, it is impossible for promotion to be used to maximum effect.

THE PROMOTION MANAGER AS HEAD OF A DEPARTMENT

The Marketing Communications Manager is a section head just as much as the head of production, sales, transport or any other department; as such, he has staff responsibilities. The size of his department depends to a great extent on whether any external services are employed.

Where the firm does not use an advertising agency or PR consultancy, the Promotion Manager must have in his department staff to prepare advertisements or news releases; similarly he must be able to handle media selection, planning, and the physical implementation of his campaign. Alternatively, he must be in touch with freelance workers on whom he can call.

Even when this work is undertaken by the external services described in chapter 4, there are still internal staffing requirements. Careful control must be kept of schedules, accurate records maintained of advertising and public relations activities, and press cuttings and voucher copies and invoices checked. Promotion may involve despatch of product literature, sorting out customer requests and perhaps passing them to representatives as sales leads, and analysing campaign response. Promotion involves a great many executive, creative and purely routine administrative tasks, even when external services are employed. Division of work between manufacturer and external services varies but, whatever the circumstances, the Promotion Manager must ensure he has staff to cope with whatever tasks he accepts as his responsibility.

SELECTION OF EXTERNAL SERVICES, AND LIAISON

The advantages and disadvantages of using an advertising agency, public relations consultancy, and merchandising or sales promotion organization are discussed in Chapter 4, but clearly the decision whether or not to use external services rests largely with the Promotion Manager, who will advise his directors accordingly. If it is decided to do so, he is then responsible for selecting suitable organizations, negotiating arrangements for handling his business, and briefing them on company requirements. After this briefing he must, throughout the campaign, work closely with the external teams in preparing and executing proposals, and in evaluating the results.

The importance of external liaison must never be under-estimated, because whether or not the advertising agency or public relations consultancy produces a good scheme depends largely on the client's Promotion Manager. The point that, in business marketing, the buyer is also a co-producer, applies equally to relationships with external services – there is no question of the Promotion Manager sitting back and leaving everything to the agency or consultancy, for even the finest organization, staffed by experts in every branch of marketing communications, can contribute its best only if it receives the client's full backing and co-operation.

DIVISION OF WORK

Some firms rely on external services for the full range of promotional media, while others undertake part of the work themselves. More usually press, television, and radio come within the external orbit (for both advertising and editorial columns), while control of other media may rest with either party. Direct mail, exhibitions, merchandising, sales promotion and created media are frequently under the promotion department's direct control, even when agencies or consultancies are employed. Some firms divide their appropriation into two parts: an 'above the line' budget to be spent by external services, and a 'below the line' budget retained for in-house use. There is no standard practice about where the client's work ends and the agency's or consultancy's starts, and much depends on whatever arrangements the Promotion Manager considers most effective in the circumstances under which his firm operates.

THE PROMOTION DEPARTMENT – ITS SIZE AND STRUCTURE

Organizational structures within Promotion departments vary enormously: firms may or may not employ external services and, either way, Promotion Managers may rely on only a few staff or alternatively may have large departments employing numbers of experts, equivalent to a fully staffed agency or consultancy. The Promotion department may in fact contain a number of specialists who are the external experts' counterparts. In such circumstances, advertising agency proposals are checked by the Promotion Manager's own advertising experts, public relations by PR specialists and so on, with the Promotion Manager in overall control and taking an overall view. Alternatively, these in-house experts may undertake the full promotion task without outside assistance.

A company marketing several products, or operating in autonomous divisions, may well have separate promotion departments, each under its own Promotion Manager and co-ordinated by a Promotion Director. Each department may mount its promotional activities without external assistance, but in other cases may employ one or more agencies or consultancies. The Promotion Director must ensure that, rather than appear as fragmented campaigns, these individual efforts reinforce each other.

This structure may be extended, on the advertising side, to include the media independents described later – the companies which undertake responsibility for buying media on behalf of advertisers, independently of the agency providing the creative work. One company used four different agencies for its four operating divisions: since all advertised heavily on televison, the company then employed a media independent to co-ordinate the campaigns and prevent the divisions from pre-empting each other's television spots, thus wasting valuable resources fighting each other rather than competitors. The same need to avoid conflict of interests applies to advertising or public relations activities in other media.

Many different organizational patterns are practicable, and there is no question of one being better than others: firms adopt the organizational structure most suited to circumstances and adapt it as business conditions, and the firm itself, change. The Promotion Manager must also consider future products and, in his role as a departmental head, recruit and train new staff and/or review external service arrangements accordingly.

IN-HOUSE OR EXTERNAL SERVICES?

There are advantages and drawbacks to both in-house and external operations. What is not immediately apparent, however, is that one is the converse of the other: the advantages of external services, reviewed in Chapter 4, are the drawbacks of undertaking the work within the promotion department. Conversely, the advantages of in-house work are the drawbacks of external services.

There is one further advantage to external services: added flexibility. Should a firm employ additional in-house staff in anticipation of an increased workload, it may incur redundancy costs if the anticipated work does not materialise. Using external services means that they, rather than the client organization, carry the risk. Much the same applies to quality of work: should the advertising or public relations produced not meet the required standards, it is relatively easier to change agencies or consultancies than the staff of a department.

RELEVANT ORGANIZATIONS

INCORPORATED SOCIETY OF BRITISH ADVERTISERS
(44 Hertford Street, London W1Y 8AE)

ISBA is dedicated to looking after advertisers' interests. Its main area of operation is advertising, but activities extend into related fields, including exhibitions, sponsorship and research. The benefits of ISBA membership are best summarised by a quotation from its own literature, which points out that it:

" –provides a constant service of up-to-date information.
 –gives invaluable help and advice when needed.
 –helps to protect your company's interests, at home and abroad, by acting as the advertiser's collective voice.
 –enables your company to shape events in the national and international marketing scene.
 –works with your company to improve its marketing skills."

ISBA has working committees devoted to different aspects of advertising, including exhibitions, industrial, international, outdoor, press, radio, TV, screen, research, sales promotion, and standards and practices.

The Society publishes a monthly newsletter and other publications of specific business-to-business interest, including industrial and exhibition supplements and numerous informative booklets – recent titles include guides to advertising overseas, industrial publicity, press supplements and the advertiser, sales promotion, and sponsorship.

CHARTERED INSTITUTE OF MARKETING
(Moor Hall, Cookham, Maidenhead, Berks SL6 9QH)

The Institute is a professional membership organization: it requires its members to recognise their responsibilities and adhere to the Institute's code of practice.

THE ROLE OF THE SUPPLIER ORGANIZATION

A number of Institute activities have direct business-to-business relevance. In addition to its education and examination activities, it mounts a wide range of practical training courses, many specifically orientated to industrial marketing. The Institute also has many events organized at local branch level, and there are various specific industry groups, including construction, hotel, travel and agriculture.

The library and information services subscribe to all major published marketing intelligence services, and have an on-line search facility linked to major external databases. Using these, the information department's staff can provide members with information on specific products and markets, both industrial and consumer.

The Institute manages the Marketing Initiative, which is part of Lord Young's Enterprise Initiative, for the Department of Trade & Industry (described on page 44), and maintains a register of Marketing Consultants: these undertake some 90 per cent of the projects commissioned through the Marketing Initiative.

CHAPTER FOUR

The Role of External Services

Whether undertaken in-house by companies themselves, by the external services discussed in this chapter, or shared between the two, the component tasks of effective marketing communications (listed in Chapter 3, and examined in detail in Part 4) remain the same. This chapter, rather than review these tasks, examines how external service organizations set about them in partnership with their clients.

These service organizations could include advertising agencies, public relations consultancies, and merchandising or sales promotion firms which, for simplicity, are henceforth termed consultants. These could in their turn call on other services such as art, design and photographic studios, direct mail houses, exhibition stand designers and contractors, market research firms, typesetters and printers, TV/video and film production companies, sound recording studios and a host of others. Alternatively, any company undertaking its promotional activities in-house could call on these secondary services direct.

THE ADVANTAGES OF EXTERNAL SERVICES

Companies employ an advertising agency, public relations consultancy or other external services, instead of relying on in-house departments, for various reasons, including the following.

AN EXPERT TEAM

Consultants provide a team of experts, including specialists in many different aspects of promotion, to work in partnership with the client's own staff. The team includes experts in planning, in media and messages (for both advertising and editorial columns as necessary), in created media, in print and production, and in other promotional activities. Use of external services, however, brings many other advantages.

THE WORK-LOAD PROBLEM

Clients could recruit staff direct, but this could be uneconomic if there is insufficient work to keep an expert on a specialist promotional area fully occupied. The consultant firm on the other hand, by spreading work across a number of clients according to their need for expert advice, can afford to employ full-time specialists. Should a client try to overcome the work-load shortfall by use of freelance workers, they would be unaccustomed to working together, whereas the consultancy already has the experts available and working as a team. The client, on the other hand, has the multiple tasks of locating, evaluating, selecting, engaging, briefing and then co-ordinating independent specialists.

A DETACHED VIEWPOINT

A third advantage of external service is the consultant's fresh approach to a problem, since consultancy staff are detached from the client's day-to-day operations. Internal staff often become so involved in detail that they fail to recognize underlying problems.

OTHER EXPERIENCE

Consultancy personnel handle a variety of clients, and so are not restricted to any one company's problems. With their wider experience, they are unlikely to take a narrow view. Furthermore, experience gained in solving one marketing problem is frequently relevant to others, and each client thus benefits from the consultant's experience in other fields. This advantage is of particular importance today when marketing practices change so rapidly. Client companies also keep themselves up-to-date but, because they operate in restricted product fields, their experience is inevitably limited.

BUYING POWER

The consultant's total promotional expenditure necessarily exceeds any individual client's. When buying on clients' behalf, it can thereby bring considerable pressure to bear on suppliers – far more leverage than most clients can exert on their own. This buying muscle can be exerted on purchases of advertising space, artwork, created media, market research, merchandising material, printing, sales promotion incentives, typesetting and indeed all items bought for clients. This financial leverage, coupled with the expertise of the marketplace mentioned earlier, and the knowledge of which suppliers to approach, can result in considerable savings.

REDUCED COST

When using an advertising agency, a further advantage can arise from the commission granted by media-owners, which helps reduce the cost of agency service. Recognized advertising agencies receive commission, ranging from ten to 15 per cent, on almost everything they buy on their clients' behalf.

Where the commission provides a sufficient profit, after covering operating costs, the agency may work on commission alone. In such cases, the advertiser reaps the benefit of agency service without charge. If the agency, on the other hand, finds its expenses in handling the client's advertising exceed the commission received, or leave an insufficient margin of profit, it charges a service fee to obtain the additional income necessary. Even where the advertiser pays a service fee, however, this is often less expensive than taking all the experts onto his own staff. Conversely, should the client consider the agency commission more than provides sufficient profit, he may – when negotiating arrangements – call for the commission level to be reduced.

Public relations, merchandising and sales promotion consultancies usually work on a fee basis, their charges being directly proportionate to expenses incurred and the hours spent working on clients' behalf. If any suppliers grant commission, however, this would be taken into account when calculating the service fee.

OTHER SAVINGS

Other less vital benefits of external service can also result in welcome savings in time, effort and money. Any company mounting its campaign direct is necessarily involved in the clerical and administrative chores of bookings and orders, despatching news releases, and implementing the detail of the campaign.

The company then receives individual invoices for all advertisements booked, artwork and production costs, expenses incurred in public relations activities, and charges for created media.

Organizations using external services, on the other hand, are relieved of these administrative booking and despatch headaches, and receive comprehensive accounts covering these many items which can be settled with a single payment. There are additional clerical savings in that typed copies of promotional programmes are provided, including media schedules, press circulation lists, and the text of advertisements and news releases, as a normal part of external service. External services can make the client's life operationally easier.

A FINAL NOTE

Chapter 3 pointed out that the advantages of external service are the drawbacks for any client undertaking the work within his own organization. Conversely, the disadvantages of external service discussed below are the advantages of in-house work.

THE DRAWBACKS OF EXTERNAL SERVICE

For advantages there are necessarily drawbacks although, when employing external services, these are in most cases outweighed by the benefits.

DIVIDED ATTENTION

One drawback is that, as external staff work for several clients at the same time, they clearly cannot devote their attention to all of them simultaneously. If one client faces an urgent problem, other pressures may prevent external personnel from dealing with it, whereas a manufacturer with in-house staff knows his problems receive undivided attention all the time.

THE TIME LAG

External service is, for reasons explained later, sometimes slower than direct working, and an organization with a promotional programme subject to unexpected changes might find it more practicable to do the job in-house. If the content, timing and destinations of a company's promotional messages are all under constant review, perhaps because of a fast-changing market situation, this could well apply.

Divided attention and the time lag apply to all types of external service. Two further possible drawbacks are specific to advertising agencies.

COST

A possible drawback of agency service may arise from the relationship between commission received, service fee charged, and the amount of work involved. The commission on some types of advertising may be so small and the service fee so high that it becomes uneconomic to employ an advertising agency. Much depends on the type of advertising, for where costs are low (as with many business media) the agency receives little income from commission. On the other hand, it takes as much effort to prepare an advertisement for a technical journal as for a national newspaper, yet the former task brings less revenue than the latter, simply because the agency receives commission on a far smaller sum.

BUILT-IN INERTIA

Income *versus* workload problems may extend further, since an agency receives roughly the same commission on a given sum, whether spent on a single advertisement or on hundreds, but its operating costs differ considerably. A business-to-business firm, for example, might find a series of smaller advertisements in a range of professional publications far more productive than one large advertisement in a general newspaper, and would consequently prefer to advertise this way. This could prove extremely uneconomic for the agency, however – each publication on the schedule necessitates typing an order, preparing copy and type mark-up, checking proofs and vouchers, and paying an invoice – the administrative costs would leave little or no profit. The commission system thus has a built-in temptation for agencies to achieve maximum income for minimum effort.

The same argument applies to changes in message content. The agency incurs lower staff costs by preparing one advertisement and letting it run for a year than if it changes the content each month. The commission income remains the same, yet monthly changes of copy means 12 times as much work, with consequent higher staff costs and lower profit.

Agencies – and indeed all service organizations – rightly need to make a profit, and to some extent charging a higher service fee can recoup the additional costs involved. The higher the service fee, however, the more attractive it is for the client to run an in-house department, or to transfer to a rival firm charging a lower fee.

Agency/consultancy directors are well aware of these drawbacks, and take positive action to overcome them. External management is thus of great importance in ensuring promotional expertise is applied to maximum effect on clients' behalf. Equally, responsibility rests to some degree with the client: possible drawbacks should be ironed out at service selection stage, and client/consultant relationships should be compatible.

SELECTING EXTERNAL SERVICES

The selection of external services, whether advertising agency, public relations consultancy, merchandising or sales promotion organization, calls for careful consideration. The various aspects to be evaluated include the following.

RANGE OF SERVICES OFFERED

This is largely a straight cross-checking procedure – what services are required, and what services does the consultant provide? There should be a close match because, if the consultancy lacks any necessary services, the problems then arise of locating, evaluating, selecting, engaging, and then co-ordinating independent freelance workers.

QUALITY OF WORK

That the consultant provides the necessary services is insufficient in itself: the standard is as important as the range. Evaluation of quality standards is a skilled task, to which Chapter 25 is devoted.

QUALITY OF STAFF

Quality of work depends on quality of staff, and it is advisable to consider staffing *in depth*. What level of expertise exists within the service organization, beyond the executives who will handle the business? One consultancy commented that it never recruited office juniors – only future directors!

RELEVANT EXPERIENCE

A major advantage of using external services is experience in other fields. When selecting a consultant, staff experience – and the relevance of that experience to the business area in question – is an important consideration. Do the staff in fact have *business-to-business* experience? Is this in a related industry, so that the client can benefit accordingly?

ACCOUNTS HANDLED

Experience in other fields arises through the consultancy's accounts, as much as staff experience. The client list should be considered under three headings:

- *Relevance* – the service company may handle accounts which, although not competitive, give valuable knowledge of the target market, and practical experience of media likely to reach them;

- *Competition* – this is a controversial matter, as some companies completely rule out employing any consultant handling a competing account. Others look at the firm's operating structure, since it may function on a group system whereby it divides into autonomous sections each amounting to a self-contained service unit (organizational structure is discussed in more detail below);

- *Other* – it is advisable to study the client list in the broadest sense. Many make impressive reading, comprising leading companies, all of which demand – and presumably receive – a high standard of promotional service.

INFORMED OPINIONS

Informal contact with those having practical experience of the consultant's services – this could include other clients, and those working for media, printers or other suppliers – can yield much useful information. But do remember the old adage – 'No client is ever satisfied!' No account can ever be handled *perfectly*, so what inevitably goes wrong should be considered in the light of all the good work done. If numerous contacts all report adversely, however, then dissatisfaction may be far deeper than with the minor snags which necessarily crop up in all working relationships.

SIZE AND IMPORTANCE OF CLIENT'S ACCOUNT

These two criteria should be reviewed together, and either of two extremes avoided. One is to be a very small fish in a very large pond: if an account is too small by the consultant's standards then, when different clients compete for attention, the big spenders may receive priority. Equally, it is best to avoid being too big, since one advantage of external service is a detached viewpoint. This sometimes necessitates the consultant drawing clients' attention to some unwelcome home truths. If a client accounts for too high a proportion of total billing, this may inhibit the consultant's plain speaking, for fear of possibly upsetting the client and thereby losing the business.

COST

Cost must of course be considered in the light of the quality of work delivered but, whatever the nature of the service organization, and whether engaged on a commission and/or service fee arrangement, it is essential there is a clear understanding between both parties as to precisely what is (and is not) covered by the consultant's remuneration.

Is provision of desk or field research to be charged, or covered by the consultant's normal remuneration? What about other expenses incurred? The fundamental basis of charges is staff time, which in turn affects costs. Accordingly, it is more expensive to have weekly rather than monthly meetings. Conversely, it costs less if the client visits the consultancy rather than *vice versa*, since the service charge will cover not only presence at meetings but also travelling time and expenses. A clear understanding of working arrangements prevents subsequent misunderstandings about the cost of external service.

TERMS OF CONTRACT

Legalities are also important, and the best advice is to read the small print. Should working arrangements not prove satisfactory, for example, what notice must either party give to terminate the contract? Who owns the copyright of artwork and of created media? How frequently will accounts be presented, how promptly must they be settled, and what are the conditions of payment? Is a payment required in advance, to cover operating costs? Many arguments can be overcome by a clear understanding of such matters.

ORGANIZATION STRUCTURE

Any client should check on operational arrangements, particularly if the consultancy handles a competitive account. Some are organized on a pyramid system, whereby contact executives are responsible for a number of clients (rather than for staff members) and specialist staff all work on several accounts, each of which may be under the control of a different client service director.

Others operate on a group system, whereby the firm divides into two or more separate units, each amounting to a self-contained service operation. The group system adopted by many large consultants has various advantages: each account group becomes a profit centre, it encourages a competitive spirit, enables the consultancy to handle competing accounts (provided clients agree), and staff can be switched between groups from time to time to bring fresh input to the accounts handled whilst still maintaining continuity.

OPERATING ARRANGEMENTS

Equally important are arrangements for handling the client's business, as frequency of meetings and their location directly affect costs. Furthermore, is it the consultant's practice to issue contact reports after each meeting, summarising the actions agreed, allocating responsibilities and specifying dates?

As suggested earlier, it is worth examining operational aspects in depth. The client may meet top executives from time to time, but who will actually *work* on the account, and how can the client ensure his affairs are not delegated to the most junior junior? Open discussions well in advance about practical working arrangements for handling the business, prevent time-wasting arguments later.

PROFESSIONAL MEMBERSHIP

The range and standard of services provided necessarily differs from firm to firm, and professional membership can be an important criterion in service selection. Whilst there is nothing to prevent someone with no real knowledge or experience proclaiming himself an advertising agent or public relations consultant, it is very different if this individual wishes to claim he is in membership of the relevant professional organization. The official bodies listed below lay down vigorous standards for accepting firms into membership, and can also assist intending clients in selecting and drawing up a shortlist of suitable member firms. From that point on, responsibility necessarily rests with the client: it is essential to meet relevant staff, to ensure both parties to the contract are compatible and agree how to best work in partnership.

SERVICE ORGANIZATION PROCEDURE

When a company appoints a consultancy, the first task for their staff is to find out all about the client's business operations and marketing problems. These investigations (discussed in Part 4) necessarily duplicate those undertaken by the Promotion manager, as external staff need an equally clear understanding of their client's company background and marketing objectives. Consultants devote great care to making in-depth investigations for, until the client's marketing problems have been accurately defined, staff are in no position to solve them. The promotional budget's size and duration are also important to external advisers, as are details of what the appropriation is to cover. Is the client undertaking part of the campaign in-house and keeping back a 'below the line' budget for this purpose? Are production charges included or only media and other direct costs? Practice varies with the firm, and so the consultant must establish what money is available, and what it is to cover.

Ideally, the client gives his consultants a thorough briefing: the quality of the work they produce depends to a considerable extent on the client's skill in giving all the information needed to prepare proposals on his behalf.

Once the consultancy has a correct understanding of the situation, staff can start preparing a promotional campaign to help their client achieve his marketing objectives. In many cases, to ensure that its understanding of the problem is correct, the consultant prepares a 'Facts Book' detailing the situation, which the client double-checks for accuracy.

PLANNING THE CAMPAIGN

The consultant's 'Account Executive' plays an important part in defining and solving the client's problem. This title is somewhat misleading since, although he is responsible for expenditure, he has little to do with accounting as such. This executive has, however, full responsibility for *all* aspects of handling the client's business or 'account'. He is usually appointed soon after the consultant is selected or, on occasion, his inclusion in the team pitching for the business is one reason why the client selected the particular consultancy. Either way, the Account Executive attends the meeting at which the consultancy is formally briefed on the problem. It is true to say that no client, however well-meaning, ever gives a perfect briefing and it is the Account Executive's responsibility to ensure, by asking the necessary questions, that his organization has all the information it needs to solve the client's problem.

The Account Executive has a dual function, as he represents the consultant to the client, and the client to the consultant. He is the individual to whom consultancy staff turn for information about the client's business operations; equally, it is through him that the client's problems are channelled to appropriate specialists, and their work co-ordinated. There may be different executive levels: some larger consultants have Account Executives backed by Assistant Executives who handle the day-to-day work. At a higher level are Account Supervisors, each responsible for a number of Account Executives. At an even higher level may be Account Directors with overall responsibility for all clients handled by their Account Supervisors and Executives.

Another variation is that executive staff often have responsibility for a number of accounts rather than just one. To encourage cross-fertilization of ideas, and to prevent getting in a rut (quite apart from solving client's workload problems by spreading staff costs across several accounts), many consultancies deliberately give their executives varied responsibilities. There are also consultancies where the term 'Account Executive' is not used, executive staff being referred to as 'representatives' or 'managers'. For simplicity, however, we will use the term 'Account Executive' to identify the executive role.

Once the client's problem is clearly defined, consultancy staff can consider possible solutions: a task in which the Account Executive plays a vital role. He usually starts by convening a 'Plans Board', comprising senior representatives of all important areas of expertise. The Plans Board (which may be formal or informal) may also include other Account Executives for the benefit of their experience and advice. Other senior members of various departments may also participate in discussions, even though they are not involved in the account's day-to-day operation, to give the client maximum benefit of the consultancy's combined talents.

Members of the Plans Board discuss their client's overall problem from every aspect, and finally agree how best to resolve it. Since any promotional campaign represents a combination of interlocking decisions about marketing, media and messages, print and production, and other aspects of promotion, clearly the basis of the solution must be agreed by the Board as a whole.

ACCOUNT PLANNING

Some consultancies solve their clients' promotional problems differently, by separating out the planning function. They consider campaign strategy too important and too time-consuming to be prepared by busy Account Executives in their 'spare time'. Accordingly, this is made the full-time responsibility of an Account Planner, whose task is to discipline the first essential of effective promotion – developing the strategy on which message and media proposals are based, and by which they are evaluated.

The Planner's first task is to analyse all available data, and propose any new research necessary to fill any gaps in this information. In the light of these collated findings, the Planner then drafts a promotional strategy for discussion by the account team or Plans Board, before it is presented to the client. Later still, during the campaign's implementation and execution, the Account Planner evaluates target market reactions, to see whether promotional objectives are being achieved. In due course he will recommend any necessary strategy modifications in the light of this new information. Account planning also extends beyond current operations, assessing long-term market trends in order to develop long-term strategies. The multi-skill planning function is increasingly recognized in the formal structure of more and more service organizations.

THE RESEARCH DEPARTMENT

When the Plans Board first discuss their client's marketing problem, it may be apparent that there is insufficient information on which to base proposals, and members therefore call on the Research Department to rectify this situation. The department already has a representative on the Board for the benefit of general advice, but when more detailed information is required the Research Department then functions in its own right.

Considerable information is already available in published form, and so any field research is always preceded by desk research, checking through existing information sources. In some firms desk research staff form a separate department and may be known as 'Information' or 'Library', while a second department – usually formally titled 'Research Department' – looks after field research.

Desk research always precedes field research, as a matter of procedure, but if some vital questions remain unanswered, or some available information is very dated, or if different sources contribute conflicting data, then field research becomes essential. The Research Department will then take action: its task is planning and control, rather than actual fieldwork. The department will select the most suitable market researchers, and work with them in planning and supervising the research. It then carefully interprets the results and makes recommendations for action.

Many 'Research Departments' have become Account Planning sections, described earlier. Research staff found insufficient job satisfaction in simply collecting data: they wanted to ensure practical use was made of the valuable information they had gathered. This wish coincided with the management view that promotional strategy could not be drafted by busy Account Executives on a spare-time basis.

Once field research findings have been carefully checked and interpreted, the Plans Board will meet again to consider overall promotional strategy. As soon as the campaign plan has been agreed, individual departments then work independently to finalise their ideas and produce detailed proposals in line with the agreed broad plan.

DETAILED PROPOSALS

All major departments contribute, through their representatives on the Plans Board, to high-level discussions of each client's overall campaign. Once the general strategy is agreed, each department then commences detailed planning of its component contribution to the overall solution.

Much depends on whether the service organization is an advertising agency, public relations consultancy or merchandising or sales promotion firm, but the many experts – whether in existing media through advertising or editorial columns, or in created media – all share a common aim: to devise effective promotional messages and deliver them to the client's target markets as effectively and economically as possible, through whatever media are their particular specialism.

The experts' skill lies not so much in detailed knowledge (although this may demand years of experience), but in applying this knowledge to each client's particular problems. This vital area is examined in detail in Part 4.

REVIEW OF PROPOSALS

As soon as detailed proposals are ready for consideration, the Plans Board meets to review the work. The committee may possibly change its name, and be retitled the 'Review Board'. In some instances, the Review Board comprises the same executives as the Plans Board, and would probably continue under the same name. In other cases, individuals as well as title change. Whatever the practice, the Board's objective is to make a meticulous check of the proposals, to ensure that all aspects of the campaign interlock, that there are no discrepancies between the various departmental contributions, that the proposals conform to the Plans Board's agreed strategy, and that the work is of the highest quality.

Consultancy procedure is thus investigation, problem analysis, agreement on a basic solution, preparing a detailed plan, and careful checking of proposals. The various stages reflect the care consultants take, even if procedures are not always on a formal basis. A 'Plans Board' may indeed be completely informal, with the Account Executive discussing matters with the appropriate experts, after normal office hours and away from the distractions of the telephone and other interruptions. Some consultants argue against formal Plans or Review Board procedures, on the grounds that they impose a standard style irrespective of clients' individual requirements, and stifle initiative and it is for this reason that meetings are often completely informal.

PRESENTATION OF PROPOSALS

As soon as the Review Board has approved the detailed proposals, they are made ready for presentation. It is essential that both media and message proposals are presented together, and their relationship explained, for no client could approve a media proposal without knowing the messages to be featured, nor approve messages without knowing the media to carry them. Message and media proposals are accordingly presented jointly, together with other components of the plan.

Campaign presentation is of major importance. It should not be a selling exercise, but rather a careful explanation of the component parts of a complex plan and how they inter-relate. Presenting proposals is, in fact, the very reverse of the consultant's first task. The client's problem, when first discussed, was broken into specialist areas for detailed work by appropriate experts, whereas at presentation stage the component parts of the solution are united and presented as a co-ordinated plan.

The Account Executive usually outlines the market situation and the overall approach to the client's problem. He then introduces individual team members who present their specialist components of the campaign and justify the thinking behind them. Finally, the Account Executive summarises the major points made and the reasoning behind the presentation.

Effective presentation is vital, since a client's acceptance of proposals depends on his clearly understanding the campaign plan's many complex and interlocking components. There have been instances of proposals being rejected, not because the plan was faulty but because the presentation failed to explain it adequately. For this reason, consultants usually take considerable pains to ensure that their clients have clear understanding of campaign proposals.

When preparing for a major presentation, consultant staff may rehearse beforehand, and go to the extent of scripting the proceedings, listing the order of speaking, setting down the words to be spoken by each executive, and specifying the visual aids to be used. Some consultants put the entire presentation on video and screen this to their client, rather than risk the slip-ups that might occur in a live presentation. Many now use sophisticated electronic techniques rather than standard visual aids. This procedure can ensure that the campaign proposals are faultlessly presented. The more complex the proposals, the greater the need for lucid presentation of all the details and the reasoning behind them.

EXECUTION OF PROPOSALS

Before formally approving the proposals, the client checks to ensure they are sound and dovetail with his company's marketing activities. Once the consultant has the client's agreement, the promotional proposals can be put into effect. The detailed procedures of both approval and execution are described in Part 4.

THE CONTROL DEPARTMENT

The Control Department is often described as the nerve centre of any service organization. Its function is revealed by the various names by which it may be titled – 'Progress', 'Traffic', 'Control' or 'Copy Detail'. It controls the progress or traffic of detailed work, and smooth functioning depends to a great extent on this department's efficiency.

The control department plans the workflow through the organization, anticipates the time needed for each stage, and allows a safety margin to cover unexpected delays and, if necessary, revision of material. A time-chart is prepared, scheduling so many days for each task, and actual progress then monitored to ensure no delays occur. If someone early in the chain fails to meet their deadline, other unfortunate individuals have to race against time later. Haste seldom results in quality, and greatly increases the risk of costly errors. A good Control Department thus directly increases the likelihood of high quality proposals, as well as increasing efficiency.

When a major new campaign must be prepared and presented, Control's remit extends back to earlier stages, to ensure proposals are ready in good time for submission (and prior checking by the Review Board). Once the proposals are approved, the department also supervises their execution.

VOUCHERS, CHECKING AND ACCOUNTS

Just as the promotion manager checks that his company receives value for money, so does the consultant. The Voucher section checks that the correct advertisement appeared in the position booked on the appointed day, with printing quality up to standard. Not until the voucher copy has been checked and approved is the media-owner's invoice passed through for payment.

Public relations personnel similarly monitor the media, to check editorial references to their clients.

OTHER DEPARTMENTS

Whatever variations there may be in size and organizational structure, the general pattern of consultancy procedure remains the same: problem analysis, preparation of proposals to solve the defined problem, and execution of the approved proposals.

Many service organizations have, however, broadened their range of services by developing other departments, staffed by experts capable of solving specialist aspects of clients' marketing problems, thereby breaking down the barriers between different areas of promotion. Some advertising agencies, for example, have specialist merchandising, public relations or sales promotion departments.

Others develop these activities differently, through specialist subsidiary or associated companies which offer their services to all, rather than restricting them to the consultant's immediate clients. These companies, as well as operating profitably in their own right, also play an important part in attracting new business for the parent organization.

SPECIALIST ORGANIZATIONS

Some service organizations, rather than diversify their departments, concentrate their abilities: some advertising agencies or public relations consultancies now specialise in technical or financial promotion. Writing advertising copy or news releases for industrial products frequently demands technical knowledge the average consumer writer does not possess. Similarly, technical illustrations may prove beyond the average creative expertise and business media differ markedly from those used to reach consumer markets. Specialist organizations, whose staff have the necessary technical expertise, now make an important contribution to promotional planning.

Some advertising agencies concentrate their expertise in a different way. Rather than provide the full creative, media and production service, they restrict their activities to one of these three functions. It is thus possible to call on specialist services for creative work only, while 'Media Independents' undertake responsibility for buying media on behalf of advertisers, independently of the agency providing the creative work. Other service organizations concentrate on different specialist areas of promotion.

'MERGER MANIA'

The world of marketing communications has always been fast-changing, but in recent years has become increasingly turbulent. Many consultants, to broaden their portfolio of client services, have taken over others as well as setting up specialist subsidiaries.

Some larger firms have become conglomerates of autonomous companies and, as well as operating on a full service basis, also offer a 'cafeteria' or 'a la carte' service, through which clients select whichever services they wish.

PROFESSIONAL AND OTHER ORGANIZATIONS

A number of useful reference sources and organizations can assist in locating suitable external services of high calibre. These include the following.

ASSOCIATION OF BUSINESS ADVERTISING AGENCIES
(15 Theed Street, London SE1 8ST)

The ABAA is a body of specialist agencies which handle industrial or business-to-business accounts as their main activity. Generally they offer full marketing communications support to their clients, ranging from press and television advertising to below-the-line and exhibitions or press relations, either directly or in association with specialists in these fields. The agencies forming ABAA are virtually all dedicated to business advertising: they must derive more than 60 per cent of their income from business campaigns, and be deliberately set up to handle this kind of advertising.

ASSOCIATION OF MEDIA INDEPENDENTS
(34 Grand Avenue, London N10 3BP)

The AMI represents media specialist companies. Members must be recognized by the media organizations, be independent of advertisers and agencies, and satisfy the Association's Council of their professional and financial standing. More than two-thirds of the turnover of the Independent sector is handled by AMI members.

BRITISH RATE & DATA'S ADVERTISER & AGENCY LIST
(Maclean Hunter House, Chalk Lane, Cockfosters Road, Barnet, Herts EN4 0BU)

Published quarterly in January, April, July and October, the BRAD *Advertiser & Agency List* is a source of information on all aspects of advertising and commercial publishing. It provides information about advertising agencies, their clients, brand names and national advertisers, and also includes details of incentive premium and sales promotion companies, market research companies, publishing groups, representatives, and direct mail companies.

DEPARTMENT OF TRADE AND INDUSTRY
(1–19 Victoria Street, London SW1H 0ET)

The DTI has launched an 'Enterprise Initiative' to help small and medium-sized businesses become more efficient. Any independent firm with less than 500 employees can apply for assistance. The Initiative brings together in one package a range of DTI services designed to help solve business problems. In addition to regional grants and funding for research and technology, there are grants for 'Business Development Initiatives', to offset part of the cost of consultancy studies in several areas of operation: these include all aspects of marketing.

The Chartered Institute of Marketing (described on page 28) has been retained by the DTI to handle the management and control of the Marketing Initiative provision within the overall Enterprise Initiative.

The DTI has also published 'Single Market' information packs, in preparation for the removal of frontier restrictions in 1992. These include *An Action Checklist for Business*, a series of factsheets, and information about *Spearhead*, the DTI's single market on-line database. There is also a programme of regional breakfast presentation seminars at some 20 centres throughout the country.

INSTITUTE OF DIRECTORS
(116 Pall Mall, London SW1Y 5ED)

The Institute has published a number of useful booklets, including:

– *The Director's Guide to Choosing and Using an Advertising Agency.*
– *The Director's Guide to Choosing and Using a PR Consultancy.*

INSTITUTE OF PRACTITIONERS IN ADVERTISING
(44 Belgrave Square, London SW1X 8QS)

The IPA is the professional organization representing advertising agencies within the UK, and includes within its activities many of specific business-to-business interest. It has published a series of booklets under the general heading of *'How to Succeed in Industrial Advertising'*, which cover:

1. Getting the most out of the client-agency partnership
2. Getting the most out of the advertising budget
3. Getting the most out of the media spend
4. Industrial advertising and marketing in Europe
5. A plain man's guide to industrial market research

The IPA also has a Business-to-Business Committee, and has conducted a survey of *Business-to-Business Advertising* among its members. The Committee is working to develop closer links with advertisers through the Incorporated Society of British Advertisers (see page 28) and mounted a joint IPA/ISBA Business-to-Business Workshop. Other plans include provision of specialised training opportunities for business-to-business practitioners, open to all IPA agency executives.

MARKETING AND PROMOTION ASSOCIATION
(133 Regency Street, London SW1P 4AG)

This non-profit Association (Limited by Guarantee) offers advice and help to companies and individuals on all matters relating to marketing and the communications industry. Many problems are referred to the Association by the CBI, DTI, Government departments and others.

'PORTFOLIO' SERVICES

There are a number of organizations which maintain, on a commercial basis, portfolios and show reels illustrating consultants' work, records of their range of services and client lists, and can thus assist in locating suitable external services.

PUBLIC RELATIONS CONSULTANTS ASSOCIATION
(Premier House, 10 Greycoat Place, London SW1P 1SB)

The PRCA was formed to encourage and promote the advancement of firms engaged in public relations consultancy. It maintains a close fraternal relationship with the Institute of Public Relations (described on page 175).

The Association has a regular programme of activities, issues publications, carries out research into consultancy practice and usage, informs and assists its members and generally promotes the use of public relations consultants to outside organizations.

The PRCA has published a booklet entitled *'Selecting and employing a Public Relations Consultancy'*.

Of particular interest is the Association's Industry and Technology Group which includes more than 25 top consultancies specialising in business-to-business PR. The Group acts as a focal point for companies wishing to find out more about the benefits of industrial and technical public relations, as well as working to maintain high standards among its member consultancies.

The Group has published a *'Business-to-Business is our Business'* dossier giving details of member consultancies' backgrounds, clients and achievements in more than 60 sectors of industry and technology. Separate sheets devoted to each member firm contain a datafile description of the business, its experience, client list, and some case histories. All members provide further information and copies of their promotional literature, on request.

PUBLIC RELATIONS YEAR BOOK
(Marketing Department, Financial Times Business Information, 7th Floor, 50–64 Broadway, London SW1H 0DB)

This Year Book, published by the *Financial Times* in association with the Public Relations Consultants Association (see page 45) is a listing and profiling of some 170 consultancies in the UK and overseas. It also contains a number of topical articles including '*How to choose a consultancy*'. A *Who's Who in Public Relations* section provides biographies of more than 500 top PRCA members and the Client Index indicates the current consultancies retained by leading companies. There are numerous other helpful reference sections.

CHAPTER FIVE

The Role of the Media-Owners

This chapter examines the owners of *existing* media available for marketing communications, through both advertising and editorial columns. Individual media (both existing and created) are examined later, but this chapter first examines existing media as business operations.

THE FINANCIAL CIRCLE

Most media-owners sell two products: one consumer and the other business-to-business. Newspaper and magazine publishers, for example, sell copies to their readers, and advertising space to agencies and their clients. In some instances, industrial and technical journals for example, both products are business-to-business. Whether or not the publication appeals to consumer or business markets, both products are financially linked. If a press medium is of editorial quality which attracts high readership, the owner receives considerable cover revenue, and can also sell space to advertisers wishing to reach that audience. High cover and high advertisement revenue permit the media-owner to produce a high-quality medium and promote it effectively: this increases readership even further, and so completes the financial circle – in this case an upward spiral. When increased advertisement revenue makes possible lower cover price and/or more pages of editorial, thus increasing sales even further, the financial circle recommences.

Conversely a poor quality medium attracts few readers. Without a worthwhile audience, the media-owner finds it difficult to sell advertising space, which results in poor advertisement revenue as well as poor cover revenue. In consequence, the media-owner has insufficient funds to produce a medium which consumers wish to buy, and no funds to promote it to them. In this case the financial link is a vicious circle, with a downward spiral.

There are of course external factors, such as the state of advertisers' markets and the relative editorial appeal and advertising efficiency of other media, but the internal financial circle directly affects any media-owner's business operation.

THE MEDIA-OWNER'S STRUCTURE

Just as a clear appreciation of how external services operate helps the client work in partnership to best effect, it is equally important to understand the day-to-day operations of the media, to use their editorial or advertising columns to best advantage. All media-owners differ in individual structure, but it is nevertheless possible to outline a basic format around which individual media-owners make variations suited to their particular circumstances.

This review of media-owners' various departments, and the interrelationship of their activities, is mainly in terms of the press, since this is the medium most business firms are likely to use for both advertising and public relations, and is also the largest in terms of advertisement revenue. The principles hold for other media, however, where the financial circle is equally applicable.

EDITORIAL

Magazines and newspapers are read for their editorial and television is watched largely for entertainment or information, and it is the Editor's skill in interpreting and satisfying target audience interests on which the size and composition of the media audience depends. This in turn influences the possibilities for using editorial and advertising columns as effective means of marketing communication.

Editorial frequently sub-divides into special sections appealing to particular groups within the overall media audience. Many newspapers and periodicals, for example, have special financial or management pages, while on television and radio there are similar specialist programmes. Some special sections appear regularly (whether daily, weekly or monthly) while others appear only on special occasions.

Features are sometimes published as special supplements and, whilst many are valuable, a word of warning is also necessary. Some less experienced manufacturers, persuaded to advertise in 'special issues', discovered later there was minimal editorial content and the so-called supplement in fact contained only advertisements! Needless to say, readers pay little attention to such 'supplements', and advertisers receive poor value for money. A few publishers even directly horse-trade editorial coverage in return for advertising income – this is a very different matter to well-prepared feature articles, possibly with advertising support, resulting from public relations activity. Reputable publishers produce many excellent supplements, however – well-written and well-promoted, so that sales actually increase, many additional readers buying the publication expressly for the special supplements. Such features often have a long life, being kept for reference.

The Incorporated Society of British Advertisers, described on page 132, has published a *Guide to Press Supplements & The Advertiser*.

It is important – for both advertising and public relations purposes – to acquire an in-depth knowledge of each medium's editorial make-up. Unless the Promotion Manager (or his consultants) knows which features appear on which days, how can he decide where and when to place advertisements, or whether a publication merits inclusion on the News Releases circulation list and, if so, when to send it?

To undertake effective public relations, the Promotion Manager must know the name not only of the Editor but also of individual journalists, together with their specialist areas. He must also know when their various features go to press – how else can he ensure news releases arrive on the right desk at the right time?

Journalists are busy people working against deadlines, with better things to do than waste their time attending unnecessary press conferences or ploughing through piles of badly written news releases in the hope of finding something of interest. They do, however, welcome genuine news items, or even feature articles, and (Chapter 16) gives practical guidance on how best to give journalists the information they need.

Editorial is not always the justification for a medium, however. Outdoor advertising, for example, has no editorial content and exists solely as a promotional medium. Advertising also serves as editorial with some media: the 'editorial' of an exhibition is of course the advertisers' stands. Advertising serves the media audience just as much as it serves advertisers and media-owners: exhibitions provide a clear example of this but the principle applies equally to other media.

PRODUCTION

Editorial, together with relevant illustrations, must be converted to actual copies, and readership depends not only on editorial being of interest but also on the standard of printing.

It is important to keep up-to-date with developments in printing technology, since these changes directly affect the speed and efficiency with which promotional messages are delivered to target markets. These changes are important for both advertising and public relations reasons – as copy handling periods become shorter, there are new opportunities for urgent advertisements or news releases. Technological changes also permit regional editions of national media, which in turn present new public relations and advertising opportunities. New printing methods also call for different types of news photographs and advertising material.

Television and radio programmes must similarly be produced and transmitted. Outdoor advertising sites must be constructed and the posters themselves pasted up. For some media, such as direct mail and exhibitions, production constitutes the main part of the medium. Technological changes are equally relevant to these and other media.

CIRCULATION

Successful publishing demands more than writing and printing alone, for printed copies are valueless until delivered to actual readers. This is the circulation task, and the sheer physical work involved is considerable. Printed copies flowing from the press must be bundled and addressed, and special transport frequently arranged: fleets of delivery vans, special trains and even aircraft.

Copies must be distributed to wholesalers and newsagents, and the Circulation Manager's aim is to ensure his publication is well displayed and available in sufficient quantities. In this respect, the role of circulation representatives parallels that of most salesmen selling to retailers.

In addition to the routine distribution operation, complex enough as that is, the Circulation Department may make special arrangements for extra sales at important events or exhibitions.

Technological change is having its effect here also. It is now unnecessary to print in one location and then physically transport heavy bulk supplies to other parts of the country. New technology means that material written and typeset in one location can be printed at another (perhaps where there is spare printing capacity), thus speeding the circulation process at the same time as cutting distribution costs.

With some media, on the other hand, there is no circulation by way of a separate physical activity. With direct mail, for example, circulation is really an extension of production, while with exhibitions it is the audience which comes to the medium rather than *vice versa*. Television and radio programmes are transmitted, rather than physically transported.

To increase audience numbers, many media-owners establish promotion departments. Circulation, subscriptions and promotion may operate as separate departments, or may be joined to provide overall publishing services.

SUBSCRIPTIONS AND CONTROLLED CIRCULATION

Some publications, particularly magazines, post copies direct to readers (who may be either private individuals or business-to-business libraries and companies) on a subscription basis, as well as distributing through newsagents. Subscription circulation is important for two reasons: first as a source of revenue, and secondly because it implies regular readership, which is of great interest to potential advertisers. Subscription analysis, as a form of research, can provide valuable information about the numbers, location and types of readers.

With controlled circulation magazines, where copies are posted (free of charge) to named individuals in defined categories, this research aspect outweighs the subscription revenue forgone. Controlled circulation publishers rely on the assurances they can give about circulation and thus readership to bring an advertisement income which more than compensates for lost subscription revenue, and in this respect readership data is all important.

The same considerations apply to specialist journals received by members of professional bodies, in return for their membership subscription.

Such research is increasingly sophisticated as the relevant databases are computerised.

PROMOTION

The Promotion Department plays a key role with both subscription copies and those sold through newsagents. Other media without the equivalent of circulation or subscription departments rely equally on effective promotion. The size of television and radio audiences depends not only on the production and transmission of programmes but equally on their promotion, as does the number of visitors attending an exhibition. The Promotion Department may also sponsor special events, or mount competitions and awards schemes, as part of the medium's overall promotion programme.

Any media-owner planning promotional activities is a manufacturer in his own right, with merchandise to sell, who must plan his campaigns with as much care as other producers. The media-owner may well have an Advertising Manager (responsible for promoting the medium) in addition to an Advertisement Manager (responsible for advertising revenue).

The Advertising (or Promotion) Manager may plan a number of parallel campaigns. One will be aimed at target audiences, persuading them to buy a publication, attend an exhibition, or watch or listen to a TV or radio programme. Other campaigns may be business-to-business: just as consumer manufacturers have a second campaign aimed at retailers and wholesalers, so media-owners mount campaigns to wholesale and retail newsagents, persuading them to stock and display their publications.

Media-owners differ from other suppliers in needing a third campaign (again business-to-business) to potential advertisers and their agencies, to obtain advertisement revenue. Most media-owners back up the efforts of their media representatives with considerable promotional activity, including direct mail shots, trade press advertisements, and sales aids for media representatives to use in their presentations.

The Promotion Department will also publicise the work of ancillary services such as research, or merchandising.

RESEARCH

A great deal of advertising research is undertaken centrally, through the industry-wide databases. These sources provide valuable information about reading (or viewing or listening) habits, readily available to all, and serve as an important tool in media selection. This information can be equally valuable to PR practitioners, but its public relations relevance is sometimes not fully appreciated.

Given the existence of central databases, why should a media-owner undertake further research? Quite simply, to provide additional information not contained in the central research, which might persuade advertisers and agencies to view his medium more favourably.

Much media-owners' research is at one of two levels. The first provides information about the medium's coverage of a given market. Research at the second level provides data about the market covered. This persuades manufacturers to mount a campaign in that market, when the media-owner then uses his first-level research to ensure he gets his share of advertising expenditure.

Media-owners' readership and market surveys provide much valuable information, and the Research Department's objective is to provide additional data which assists promotional planning. This information is often obtained by media-owners subscribing to the many research services available, or perhaps by commissioning special computer runs of the central surveys to provide additional tabulations not available in the surveys' standard formats.

An increasing number of rival media-owners, rather than fight each other for shares of a static market, now work alongside immediate competitors to provide co-operative research data about their medium overall, and its advantages over other media. Developments of this kind include research into the business press, direct mail, exhibitions, general magazines, regional press, cinema and video, posters and radio.

This additional research data equally assists media representatives in their selling task. Their need for market information has led to some research departments serving a different function, providing a support service for the Advertisement Department. The research task here is to assemble practical data that advertisement representatives can use in their contacts with advertisers and agencies. Where research serves this internal role of helping secure additional business, the department may be titled 'Sales Research', 'Marketing Services' or 'Business Development' and operate independently of the Research Department, which devotes itself to media research.

MARKETING AND MERCHANDISING

A media-owner's marketing survey is sometimes linked with information about merchandising services provided to assist advertisers in ensuring successful campaigns. This marketing and merchandising manual thus includes details of conference facilities, reader reply cards, reprints, trade mailings and many other services which, when criteria for media comparison are reviewed in Part 3, are grouped under the generic title of 'Facilities'.

THE ADVERTISEMENT DEPARTMENT

This department's objective is to maximise advertisement revenue. For television, radio or posters, or other media with no sales or subscriptions income, advertising is the main revenue source on which the media depends for existence – although sales of editorial or programme material to other media-owners may bring additional income. Even when a medium is not wholly dependent on advertisement revenue (a publication sent to association members in return for their subscriptions, for example) this income is still important in that it finances larger and better printed issues. Better value for money applies equally to publications sold in the normal way, as advertisement revenue may facilitate both lower cover price and thicker issues.

The executive responsible for sales of advertising space (or time) is usually titled the Advertisement Manager or Director (as distinct from the Advertising Manager, whose task is to buy advertising). Before starting the sales operation, the Advertisement Manager – and his representatives – must ascertain just what is available to sell. For press media, the Advertisement Manager agrees with the Editor the amount of advertising space he can sell, and negotiates precise sizes and positions. The rates at which these advertisement spaces and positions will be sold must also be decided.

This exercise, often undertaken on an issue-by-issue basis, is no one-way process of the Editor simply telling the Advertisement Manager what is available. The level of financial support achieved by advertisement sales directly affects the number of editorial pages that can be included and thus the issue size. With other media, a similar process applies: exhibition organizers must know the total space available within the exhibition area, and the size of individual stands, while television and radio representatives must know the amount of advertising airtime and the positioning of commercial breaks. Once advertising availability is known, the Advertisement Manager can set about achieving sales.

THE ADVERTISEMENT MANAGER AS A DEPARTMENTAL HEAD

The Advertisement Manager is section head just as much as the Editor, Production or Circulation Manager, or a manufacturer's Promotion Manager.

Accordingly he must estimate the number and frequency of sales calls to be made: this directly influences the number of representatives required. The level at which contact must be made is also important, since some selling tasks call for representatives with special experience and skill.

DIVISION OF WORK

The Advertisement Manager must compile and analyse a list of potential advertisers and – when appropriate – their agencies. The next task is to provide each representative with a call list. Dividing the total list can be done in various ways, and the Advertisement Manager must decide the most appropriate for his medium: perhaps a straightforward sharing basis, each representative being responsible for a number of advertisers and agencies. Alternatively, calls may be allocated by advertising category, some representatives handling classified advertising, for example, and others display. There may be further sub-division within each category, one representative specialising in, say, financial or information technology advertising. Again, calls may be split by area, with sales staff being responsible for all advertising within defined territories. Should there be insufficient work to justify a full-time representative in a given area, the Advertisement Manager may arrange for representatives to make field trips from time to time. A final point is that some media-owners prefer to contract out of advertisement selling altogether, and appoint specialist contractors to sell on their behalf. These various methods of dividing the advertisement sales task are not mutually exclusive, but frequently overlap.

The Advertisement Manager must also prepare in good time to meet possible future expansion: he must consider the future work-load, and recruit accordingly. A new representative, however experienced, will still need training to acquaint him fully with the new medium he is selling.

STAFF TRAINING

Advertisement representatives differ markedly from ordinary salesmen. Most salesmen can hand a sample to potential customers for their inspection, and promise that the delivered goods will be identical. When selling an advertising medium this is not possible, for the representative has nothing tangible to hand to the buyer. He can perhaps show a specimen copy, but this is only a single copy of an issue already published, whereas advertisers buy space not in a single copy but in thousands or even millions of a future issue with entirely new editorial matter. The only use of a specimen copy is to show the format of the publication. And for some media, such as television, posters or exhibitions, it is not even possible to show a specimen copy.

What the advertisement representative is really selling is a *means of communication* rather than something that can be picked up and handled like a piece of merchandise – communication with a number of people, of a certain type, in a particular atmosphere or mood, at a certain cost, by a specific means, at some stated time in the future. The representative may be aided by readership or viewing statistics, but these are based on what has happened in the past. Advertisers book future space or time, judging what they will get on the basis of previous performance. The advertisement representative must sell the intangible factors of a means of communication.

Staff training is an important but controversial area since the calibre of representatives employed by certain media has been the subject of considerable criticism – some media-owners are equally critical of client and agency staff! If a representative is to assist advertisers and agencies in making maximum effective use of his medium (rather than simply selling space in it), he requires a wide-ranging knowledge which reflects the tasks of both advertiser and agency, described in Part 4. A good media representative merits his title – he represents a valuable source of information about the industry his publication serves and to which advertisers are selling. His expertise – and therefore the training required – should cover:

- *The product* – representatives must be fully acquainted with the physical means by which the medium delivers advertisers' messages, mechanical production data regarding the advertisement material required and copy dates, together with details of advertisement sizes, positions and rates;
- *Editorial policy* – although the publication's physical format remains the same, editorial content changes with each issue. This presents opportunities for selling special positions to existing advertisers, or for attracting new advertisers previously not interested. Representatives must be fully conversant with overall editorial policy and all future features: in this respect, training is never-ending;
- *Media audience* – one of the first tasks of both advertiser and agency is to define their target market and, in evaluating media, make a straight cross-check – what market groups will the medium deliver, and in what numbers? Representatives must therefore be ready to provide readership or viewership statistics, and other research information, about the audience the medium can deliver;
- *Potential advertisers* – like all others selling business products, media representatives must be 'two-businesses people' and knowledgeable about their clients' businesses as well as their own. Representatives must appreciate the promotional problems of those on whom they are to call. What is their campaign objective? Which groups constitute their target market (and what coverage of these groups does the medium offer)? What promotional campaigns do they mount already? If media representatives are to be of service – and thus obtain the orders they seek – they must fully understand their clients' objectives. Company executives (and their consultants) have an important complementary role to play here – full discussions with media representatives can be effective in helping them ensure their medium makes maximum contribution to achieving the advertiser's objectives. Even when all planning and buying is handled by the agency, many promotion managers find it productive to maintain direct contact with the media;
- *Competition* – representatives sell against rivals, so a clear understanding of competitive media is important. Representatives should appreciate the drawbacks (and merits) of indirect as well as direct competition: specialist publications, for example, compete not only with rival journals but also with direct mail and exhibitions;
- *Media selection and planning* – media representatives who understand the criteria by which media are evaluated, and the principles on which schedules

are planned, can help ensure their particular medium makes its maximum possible contribution to achieving advertisers' objectives;
- *Creative skills and constraints* – where advertisers are inexperienced, representatives may have to create and produce advertisements for their use, for without this help they could not buy space in the medium. This aspect of the representatives' work is discussed below, as are the legal and voluntary constraints affecting creative content;
- *Selling techniques* – while salesmanship is important, it must be based on sound knowledge and reasoning. A few media representatives mistakenly believe that glib sales talk (or unnecessary offers of entertainment) can compensate for lack of basic reasons for buying space in the medium.

SUPERVISION AND CONTROL

The Advertisement Manager must keep himself informed of his representatives' progress. Some media representatives, like their colleagues on the client side, submit regular call reports, so the Advertisement Manager knows the current position regarding orders received or pending, and can maintain up-to-date records.

THE DIRECTION OF SELLING

Selling advertising space is a business-to-business operation, so analysis of the prospects' decision-making process is as important for the media-owner as it is for any business organization. Much depends on the relative dominance of client and agency. In some cases the agency is the dominant partner, with the client playing a passive role in briefing the agency on the problem, and checking and approving their proposals. With some companies, however, particularly those with strong marketing orientation, the client adopts the more dominant role.

The Advertisement Manager and his representatives must accordingly decide whether their sales efforts should be directed to the advertiser or to his agency or to both, and which individuals in these organizations to contact. The detailed structures of the advertiser and his agency and their inter-relationship, described in previous chapters, are significant in this respect.

The executives concerned influence the sales approach as well as the direction of media selling. When called on an advertiser direct, for example, much depends on his specialist expertise (or any weaknesses in his knowledge). Any Promotion Manager should have an all-round understanding of marketing communications, but will clearly be more expert on some aspects than others, and his questioning will reflect his special promotional interests. A company executive with a technical background, who handles marketing communications alongside other responsibilities, will have a different viewpoint to one whose background is purely advertising or public relations. The former could welcome general guidance from an experienced media representative. If the latter, one who trained originally as a copywriter or visualiser will be influenced by the medium's creative possibilities, while one with a research or media background will make a more statistical evaluation. A Promotion Manager experienced in public relations will make yet a different assessment. The media representative's approach must vary accordingly, and for this reason a thorough personal knowledge of prospects is essential. The same is true when calling on an agency account executive.

In many cases, clients ask media representatives to contact the advertising agency: some then meet the problem of deciding *who* to sell to – Account Executives, Directors, Supervisors or Planners; or Media Assessors, Buyers, Directors, Group Heads, Planners, Researchers or the other titles found in agencies. Many media-owners therefore maintain central records to draw up a 'structure chart' for client/agency relationships. The record shows which people influence media decisions, and lists the names of the Promotion Manager, Account Executive, Media Planners or Buyers and so on. More important, 'weights' are allocated to each (just as media planners often assess media) according to the relative influence each has on media decisions. Where several representatives call on the same agency, the Advertisement Manager may construct an overall organizational chart based on the combined views of all the representatives concerned. This practice parallels the selling operations of many business suppliers, and reflects yet again that purchase of advertising space is a business-to-business decision.

CONFIRMING THE ORDERS

Media-owners maintain some form of 'Space Register' showing the amount of advertising space sold and still available in future issues, sub-divided into run-of-paper (which might appear anywhere in the publication) and special positions.

Immediately an order is received it is carefully checked for accuracy of vital facts (such as size, position, costs, discounts etc), and to ensure it is duly signed and correct in every way. The Register is then checked to see if the space requested is still available. For run-of-paper insertions, this is a straightforward check that total bookings do not exceed the space available. Checking special positions is more complex, however: such positions can be sold only once, and ill-will would arise if the same space were promised to two advertisers.

The Space Register often functions even before an order is received, for its accuracy may determine whether or not the order is obtained. Many media representatives check the Register during telephone sales and make immediate bookings based on the information given: such data must be literally up-to-the-minute.

Publishers maintain Space Registers, and owners of other media have similar systems. Exhibition organizers keep records of stand space sold and available, while television and radio contractors have a 'Time Register' showing the booking position for commercial breaks. Poster contractors know when each site will become available, and for how long a period.

Once the order has been checked against the Register, an appropriate entry is made and the order duly acknowledged. This could be either by returning a tear-off slip incorporated in the order, or by sending the media-owner's own acknowledgment form. Two steps then follow: production staff must obtain the necessary material, and the Advertisement Department decide the most suitable make-up and where best to place each advertisement.

PRODUCTION AND CREATIVE SERVICES

As soon as an advertiser's material is received, the prudent media-owner checks it without delay: should the material be at fault, prompt notification enables the client or agency to rectify the mistake.

Even when a complete advertisement is provided, its appearance in the medium still involves production work. A press advertisement, for example, must be inserted in the appropriate position and correctly printed. Other media involve similar straightforward production work.

Frequently, however, less experienced advertisers require additional services. When only typed or even hand-written text is supplied, the media-owner must lay out and typeset this material, for without such production services it would not be possible to carry the advertisement. Facilities for inexperienced advertisers often extend to special media staff who prepare copy and design proposals for advertisers' use. Alternatively representatives themselves may prepare creative suggestions.

Other media equally provide creative and production services. Direct mail houses offer creative advice to those using their medium, while many television and radio contractors quote all-inclusive rates for special 'budget' commercials, and the same facility applies to cinema advertising.

Some media-owners provide such creative services to safeguard their own interests because of advertisers who ignore their medium's creative possibilities and, in extreme cases, produce advertisements that are actually *negative* in effect. Such media-owners therefore adopt the more positive attitude of ensuring that their advertisers mount effective campaigns and they no longer take the passive role of providing help only when asked. This action is, of course, self-defence since if advertisements do not bring results the media-owner will not get repeat orders.

PREPARING THE MAKE-UP

The make-up problem does not arise where advertisements have been booked for special positions, as their location within the publication is determined by the booking. Many advertisements, on the other hand, are run-of-paper bookings, whereby the Advertisement Department is left to place them in the most suitable position. This is a service the advertiser expects, but such action is also in the department's own interest for a well-placed advertisement will achieve a better response, thus increasing the likelihood of a repeat order. Clearly an advertisement for office accommodation is better placed on the property page and financial services on the financial page, than *vice versa*. Such obvious cases speak for themselves but placing advertisements in position is usually more difficult, particularly when the Advertisement Department tries to satisfy all the competing calls for front half of publication, right-hand page, outside edge, top of column, and similar requests. Once the detailed make-up is decided, however, the media-owner then proceeds to the next stage.

FINAL PROOFS

Production staff tackle two separate tasks simultaneously – editorial and advertising. The Advertisement Department's make-up serves as production's guide in placing advertisements in position next to the most favourable editorial. Further proofs are produced, but for internal use only, to ensure all is in order and no mistake has slipped through the previous careful checks. The make-up sheets may show, for example, a 25 cm × 2 columns advertisement appearing on a given page, which editorial staff have designed allowing only for 20 cm × 2 columns. Or perhaps, through a production slip, material of the wrong column width was sent in error which, through an equally unfortunate mistake, was not noticed on receipt. Again, page proofs may reveal two coupon advertisements placed back to back: neither advertiser could receive maximum results and the Advertisement Department would have to give both advertisers a rebate, thereby losing valuable revenue.

Page proofs may also reveal other unfortunate positioning to be corrected: a computer system advertisement may have been placed on the computing page but, if the lead story features details of a major systems failure, the Promotion Manager would rightly be distressed to find his advertisement adjacent to editorial that must inevitably reduce reader response. Such calamities are rare, but the possibilities nevertheless exist: hence the rule for the media-owner – just as much as for the advertiser and agency – is meticulous checking and double-checking to avoid any possible errors. All going well, however, publication can proceed with no last-minute changes.

PUBLICATION

Copies of magazines and newspapers must be printed and physically distributed to newsagents or subscribers, television and radio programmes and commercials transmitted, and cinema films screened. Although the Advertisement Department is not directly involved, its activities nevertheless depend on successful completion of this vital stage: actual communication of advertising messages to the media audience.

INVOICING AND VOUCHER COPIES

Immediately the issue is published, the Advertisement Department must pass to accounts staff all the information necessary to invoice advertisers (or their agencies) correctly. The invoicing section must ensure all advertisements are charged at the correct rate for each appearance. An efficient Accounts Department avoids loss of advertisement revenue through failure to invoice, and directly affects speed of payment. Invoice queries can cause ill-will with advertisers and agencies and also hold up payment which, in turn, can cost money in bank charges.

Equally important is a smoothly operating voucher service, for the advertiser (or agency) will want to check that their advertising appeared as booked, before settling the account. With media not able to provide a voucher copy (or physical proof of appearance such as a tear sheet), the media-owner may send a 'Certificate of Transmission' (or of posting) or some other assurance. Failure to send the necessary voucher or documentation delays payment until this omission is rectified.

FOLLOW-UP

Even after each advertisement has been invoiced, the operation is not yet complete, for follow-up is essential. The representatives who obtained each order should check the advertisements with as much care as the advertisers and their agencies devote to them. Did the advertisements print well? Did the exhibitor have an attractive stand? What ratings did the TV commercials receive? Evaluation of results is a major consideration for both advertiser and agency, and media representatives must be equally concerned with those advertisements which have just appeared. This also provides the ideal opportunity to seek repeat orders.

THE NEW ISSUE

Every new issue presents opportunities to follow up previous advertising and affords scope for new sales, which means the Advertisement Department's operation has now returned to the point at which it started.

PART 3

The Tools of Marketing Communications

Part 3A: Marketing Communications Media
Part 3B: Existing Media – The Advertising Route
Part 3C: Existing Media – The Editorial Route
Part 3D: Created Media

Part 3A: Marketing Communications Media

CHAPTER SIX

The Range of Media, and Criteria for Comparison

Part 3 examines in detail the numerous marketing communications media outlined in the earlier overview. Before so doing, it is relevant to establish some order of importance, and to compare and contrast expenditure figures.

ISBA, the Incorporated Society of British Advertisers (see page 28), gives the following percentage share figures for advertising expenditure in 1986:

TV		29.0
Regional Press		20.0
National Press		15.0
Direct Mail		8.3
Exhibitions*		
General	4.5	
Agricultural Shows	1.9	
Private Exhibitions	1.1	7.5
Business Press		6.5
Magazines & Periodicals		5.0
Directories		4.7
Posters & Transport		3.4
Radio		1.6
Cinema		—

*For those particularly interested in this marketing communications medium, ISBA undertakes an *Annual Exhibition Expenditure Survey*, details of which are on page 132.

Business marketing communication differs markedly from that undertaken for consumer products or services, however, and a 1987 survey of expenditure on business-to-business media by British Business Press (see page 104) shows a very different picture. The BBP research '*Better Business Advertising to the Boardroom*' gives the following percentage figures:

Business Press	34.5	
Brochures, catalogues	14.4	
Exhibitions	14.1	63.0
Direct Mail	8.1	
Public Relations	6.0	
Directories	5.5	
Regional Newspapers	2.9	
National Newspapers	2.8	25.3

Videos/AV	2.8	
Premiums	2.1	
Point-of-Sale	1.5	
Posters	1.4	
TV	1.2	
Sponsorship	1.0	
Radio	0.5	
Others	1.2	11.7

Another source gives the following broad breakdowns for promotional expenditure on business-to-business media:

Media (mainly press) Advertising	40.0
Sales Literature	27.0
Exhibitions	15.0
Direct Mail	9.0
Public Relations	9.0

The figures cannot be directly compared, however, as — quite apart from different classifications and survey periods — the range of media covered differs: the ISBA figures, based on Advertising Association statistics, are understandably restricted to *Advertising* (defined as paid-for media) whereas the BBP survey covers media which, although they call for expenditure, involve no contractual obligation with a media-owner: these include videos/AV, brochures and catalogues, premiums, point-of-sale, public relations and sponsorship.

All three sources exclude the cost of the sales force — this, as already established, is a powerful marketing communications medium, quite apart from its selling function. Also excluded are telephone selling and the other three P's — Product, Price and Place.

The purpose of this review is not to argue which percentage shares are right, but only to prove the point that marketing communication for business purposes *does* differ from that undertaken for consumer products and services. All these means of communication are examined in detail in the chapters following, under the following broad headings:

Part 3B: Existing Media — the Advertising Route
Part 3C: Existing Media — the Editorial Route
Part 3D: Created Media

As regards created media, if existing media do not fully meet an organization's marketing communications needs, the Promotion Manager may have to create his own.

Before examining these media, however, it is necessary to establish criteria for comparing them.

MEDIA EVALUATION – CRITERIA FOR COMPARISON

There are various criteria by which promotional media can be evaluated to select those most suitable. Chapter 25 reviews criteria for evaluating complete campaign proposals, but this chapter first analyses how to compare individual media.

A first essential is to distinguish *quantitative* from *qualitative* criteria. Quantitative data refer to *numbers* of copies sold or read or viewers reached, while qualitative criteria reflect *opinions* about the relative value of editorial rather than advertising columns; of interactive rather than one-way communication; of product demonstration; or of high quality colour reproduction.

The qualitative/quantitative distinction is essentially a simple one, but much media research how attempts to quantify qualitative aspects through '*U & A*' studies, which measure Usage and Attitudes. Some research surveys described later quantify readers' usage of publications, and whether they read every issue, read regularly, and read half or more. Attitudinal questions quantify readers' opinions of media as, for example, best source of new ideas, best reports of the market, easily readable specialist information, best editorial coverage of the industry, and usefulness of advertising.

The various quantitative and qualitative criteria vary in importance according to each firm's marketing objectives, and so the following review is not in any universally correct order of priority.

QUALITATIVE CRITERIA

THE MEDIUM

This criterion concerns the means by which a given medium delivers promotional messages – do people read it (if so, in black and white or colour?), watch it or listen to it? Equally, what is the *quality* of delivery – not all press media, for example, offer high quality printing or good colour reproduction.

Does the medium permit a detailed message, can it demonstrate a product, and to what degree is it interactive? Press media offer one-way communication of detailed messages, while television and cinema both permit product demonstration but not detailed messages; neither can however match the exhibition medium for two-way communication which enables prospects to try products for themselves and put questions to sales representatives who, in their turn, make personal contact with customers. Direct mail gives no personal contact but can 'demonstrate' by distributing samples, together with detailed product specifications. Some media facilitate customer action: direct mail can also include reply-cards to stimulate response, thus paving the way for calls by sales representatives, while merchandising and sales promotion can encourage response by offers of tangible incentives.

A detailed study of the actual means by which media deliver messages is therefore vital. Equally important is keeping this knowledge up-to-date, in the light of changing media technology.

ENVIRONMENT

Editorial policy reflects readers' interests, so any Promotion Manager should check previous issues to see the frequency of editorial references to his product area, since this gives a strong indication of whether readers are likely to be in the market for such merchandise.

A medium's editorial can influence mood in another way, through its atmosphere of authority or expertise, with consequent benefit to products featured in both editorial or advertising columns.

The customer's state of mind when receiving promotional messages directly enhances or weakens campaign effectiveness. It is therefore important to distinguish between media where messages are intrusive and those where they are acceptable or, better still, have positive interest value. Messages in editorial columns, resulting from public relations activity, benefit from third party endorsement. Specialist publications give the double benefit of reaching selected readers and delivering promotional messages when these likely purchasers are in a receptive mood, and the same is true of many exhibitions. This principle can be extended to specific positions within a medium: an advertisement on a newspaper's management page selects managers out of the total readership. Furthermore, it delivers the promotional message when they are mentally 'tuned in' to the subject of management and thus likely to be responsive to advertisements featuring management products or services.

When evaluating media, many executives mistakenly think in terms of their promotional activities, rather than concentrating on potential buyers. Rather than ask 'What will the promotional message do to people?' emphasis should shift to 'What will people do to the message?'. The answer to this question depends not only on campaign creativity but equally on potential buyers' states of mind when they receive the promotional message – a medium which delivers its message to the target market when they are likely to respond favourably will be highly effective. Hence the importance of U & A studies of reader attitudes to both editorial and advertising.

This benefit (and a possible obstacle) are best illustrated by those directories the nature of which means those consulting them are potential customers in the market *now* and thus ready to buy – why else should they be consulting the directory? Such media often present golden opportunities which are, alas, wasted. Those placing advertisements have presumably never *studied* copies of the actual publications which, in consequence, contain innumerable look-alike 'visiting card' advertisements: nobody has responded to the creative challenge of overcoming the obstacles of noise and clutter to attract target market attention.

ATTENTION

The attention factor must be considered from two standpoints: the duration of the promotional message and the time for which it will receive attention.

Some media permit messages with only a very brief existence: a newscaster reference or radio or TV commercial, for example, cannot receive more attention than its duration and, once transmitted, prospective purchasers cannot refer back to it (unless, in the case of advertising, the commercial is repeated). Newspaper and magazine editorial and advertisements exist for longer periods, and so can be studied at leisure.

Equally important is the amount of time prospective purchasers devote to the message. Outdoor advertising exists 24 hours a day, but **advertising** messages must usually be kept short since most posters receive only a passing glance. Sites on stations or in buses and trains, where there is a captive audience, may be studied for longer periods.

Both aspects of attention must be considered in their communications context, for brief duration is neither an asset nor drawback until related to how much information must be conveyed. Is the message brief enough for TV or radio or a poster, or must it contain detailed product information?

The balance struck between the time needed to convey the message and the attention span it will receive has direct media implications.

WHEN?

Different media deliver messages at different times. For some companies this is a seasonal consideration, promoting their products in the Summer or Winter. Others need to be more precise and seek to deliver promotional messages on a given day. Some media, such as point-of-sale displays in dealers' showrooms, deliver reminder messages seconds before the possible purchase. This is a straight cross-checking procedure – when is the most effective time for receipt of promotional messages, and when will the various media deliver them?

FREQUENCY

A second aspect of timing concerns repetition: the regularity with which a medium can deliver a promotional message. A news release will be published once at most, so the target market will not see a company's name again until there is further newsworthy information. Most exhibitions permit market stimulus only once a year. Other media, through their advertising columns, offer facilities to give monthly, weekly or even daily reminders, according to their frequency of publication. Buyer behaviour – day or week or month and frequency of purchase – thus directly influence media selection.

SPEED

A third aspect of timing concerns speed of operation rather than when and how often promotional messages are delivered. Some media require advertising or news release material far in advance of publication date. A company wishing to make an urgent announcement would choose the medium with the shortest copy-handling period, in order to deliver the promotional message as swiftly as possible.

Conversely, if future plans are subject to constant change, the company would avoid media with long copy-handling periods since this necessitates deciding message content perhaps months in advance of actual delivery.

A variation of this theme are those advertising media which demand notice of cancellation long in advance of publication date, and thus inhibit flexible planning.

Technological change is again vitally important: copy and press dates are being brought forward, thereby making media more flexible for those already using them, at the same time as presenting new advertising and public relations opportunities to other organizations.

FLEXIBILITY

Speed affects flexibility, but some media are in themselves more flexible than others. The most flexible of all (by both quantitative and qualitative standards) is perhaps direct mail, since this medium's 'tap' can be turned on or off at will as regards both timing and quantity. A manufacturer with a fixed output of, for example, 300 units per month, can seek to achieve this number of sales leads by controlling the flow and number of his direct mail shots, and adjusting his mailings according to response required and received. Direct mail is flexible in other respects, as Chapter 11 makes clear: different messages can be sent to different target groups, and at different times.

COMPLEXITY AND CONVENIENCE

Few things could make life easier than taking the entire budget and allocating it to a few large advertisements in a limited number of media. Contrast this with the complexity of administering campaigns which utilise perhaps dozens of individual media within any one media group. If seeking to reach AB businessmen it is far simpler, for example, to mount a campaign in national media than to reach them through an extensive list of specialist publications. The latter route involves additional work in devising individual messages for each market segment, quite apart from the labour involved in planning and booking the campaign. Production costs also increase – the more complex the schedule, the higher the costs in terms of time, effort and money.

Complexity and convenience considerations – when extended to multi-media campaigns involving national and regional press, direct mail supported by local dealer-based demonstrations and back-up public relations activities, supporting literature and business gifts – mean this matter must necessarily be reconsidered in Chapter 24, which is devoted to overall media planning. Within this chapter, however, it is sufficient to recognize that media choice must necessarily recognize the amount of effort required to service each medium, and may be influenced by ease of use – or even idleness!

LIFE

The life of a medium, and thus the period for which a target market is stimulated, has practical implications. Some media stimulate response within a few days (or even minutes) in one short burst, while others bring customer replies over weeks, months or even years. Television and radio, for example, deliver their full impact at time of transmission, whereas a magazine printed on high quality paper may bring results until it literally falls to pieces. There is thus an important distinction between publications that are read and thrown away, those passed to others (thus providing a 'pass-on' or secondary readership), and those kept for reference.

The practical implications of media life are twofold. One is that the organization should be geared up to respond to market demand throughout the requisite time period. The second concerns evaluation of results, since this should not be completed until after the medium has had full opportunity to deliver its target market response – too swift an evaluation would give a false impression of effectiveness.

INDIRECT INFLUENCE

Some media influence campaign effectiveness through their impact on important groups other than the main media audience. Business firms selling to 'reseller' markets place great emphasis on good distribution and display at point of sale, and any medium that helps achieve this has a marked advantage over others. The most quoted example is television, which influences retailers just as much as the media audience.

Co-operative press advertisements, featuring stockists' names and addresses, can equally influence their activities. An extreme example of such influence concerned a poster site facing an insufficiently enthusiastic dealer's showroom: this was booked for its constant reminder effect on that one individual rather than the passing public!

Promotional activities can equally encourage sales representatives, convincing them that the company is doing everything possible to give effective sales support. Where such considerations apply, this must clearly influence media decisions.

AVAILABILITY

This criterion concerns advertising rather than other forms of communication, and covers three influences on media selection. One links with *how* the medium delivers the advertising message: it concerns creative scope and thus could be asked under either heading. The underlying question is a simple one: what advertisement 'units' or formats – or choice of units – are available for creative proposals? The range of units is extensive and most media-owners are keen to co-operate, so this need be no creative restriction. Furthermore, it is always worth asking media-owners if odd shapes will be accepted.

Secondly, what advertising spaces are actually available? If the best positions are already booked, or if only a limited number of spaces are available, there is little choice but to investigate other media.

A third criterion is determined by the regulations relating to certain media, which might categorize certain products as unacceptable. For example, cigarette advertisements are not accepted on television, but such restraints are unlikely to affect business-to-business advertisers.

CONSTRAINTS

Some media-owners have their own house-rules about the advertising they accept, and impose limits on type size, for instance, or restrict white-on-black advertisements: such restraints clearly effect creative content and are accordingly discussed in Chapter 23.

Creative content is equally affected by the voluntary codes relating to various media, also discussed in Chapter 23.

CONTROL

With what certainty can a medium be relied on to deliver promotional messages? Any company with a vital need to stimulate the market at a stated time will be wary of a medium which may not transmit the message.

Press conferences and news releases, invaluable though they are, cannot guarantee to result in delivery of promotional messages: something of greater news value may squeeze them out. This drawback is not restricted to public relations, however, since some advertising media are less certain than others: the pre-empt system of television bookings, described on page 147, means that (unless an advertiser pays the very top rate for non-pre-emptible fixed spots) his commercial may be pre-empted by another firm willing to pay more money.

Equally important, how reliable is delivery *quality* – in terms of, for example, print quality or colour values? Will the promotional message in fact be delivered correctly? Advertising lacks the credibility of third party endorsement in editorial columns, but the company does control its content: news releases on the other hand, when used by the media, may not be printed in full or may even be edited incorrectly.

COMPETITIVE ACTIVITY

This overall heading covers various comparison criteria. First, it is advisable to check if rivals appear regularly in editorial or advertising columns, on which pages and with what frequency, and the nature of their promotional campaigns.

The second criterion concerns advertising: what general weight is carried? A publication carrying a vast amount of advertising may necessitate booking larger advertisements or special positions, to ensure the message attracts attention. Alternatively, creative means may serve to attract the reader's eye.

Third is the company an advertiser will be keeping: the fact that a medium features (or does *not* carry) well designed advertisements for leading firms, in itself, influences the audience mood.

The need to monitor competitive activity applies equally to other marketing communications media: how can any organization plan sales promotion or merchandising activities, unless the Promotion Manager knows what incentives rivals are offering?

FACILITIES

The range of facilities offered by media is extremely wide, but all can be grouped under the generic heading of what media-owners will do in addition to delivering promotional messages.

Many exhibition contractors, for example, have press offices in which information packs can be placed, to supplement other public relations activity. Some make available mailing lists of visitors in previous years, who can be invited to visit an exhibitor's stand. Many trade and technical magazines include reply-cards, through which readers can request further information about products featured in editorial or advertising columns.

Television contractors offer a wide range of facilities for those selling to the 'reseller' market: one rate-card, selected at random, included direct mail facilities for advertisers to promote their campaigns to distributors, help with production of TV commercials, a merchandiser circulated to the trade giving advance details of major advertising activity on TV, promotional trailers to stimulate viewer action, a retail sales force available to help sell-in to stockists, research facilities, sales conference assistance, supporting press advertisements, together with telephone-answering and reply-handling facilities.

Less ambitious, but nevertheless vitally important, is the assistance given by some newspapers and magazine publishers to inexperienced advertisers in preparing and producing effective press advertisements.

Provision of research information by media, discussed earlier, can extend to special computer runs of published data to provide new tabulations and help with media scheduling.

Some facilities are provided free as part of the media-owner's normal service, whilst for others there may be an 'at cost' charge. Such facilities can make a valuable contribution and should most certainly be used whenever appropriate. The tail should not wag the dog, however: the primary reason for using any promotional medium is to deliver promotional messages and, in evaluating media, the answers to the questions listed above are of greater importance than any secondary facilities. Of equal importance are answers to the quantitative questions following.

QUANTITATIVE CRITERIA

THE MEDIA AUDIENCE'S COMPOSITION

Market investigations, which have a high priority at the research & investigation stage described in Part 4 (Chapter 19), call for a straight cross-check between the target market to be reached and the audience covered by the various media. The closer the approximation, the more effective the medium.

One of the terms used here is *demographics*, commonly defined as a means of analysing both media audience and target markets.

For mass media, markets are usually defined in terms of sex, age and social status. The social grades commonly used are based on the occupation of the head of the household. There are six such grades which, although usually applied to consumer markets, also have business-to-business relevance. The A, B and C1 occupations are described as 'Managerial, administrative or professional', the difference being that of level, and whether they are *Higher* (A grade), *Intermediate* (B grade), or *Supervisory or clerical and junior* (C1).

Actual *users* of business products can influence industrial purchasing decisions, and the C2 and D occupations are thus relevant to media selection. They are defined as manual workers: the difference again being that of level, depending on whether they are *skilled* (C2) or *semi and unskilled* (D).

People in the sixth grade (E) – 'those at the lowest levels of subsistence' – are unlikely to influence business decisions – these include *Casual or lowest grade workers (as well as state pensioners or widows)*. Whilst some demographic categories are not of *direct* concern, they affect the wastage concept discussed later, since messages may be delivered to people the company does not wish to reach (nor to pay for).

Most business-to-business firms are concerned less with social grades and more with the job descriptions of those their promotional messages reach, and the industry in which they are employed. These and other approaches to classifying target markets are discussed in Chapter 19. Whatever the categories, the fundamental question is a basic one: which individuals comprise the target market, and to whom will each medium deliver the promotional message?

THE MEDIA AUDIENCE'S LOCATION

This cross-checking procedure applies equally to geographic location. Media coverage information may be provided in terms of Registrar-General's Standard Regions, or perhaps by television areas. Marketing areas vary, and there should be strong correlation between the company's operational area and that to which any medium delivers the message. For local or regional operators the two areas should coincide closely, while even so-called 'national' media vary in intensity of coverage across the country.

A version of the 'location' question overlaps with 'composition' by asking where individuals live or work. Markets are in consequence classified – to use more precise terminology – 'geodemographically'. ACORN (CACI's *A Classification of Residential Neighbourhoods*) divides where people live into some 39 neighbourhood types (eg, inner city terrace, retirement areas, affluent areas) and is a valuable tool for marketing many products and services, since it shows clear life-style differences between neighbourhoods.

CACI has also developed another geodemographic classification of greater business-to-business relevance, since it analyses who *works* where. Information available from the 'Workforce' classification system includes breakdowns of:

- *Total number of workers* – shown separately for males/females, and full/part-time workers;
- *Numbers working at home*
- *Socio-economic groups* – shown separately for male and female;
- *Industrial classifications* – (as outlined on page 202) showing females and office workers separately;
- *Workers in selected industry groups*
- *Employment in particular industries* – as a proportion of employment in the same industries in the base (comparison) area.

As well as information about workforces in particular areas, CACI can provide analyses of the means by which they travel to work, thus showing the catchment area of any employment location.

THE MEDIA AUDIENCE'S SIZE

In evaluating any media audience it is necessary to know its size as well as composition and location, together with the numbers in each of the various categories. Breakdowns may be required for several classifications simultaneously, to show how many people of a given occupation in a stated industry receive the message within a defined marketing area.

THE RANGE OF MEDIA, AND CRITERIA FOR COMPARISON

There are different levels of answer to this audience size question. With press media, for example, readership as well as circulation figures may be available, but much depends on research methods and definitions. The importance of research methodology is best illustrated by the difference between press readership and television viewing.

When measuring press audiences, the definition of a 'reader' is important, as editorial or advertising contact can be made over a considerable time period. Accordingly, the 'issue period' is a key concept of the National Readership Surveys. Average readership is the number of people who claim to have read or looked at one or more copies of a given publication for at least two minutes, during a period dating back from the date of interviewing equal to the interval at which the publication appears – a daily newspaper thus has an issue period of one day, a weekly publication an issue period of seven days, while a monthly publication's is between 28 and 31 days, and so on.

Television audience measurements, by contrast, are made at the time of viewing, as electronic meters record both sets switched on and individuals viewing, and numbers are quoted in terms of TVR's or Television Rating points. A Homes Television Rating is the percentage of homes tuned to a particular transmission. TVR's may also be expressed in terms of individuals viewing rather than homes with sets switched on, so that one TVR represents one per cent of the potential TV audience. A 'viewer' is defined as someone who is present in the room with a set switched on at the turn of the clock minute, providing presence in the room is for at least 15 consecutive seconds.

The press definition 'read or looked at' covers anything from thorough reading to a casual flip through, and it does not matter which issue – any issue will do. Furthermore, some publications are 'read or looked at' more frequently than others, thus influencing the numbers likely to receive any promotional message. In addition, the figures refer to an *average* copy, whereas actual readership varies with both page and position (hence the vital importance of an in-depth knowledge of each medium's editorial format). The TV definition 'in a room' is equally imprecise: it covers anything from attentive viewing to a casual glance while undertaking some other activity. Finally, any figures are necessarily dated in themselves: some readership surveys, for example, are 6–12 months old before new data is published.

While numerical considerations are important, the research methods which produce these numbers are by no means precise. This statement is not made from a fault-finding standpoint, but simply to set matters in context. Furthermore, as other chapters make clear, some media offer little or no statistical data to analyse. Promotional personnel should therefore welcome rather than be overly critical of such data as is available.

PENETRATION *VS* PROFILE

In assessing the numbers promotional messages reach, a key consideration is the degree of coverage achieved. Penetration quantifies the *proportion* of the total market covered. If a company's target market is AB businessmen, for example, it will wish to know if a certain medium reaches 40 per cent, 50 per cent, or some other proportion of *all* such businessmen.

If the penetration is, for example, 60 per cent, the question then arises – how best to reach the remaining 40 per cent? Chapter 24, tackles this problem and examines the cumulative coverage achieved by a full campaign. Within this chapter, however, the term 'penetration' signifies the proportion of the total market to which any one medium delivers its promotional message.

A medium's 'profile', on the other hand, summarises the categories of people reached. Profiles differ from penetration figures in always adding up to 100 per cent. A simple example which illustrates the difference is specialist press. A special interest publication read by half the target market has a 50 per cent penetration. The magazine's profile, however, should indicate that 100 per cent of its readers are within the defined target group.

In point of fact, the profile might well be 90 per cent target group and 10 per cent wastage (discussed below) since few media, if any, give a perfect market match. Profile information may be provided by numerous different categories: socio-economic groupings, occupations, industries, or geographical location but, whichever sub-groups are detailed, the total profile always adds up to 100 per cent.

A 'trick' question which clearly illustrates the difference between penetration and profile is 'Which newspaper gives the highest coverage of AB businessmen – *The Sun*, or *The Times*?'

The answer is not in fact *The Times*. Whilst *The Sun*'s profile includes only a relatively small percentage of AB businessmen, a small proportion of a very large readership gives a bigger number than a large percentage of a relatively small readership. Those wishing to reach AB businessmen might not consider *The Sun* the ideal medium, however, for various reasons. One might be wastage, discussed below, while others concern qualitative considerations discussed earlier.

WASTAGE

It is unlikely that any medium will give perfect coverage of a target market. Some potential purchasers will not be reached and thus 100 per cent penetration is not achieved. Equally, some of those reached will not be in the target market. Media evaluation therefore calls for eliminative assessment of that proportion of the media audience which constitutes less valuable coverage. Such considerations must clearly influence media choice, and are of relevance for both advertising and public relations purposes. Wastage should not, however, lead to undervaluation of that part of total coverage which *is* within the target group. If this coverage is properly evaluated, then coverage of others can be regarded as a bonus rather than wastage.

COST

The criterion left until last, although an essential consideration in media selection, is cost. Much depends on budget size, for some media call for large expenditures and may thus be out of reach for firms with small appropriations. Cost, although basically a straightforward question, nevertheless presents complex problems.

Of the three main marketing communications channels, advertising in existing media differs from the other two routes – editorial columns and

THE RANGE OF MEDIA, AND CRITERIA FOR COMPARISON

created media. The difference is that advertising costs are readily available on rate-cards.

Public relations activity and created media, on the other hand, are 'at cost' which varies with the job. In other words, instead of working out what he can buy for his money, the Promotion Manager calculates what it costs to buy the promotional effort needed. Needless to say (and as Chapters 22 to 24 on budgeting and planning make clear) there is necessarily some adjustment between what it costs and what can be afforded.

Advertising costings are both easier and more difficult. They are easier in that they can be looked up in the reference sources listed on page 85, but more complex in that they vary in terms of units, sizes, positions, amount of promotion undertaken, and other considerations discussed below.

PROMOTIONAL UNITS

Evaluation is made more difficult by the fact that different promotional media are costed in different units.

Newspapers for example are usually sold in 'scc.' units, by the single column centimetre: one centimetre in one column costs £X and space is sold in multiples thereof. A 20cm × 2 cols. advertisement simply means 20 centimetres in two adjacent columns, or 40 cm (and may be charged at 40 times the unit cost). Similarly a 25 cm × 4 cols. advertisement totals 100 centimetres. Magazines, by way of contrast, are usually sold by the page or fractions thereof: half-page, quarter-page, eighth-page etc, whereas cinema, television and radio advertising is sold by time – 10, 20, 30, 40, 50 or 60 seconds and so on. Outdoor advertising, on the other hand, is sold on a 'sheetage' basis whereby advertisers buy 4, 16, 32 or 48 sheet sites.

Evaluation on a cost basis is further complicated by the fact that media-owners' charges vary with three factors: size, position and amount of advertising booked.

SIZE

A large advertisement may be necessary because there is detailed information to convey, or simply to attract attention. Costs do not necessarily increase *pro rata* with size, however. Some media-owners, seeking to sell big advertisements, offer these larger sizes at a discount rate. Others, faced with heavy demand for these sizes, charge a premium. Marketplace supply and demand thus make media comparison more complex.

POSITION

A higher rate is charged to those wishing to control the position of their advertisements within a publication, rather than rely on the media-owner's discretion. The aim in so doing might be either or both of two objectives – a larger media audience or a selective one. An advertisement on the inside front cover or 'solus' (without competition from others), will achieve a larger audience, while appearance on the management page selects, out of the total media audience, those interested in management.

Some media-owners link size and position in that an advertiser wanting the front page solus, or to appear on the management page, is restricted to an advertisement of specified size. Few newspaper proprietors would, for example, permit any front page solus advertisement to dominate the page, thereby reducing its news appeal to readers.

AMOUNT BOOKED

Those booking a consecutive number of advertisements at one time usually benefit from a substantial discount, since the media-owner incurs less expense if his representatives sell 12 advertisements at one call rather than making 12 calls to achieve the same result. The same principle applies to other media, which offer similar series or volume discounts.

SPECIAL DISCOUNTS

Many media-owners list on their rate-cards a wide range of other discounts. From time to time, however, they make special offers to boost sales in otherwise slack periods: these fall into groups – bonus offers of more advertising at no extra cost, or discount offers of the same amount of advertising at reduced cost.

PACKAGE DISCOUNTS

Most media-owners, seeking to balance supply and demand, offer financial incentives to those advertisers who are flexible in their requirements. Many offer advertising 'packages' at advantageous prices. There are convenient television, cinema and radio packages, for example, and the same applies to other media such as outdoor. Should an advertiser want precise control of when his commercials are to appear, or which sites feature his posters, it would be necessary to book at full price in the normal way.

Many advertisers employ both methods – their promotional planning includes a carefully targetted component, to ensure a minimum number of messages are delivered to the right people in the right place at the right time. This planned component is then backed up by purchase of additional 'bargain packages', which offer good value for money when delivering extra messages.

GUARANTEED DISCOUNT OFFERS

Many package discount offers are linked with the media-owner's guarantee of a minimum size audience. With GHI (or Guaranteed Home Impression) bookings, described on page 147, the television contractor keeps on transmitting the advertiser's commercial until, as revealed by research, it has achieved the guaranteed minimum number of home impressions. Other media offer similar guaranteed discount packages.

COST AND VALUE FOR MONEY

Cost and quantity are frequently evaluated simultaneously, and one medium compared with others, by CPT or 'cost per thousand' calculations – the cost of reaching each thousand of the target audience. CPT is usually expressed in pounds and/or pence, and used as a general measure of media cost and efficiency. Cost per thousand is calculated by dividing, for example, the page rate of a magazine by its circulation in thousands. To illustrate this with simple hypothetical figures, a magazine charging £500 per page and with a circulation of 50,000 thus has a cost of £500/50 = £10 per thousand circulation. Another might charge £750 per page and have 100,000 circulation and here the CPT is £750/100, or only £7.50. The second magazine costs more in outlay – £750 instead of £500 per page – but the circulation is larger, giving better value for money.

Cost per thousand can frequently serve as a precise measure, but this widely-adopted criterion is in many cases used too loosely. 'Cost per thousand' has little meaning until just what it measures is clearly established. Before comparing one medium's CPT with those of its rivals, an essential basic question is – 'Cost of *what* per thousand *what?*' CPT figures for newspapers, for example, are frequently quoted for scc's per thousand circulation – but few (if any) advertisers book advertisements of single column centimetre size. Equally, few firms assess circulation alone: their interest is readership by clearly defined target groups. For this reason, CPT calculations are made specific, based on actual advertisement costs – the cost of a half-page facing specified editorial matter in one publication rather than another. Equally, it is calculated not on circulation figures but readership by selected target groups.

PRODUCTION COSTS

Production costs, as distinct from media-owners' charges, directly affect media planning. The more media included on the schedule, the higher the production charges. With some media, production costs constitute only a small proportion of total costs, while in others they demand major consideration.

In some cases, such as exhibitions, direct mail or display material, production charges are of course inseparable from media costs.

With created media, costs include not only charges for printing leaflets or producing videos, for example, but also the expenses incurred in acquiring audiences for them.

For all media, the need to keep up-to-date with the relevant technology is again apparent, since these changes directly affect production costs.

OVERALL MEDIA COMPARISON

The wide range of comparison criteria mean there is no such thing as the *best* medium. All media have their respective advantages (and drawbacks) and the promotional planning problem is to assess the contribution they can make to achieving marketing objectives. This task is considered in Part 4.

Part 3B: Existing Media – the Advertising Route

7. Advertising – an Overview, and General Databases.

8. Press Media.

9. Specialist Readership Surveys.

10. Exhibitions.

11. Direct Mail.

12. Outdoor Advertising.

13. Television.

14. Radio.

15. Cinema.

CHAPTER SEVEN

Advertising – an Overview and General Databases

As stated earlier, advertising is defined by the Advertising Standards Authority as 'The use of paid-for media space or time as a means of persuading people to take a particular course of action, or to reach a point of view.' In short, this marketing communications medium involves contractual relationships – the media-owner's legal obligation to deliver the promotional message, and the advertiser's obligation to pay him for so doing.

THE ADVANTAGES OF ADVERTISING

Delivering promotional messages through the advertising columns of existing media presents specific benefits when compared with word-of-mouth recommendation, the editorial/public relations route, created media such as merchandising and sales promotion, or the sales force.

DEFINITE DELIVERY

Because of the media-owner's contractual obligation to publish the advertisement, it is certain to appear – contrast this with public relations where, should there be a newsworthy event of greater interest, the promotional message may be squeezed out.

ACCURATE DELIVERY

The advertiser prepares the message content and corrects the proofs, and thus controls the promotional message delivered. Any news release is subject to alteration – the message may not be delivered in full, or may be altered incorrectly. Word-of-mouth recommendation is equally subject to distortion.

SPEED

Circumstances may call for the swiftest possible delivery of a marketing communications message. Depending on media-owners' copy dates, advertising can deliver very rapidly – far faster than most sales journey cycles permit, and swifter than word-of-mouth (which, as already established, is also subject to distortion).

SELECTIVITY AND COVERAGE

Word-of-mouth recommendation spreads indiscriminately – it may miss important target market segments, or reach groups with no interest in the product or service. Advertising, by selection of suitable media, can ensure full market coverage or deliver different messages to different target groups.

TIMING

An advertiser wishing to deliver a promotional message on a particular date can achieve this simply by booking space in appropriate issues. Other media do not permit such direct control of when the target group receives the promotional message. Sales representatives can of course deliver messages on particular days if required – but to only a very limited number of prospects. An advertising campaign, suitably planned, can cover all members of the target market on the very date required.

FREQUENCY

Marketing requirements may call for delivery of promotional messages on a regular basis – reminder advertising can play an invaluable role in keeping a company's name before prospective or existing purchasers. A news release will be published once at most, and customers will not see the company name again until such time as there are further developments of news value. Sales representatives make regular contact with prospects, but journey cycles may be three months or more: advertising can help maintain brand loyalty between sales calls.

ECONOMY

'Cost per thousand' – a concept considered in Chapter 6 – varies between advertising media but, when viewed on an overall basis, cost per contact is often measured in pennies per thousand. Contrast this with sales force activity, where costs are measured in tens of pounds per call. Advertising gives low-cost communication by mass delivery of promotional messages; it can also provide leads for sales representatives, thereby increasing their productivity.

THE DRAWBACKS OF ADVERTISING

For advantages there are, as always, drawbacks. Advertising is regarded as 'blowing your own trumpet' and lacks the authenticity of 'third party endorsement' in editorial columns. It calls for considerable expenditure of money as well as time and effort. Furthermore, there may be no suitable advertising medium which reaches the target market effectively, making it necessary to consider 'created media' such as printed material, house journals and videos. Finally, advertising cannot in itself deliver the tangible stimulus to action which is such an important feature of many merchandising and sales promotion incentives.

THE RANGE OF ADVERTISING MEDIA

There is a wide range of media which offer advertising space or time, to deliver marketing communications messages. The obvious business-to-business media include specialist magazines, directories and annuals, exhibitions, and direct mail. It is also possible to use what are often considered consumer media:

newspapers, outdoor and transport, and even television and radio. No media choice should ever be ignored, as all have possible business applications.

All these media, and the specialist databases which provide information about the audiences reached, are considered in the chapters following. First, however, this chapter outlines certain general data sources which cover the full range of advertising media.

GENERAL INFORMATION SOURCES

There are numerous data sources which provide valuable information about advertising and other media, and services. Readers are recommended to make a quick check of this section, rather than read through it in the usual way, and then return to relevant sources for more detailed study later.

ADVERTISERS ANNUAL
(British Media Publications, Reed Information Services Ltd, Windsor Court, East Grinstead House, East Grinstead, West Sussex RH19 1XA.)

The Annual is now published in three sections:

- *Volume one* – covers advertising, giving details of advertising agencies (including client lists and key personnel) plus major advertisers (shown with business details and the advertising agencies they use), together with both sales promotion and PR companies;
- *Volume two* – covers media, UK and throughout the world, with information on newspapers, magazines, television, and radio;
- *Volume three* – covers specialist services and suppliers, from animal hire to voice-overs.

BRITISH RATE & DATA (BRAD)
(Maclean Hunter House, Chalk Lane, Cockfosters Road, Barnet, Herts EN4 0BU)

This company publishes a number of information sources, including:

BRAD NATIONAL GUIDE TO MEDIA SELECTION
This monthly publication contains comprehensive updated information about the advertisement rates, mechanical requirements, circulations, personnel, etc. of all media which carry advertising. All circulation figures quoted are substantiated: The Audit Bureau of Circulations described on page 100 ensures the latest ABC figures for each audit period are automatically passed to BRAD's Editor.

To update its entries, BRAD issues every month a form to which is attached the medium's current listing; the media-owner then corrects the entry for the following month's issue. BRAD's topicality is demonstrated by the fact that each issue contains between 2000 and 3000 amended listings.

BRAD DIRECTORIES AND ANNUALS
Published in April and September, this provides for annual publications the information that BRAD supplies for other media. It is a classified directory,

giving details of advertising rates and mechanical data of all annual publications and directories in Great Britain which accept advertising. It covers both trade and consumer publications.

MEDIA EXPENDITURE ANALYSIS LTD (MEAL)
(63 St Martin's Lane, London WC2N 4JT)

MEAL provides a continuous monitor of advertising activity as an aid to promotional planning. The service is based on comprehensive coverage of display advertising in the national press, magazines, television and selected radio contractors. It also includes national advertising in an extensive list of regional newspapers.

The main media groups covered by the monitoring service include:

- Television (Channel 3, Channel 4 + TV-AM)
- Ten major radio contractors
- National daily newspapers
- National Sunday newspapers
- Weekend colour supplements
- Regional evening newspapers
- Regional morning and Sunday papers
- General and weekly magazines
- Women's weekly and monthly magazines
- Special interest magazines
- Juvenile magazines

The special interest magazines group covers business and current affairs publications, including The Director, The Economist, Financial Weekly, Investors Chronicle, New Scientist, New Society, and Management Today.

Each month more than 330,000 individual advertisements are attributed to more than 1,800 brands. Each brand is attributed to one of 370 product groups, which in turn are classified into 22 categories. These categories are listed below, together with the relevant product groups when these have business-to-business relevance:

- *Agricultural and horticultural* – this category covers the following fourteen product groups: agricultural implements and machinery, agricultural feeds, agricultural fertilisers and chemicals, animal health, cultivators and hoes, farm buildings, farm seeds, fertilisers, compost and chemicals, horticulture – commercial grower, garden furniture and tools (including swimming pools), lawn mowers, portable buildings, seedsmen and nurserymen, and tractors;
- *Charity, educational and societies*
- *Drink*
- *Entertainment*
- *Financial* – thirteen product groups are covered: boroughs and corporations, building societies, company meetings, company and public notices, credit cards, City and financial services, foreign banks and travellers cheques, insurance and assurance companies, investment and growth bonds, joint stock banks, merchant banks, prospectuses, unit trusts;

ADVERTISING – AN OVERVIEW, AND GENERAL DATABASES

- *Food*
- *Government development, corporations and service recruitment* – four product groups: development corporations (British), development corporations (foreign), government departments and service recruitment, political and trade unions;
- *Holidays, travel and transport*
- *Household appliances*
- *Household equipment*
- *Household stores*
- *Institutional & industrial* – 17 product groups: advertising marketing & research, aircraft, building & construction, chartered accountants & solicitors, container materials & transport, recruitment, fire extinguishers & smoke alarms, fork lift trucks, hand tools, home extensions, industrial fuel & lubricants (not motor fuel), industrial & marine engines, industrial plastics, other products and services, corporate & sponsorship, property & chartered surveyors, electronics & semi-conductors;
- *Leisure equipment*
- *Motors* – 22 product groups, some with business-to-business relevance, including: motors (trucks and vans), motor fuels and lubricants (agricultural), and motor fuels and lubricants (aviation);
- *Office equipment* – 12 product groups: adhesive tape, calculators, computers (business and personal), computer software, dictating machines, intercom and telephone systems, photocopiers, stationery and office supplies, storage furniture and filing, typewriters and word processors, vending machines, office cleaning and services;
- *Pharmaceutical*
- *Publishing*
- *Retail and mail order*
- *Tobacco*
- *Toiletries and cosmetics*
- *Wearing apparel*
- *Local advertisers*

MEAL information is readily available in a wide range of reports and services to meet individual requirements. Various regular services relating to these product groups and categories include:

- *Advertisement analysis* – a detailed description of advertising activity giving a record of each television station and press advertisement placed during the month. The details for each advertisement are: date, station or publication, duration or size, time-on or special position, and rate-card cost;
- *Brand expenditure by medium* – this report shows television, radio and press expenditure during each of the last 12 months and in total for the period. A percentage profile is also included to give the distribution of expenditure during the period;
- *Brand expenditure by press groups* – the report shows the allocation of brand expenditure when the main interest is in the press. For each brand the expenditure is shown during the last month and the last 12 months. Total expenditure is split between television, radio and the press. Expenditure is also shown for 13 press groups;

EXISTING MEDIA – THE ADVERTISING ROUTE

- *Brand expenditure by television regions* – this service gives a detailed analysis of total television expenditure during the previous month and the latest 12 months. This is shown in total and for both channels (ITV and Channel 4) in each region;
- *Brand expenditure on radio* – 'Key Region Radio' is a continuous monitor of brand expenditure on radio. The results are compiled from ten major radio contractors in six primary marketing areas. Expenditure is shown in £000's for each contractor and in total;
- *Brand expenditure by area* – this report shows expenditure in nine main marketing areas for television and press. It is a guide to the amount of advertising weight in each area;
- *Brand advertising by selected titles* – MEAL also provides a flexible tabulation service to meet individual requirements. The following options are available when specifying an analysis:
    a) Up to 17 columns may be specified and each may be an individual publication or television contractor. The specified media may be any which are regularly monitored;
    b) The expenditure or advertisement volume information shown for each brand may be either monthly or quarterly, together with either year to date or moving annual total;
    c) The percentage profiling of expenditure across the specified media is flexible, and may be produced with sub-totals profiled on the grand total; individual media profiled on the sub-total or the brand total, etc;
- *Tri-media Digest of Brands and Advertisers* – this report shows the advertising expenditure of individual brands in total for the latest quarter, each month in the quarter, and the last 12 months. The report also gives the proportion of expenditure in television, radio and the press for each brand and product group. Each issue includes a special index showing advertisers and their brands. The *Tri-media Digest* is also published electronically, and available through various on-line computer database services;
- *Microfilmed Advertisement Service* – copies of advertisements cut from a selection of publications are coded into the MEAL product groups and microfilmed. For the product group selected by the client, reproductions of advertisements are sent each month (supplied on A4 paper in a loose-leaf folder) thus providing a continuous flow of information on the advertising strategy of competitive brands. The microfilm library has been maintained since 1969 and can also meet *ad hoc* requests for complete product groups or individual brands.

SPECIAL REPORTS

In addition to its monthly services, MEAL also produces special annual reports. For example, *Ten Year Trends* shows product group expenditure in total, in the press and on television for each of ten consecutive years, summarised with all information shown in £000's. Other special reports cover *Top 1,000 Brands* spending £1M or more, and *Top 500 Advertisers* who account for 75 per cent of all display advertising.

These established analyses are available for all MEAL product groups as follows:

Annual subscription. Results are produced monthly and despatched within a week from the end of the month.
Ad hoc requests. Complete results are held by Client Service and readily available for current or past data within 24 hours of request.
Direct access. MEAL's database is available on line to provide ad hoc analyses. These services may be accessed directly from most terminals or by contacting Client Service.

MEDIA MONITORING SERVICES
(Madison House, High Street, Sunninghill, Ascot, Berkshire SL5 9NP)

MMS regularly monitor the magazines in the major business-to-business categories, and provide information on advertising activity and expenditure in the UK business and professional press. The MMS Monitor is published twice a year and provides an alphabetical listing of advertisers in 46 business markets, detailing magazines used, number of insertions, and expenditure (at rate card costs) – a total of more than 40,000 companies and £300 million of media spend.

THE MEDIA REGISTER
(1–4 Langley Court, London WC2E 9YJ)

The Media Register publishes regular information on TV, press and poster advertising expenditure: it is primarily a consumer monitor and does not specialise in the business area. The Register nevertheless covers a wide range of trade publications, has a business-to-business category described below, and is soon to add a substantial number of titles covering the Light Commercial Vehicle and Small Truck market.

PRESS EXPENDITURE

The Media Register applies correct rate-card value to each advertisement monitored across more than 500 titles, examining them and recording the information in detail – not only display advertising, but also all classified, even in regional publications, and large advertisers are credited with their individual share.

TELEVISION EXPENDITURE

Television advertising expenditure is notoriously difficult to estimate since most TV rate-cards are based on a ladder of increasing spot rates – the 'pre-empt' system described on page 147. The Media Register technique is therefore linked to what is actually happening in the TV air-time marketplace.

The total net revenue of the independent companies is published each month through *The Television Association.* Individual contractor's share of homes is known, and each contractor's revenue may thus be calculated. Additionally, the audiences for every spot and every contractor are measured by BARB, the Broadcasters Audience Research Board described on page 150.

Consequently, an average cost-per-thousand may be estimated for each contractor by dividing revenue by impacts (in thousands), and data calculated for three broad audience sub-groups: housewives, adults and men. TV expenditure estimates can thus be calculated for a brand by multiplying the total impacts it achieved within an area by the most appropriate cost-per-thousand, and consolidating across all advertising areas. These estimates are not yet sufficiently accurate, however, as some times of day, days of week or types of programme etc offer above-average value for advertisers seeking particular target audiences. Consequently The Media Register adjusts costs-per-thousand to generate more accurate figures, such that the multiplication of all impacts within a month within an area by the most relevant cost-per-thousand is exactly equal to the (gross) contractor revenue.

This technique yields an expected expenditure for all TV advertised brands (although some brands will spend slightly more and some slightly less than this expectation, depending on various marketplace factors).

POSTER EXPENDITURE

The Media Register publishes monthly brand expenditure estimates for roadside poster advertising, using data provided by Poster Marketing (see page 143).

PRODUCT CLASSIFICATIONS

The Media Register's classification system lists 480 product groups, attributed to 34 product categories. These categories are listed below, together with the product groups where these have business-to-business application:

- *Agricultural* – covers the following six product groups: agrichemicals and fertilisers, agricultural animal health, agricultural foodstuffs, agricultural seeds, farming implements and machinery, and tractors;
- *Business-to-business* – covers the following eleven product groups: advertising and marketing, business exhibitions and conferences, couriers, freight, office cleaning services, four groups of office supplies – furniture, services, stationery, and suppliers, recruitment agencies, vehicle leasing and contracts;
- *Charities*
- *Classified*
- *Clothing*
- *Confectionary*
- *Corporate* – covers the following six product groups: electrical, financial, general, industrial, pharmaceutical, and takeover bids;
- *Cosmetics and toiletries*
- *Do-it-yourself*
- *Drink*
- *Education*
- *Entertainment*
- *Financial* – covers 18 product groups: building societies and mortgage companies, credit cards and charge cards, financial services, insurance and assurance companies, four groupings of insurance (life and pensions, motor, home and contents, and health), three groupings of banks (joint stock, foreign, and merchant), company prospectuses, company meetings and

ADVERTISING – AN OVERVIEW, AND GENERAL DATABASES

notices, credit and loan companies, solicitors and accountants, stockbrokers, travellers cheques, and unit trusts and growth bonds;
- *Food*
- *Gardening*
- *Government* – eight product groups: development boards – British, development boards – foreign, government departments/Central Office of Information, industrial relations, local government, political, public service recruitment, and Royal Mail;
- *Household durables*
- *Household furnishings*
- *Household stores*
- *Houseware*
- *Industrial* – this category covers the following eight product groups: aircraft, electrical components, estate agents, fork-lift trucks, housebuilders, industrial construction, industrial fuel, and tools;
- *Leisure equipment*
- *Luxury goods*
- *Mail order* – this category's numerous product groups include direct response office equipment;
- *Motors* – this category's product groups include car and truck rental, and light commercial vehicles;
- *Office automation* – this category includes twenty-one product groups: answering/dictating machines, calculators, nine groupings of computers (micro/mini, mainframe, corporate, dealers, systems, printers, peripherals, software, and blank discs), miscellaneous on-line services, seven groupings of telecommunications (office phone systems, car telephones, domestic telephones, facsimile, paging systems, telex, and modems), and finally typewriters and word processors;
- *Pharmaceutical*
- *Public utilities*
- *Publishing and broadcasting*
- *Retail*
- *Small electrical appliances*
- *Sport*
- *Tobacco*
- *Travel*

MEDIA REGISTER REPORTS

Media Register information is available as a monthly summary, and as selected product group reports (complete advertisement listing for TV and the Press, or analysed by selected media titles, TV area, or advertising agency) at any frequency or to cover any time period required. Reports covering all product groups are available both on microfiche and in printed form, and will shortly be available on-line.

MEDIASCOPE

Like Prestel, ITV's Oracle has pages of marketing information, including *Mediascope* – a media facts, news and comment service.

EXISTING MEDIA – THE ADVERTISING ROUTE

MEDIATEL
(52 Poland Street, London W1V 3DF)

MediaTel is a database of media information, news and developments specially designed for media buyers and sellers. Subscribers are provided with a viewdata terminal connected to a BT telephone line, and also an alphanumeric keyboard and printer. Through the keyboard, they can then call up information frames (pages) covering all the major business-to-business and consumer media detailed below. If subscribers want a copy of any information on their display screens, it is immediately available through the print-out facility.

The Media Tel database covers all cost and audience details normally used for media planning, and all information is up-dated daily. Data available covers the following main media markets (each sub-divided): national newspapers, magazines (consumer and business), television, outdoor, cinema, radio, and overseas media. There are also other information frames covering regional media (region demographics and local media opportunities), 'Encyclomedia' (various media indices and expenditure figures) and the usual miscellaneous section which includes among other items a useful 'Minefield' warning (a chronological list by month of irregular events which may affect audience deliveries) and a 'Newsline' service which reports media events as they happen (and is the most heavily accessed section of the database).

MediaTel has a special business-to-business section, comprising:

- *Agriculture* – covering arable farming, livestock farming, agricultural suppliers, and horticulture;
- *Business* – covering business management, advertising/marketing, business finance, accountancy, business travel, and exports;
- *Doctors*
- *Industrial* – covering architecture, building, construction, chemical, electrical, electronics, engineering, industrial transport, and communications;
- *Retail* – covering general retail, home retail, durables, grocery, CTNs/stationers, licensed trade, pharmaceutical, food/catering, clothing, laundry, hairdressing/beauty, toys, jewellery, and perfumes/cosmetics;
- *Computers*

Each main category is broken down into sub-sections which include: basic facts, editorial assessments, routings to related sections, and Business Media Research Committee (see page 115) profiles where available. Circulation trends are routed from the main category index.

MediaTel was set up on Prestel, British Telecom's viewdata service, but later transferred to MediaTel's own private system. The transfer enabled MediaTel to develop more sophisticated viewdata applications. These include a keyboard search system: for example, information on any particular magazine can be accessed by keying in its title; or the media opportunities for any town by keying in its name. Key words speed up access and make the system easier to use. Additionally, various standard media calculations (cost/coverage ranking for press, and a coverage and frequency guide for radio, as examples) can now be performed on MediaTel using the new interactive service. These two-way services also allow users to manipulate data held in computer files according to their specific requirements.

ADVERTISING – AN OVERVIEW, AND GENERAL DATABASES

A new development likely to increase the MediaTel service in the future is the EDIT facility, which allows media-owners to set up and edit their own MediaTel database (minimum size 100 pages). In this way, media owners can make available to MediaTel subscribers the latest research or marketing data about their medium. MediaTel also serves as an advertising medium in its own right, with solus advertising space.

A recently launched PR-Tel service, described on page 181, is designed for PR consultancies: it includes an advance editorial features database, PR-related news, information on sponsorship, exhibitions, editorial contacts, and a financial supplement.

TARGET GROUP INDEX
(Saunders House, 53 The Mall, Ealing, London W5 3TE)

TGI is a national database directly relating media and product usage: the survey findings are based on 24,000 self-completion questionnaires received from pre-contacted informants in some 3,500 sampling points in Great Britain. The Index is produced by the British Market Research Bureau (BMRB) and available on subscription.

TGI identifies heavy, medium and light users as well as non-users in a vast range of product categories and sub-categories. A full range of demographics and media usage is reported for these groups. The product group information provides the foundation for assessing individual markets' major or potential users, and their characteristics and media habits. It similarly provides information about brand usage, listing solus users (users of the product group who use a brand exclusively), most frequent users (including solus users and those who prefer it to another brand also used) and minor users (those who are more casual in their use). These definitions establish some element of brand loyalty and the degree of involvement that users have with a given brand.

TGI reports the users of thousands of brands. As with heavy to light users of product categories, demographics and media usage are reported for brand users. By using TGI, companies know who their customers are and what they read, watch and listen to. They also have the same information about competitors.

The index measures the following product and media habits:

- *Products* – heavy-to-light usage for over 2,500 brands in more than 200 fast-moving consumer product fields. Additionally, usage of over 150 other 'brands' is covered in the field of banking, building societies, airlines, holidays, cars, grocery and other retail outlets. Brands with more than a million claimed users are broken down demographically and by media;
- *Media* – audiences to 160 newspapers and magazines, weight of ITV viewing and half-hour viewing behaviour for television, weight of listening to commercial radio and exposure to outdoor media and the cinema. The TGI is designed to be complementary to JICNARS, the industry's readership survey described on page 105;
- *Characteristics* – the full range of standard demographics including social grades, household income, together with special breakdowns such as age of educational termination, working status, home ownership, length of tenure in homes, size of household and marital status;

- *Lifestyle* – respondents are asked their agreement or disagreement with 186 lifestyle statements, and all data in the questionnaire can be cross-analysed by the answers to these statements.

THE TGI REPORTS

There are 34 separate TGI volumes, and it is possible to buy individual volumes or even data relating to separate product fields. Volumes 1 and 2 are those most likely to be of business-to-business relevance since they concentrate on demographics. (The other 32 volumes are devoted to confectionery, consumer durables and appliances, clothing and shopping, drink, financial services, food, holidays and travel, household goods, leisure, motoring, pharmaceutical and chemist products, tobacco, toiletries and cosmetics.)

AB TARGET GROUP INDEX

The AB TGI seeks to give a higher degree of detail than does the broad index within those areas of product purchasing and lifestyle especially relevant to heads of household/housewives of the high (AB) socio-demographic status. It also provides this information based on significantly larger sample sizes than are found on the main survey.

The survey is based on a sample of 5,500 AB adults a year, entirely separate from those interviewed in the main TGI. Respondents are initially interviewed by telephone in order to collect classification data, and then sent a self-completion questionnaire.

There are eight volumes, devoted to:

1. Demographics;
2. Holidays and travel (including business travel in UK and abroad);
3. Sports and leisure;
4. Clothing;
5. Personal possessions, cosmetics & gifts;
6. House, home and car;
7. Drink;
8. Finance (covering banks, bank cheque cards, cash dispenser cards, credit cards/charge cards, store cards, building societies, life assurance, private health insurance, stocks and shares, unit trusts, savings and investment, pension schemes, travellers' cheques/foreign currency, mortgages, and loans.

TGI is a 'single source' measurement and all elements of the survey can be cross-referenced, eg, media usage relating to product usage, brand usage relating to audiences or demographics. BMRB has its own computer terminal facilities for conducting any special analyses on behalf of TGI subscribers. Alternatively, for those requiring direct contact with a computer bureau, various companies offer post-survey analysis on the TGI. Understandably, access to the tapes is permitted only to those who have purchased the relevant TGI volumes.

OTHER SOURCES

Other publications: some media-owners and trade and professional bodies have their own publications which they use to communicate items of interest and, in addition to these special interest publications, articles of specific interest appear from time to time in a host of other publications, both newspapers and magazines.

Activities: there are also various conferences and courses at which useful information and details of new developments can be obtained. Some of the organizations which mount these are not only sources of media information, but powerful influences on the way business media will develop in the future.

These comments about publications and activities apply equally to other marketing communications media.

CHAPTER EIGHT

Press Media

This review of advertising commences with the press medium, since this is the largest in terms of expenditure and also one of those most relevant to business communications. This media group divides into numerous sub-categories, including:

MAGAZINES

- Special interest magazines
- Business press
- Professional magazines
- Industrial and technical periodicals
- Trade press
- Controlled circulation distribution
- General magazines
- Free magazines

NEWSPAPERS

- National daily newspapers
- National Sunday newspapers
- Colour supplements
- Regional newspapers
  – Paid-for
  – Free

OTHER PRESS MEDIA

- Product information cards
- Directories

These divisions are not rigid, however, as some media could appear under more than one heading, or even shift from one category to another. Some publications, for example, are magazines in newspaper format, others were launched as newspapers but then became magazines, and supplements can be considered under the twin headings of newspapers and magazines. The national press increasingly offer regional advertising facilities, while regional newspapers have co-operative facilities for national advertisers.

To use any publication to best advantage, an in-depth knowledge of each individual title's format and editorial is essential. Circulation and readership figures apply to *average* issues, but both can vary from day to day, and readership also page by page. Should a newspaper regularly publish, for example, an information technology feature every Tuesday, readers with an interest in this area might buy Tuesday issues more regularly than other days' copies. An advertisement could be made more effective by booking that particular day of the week, and paying a premium to place it on that page, thus selecting out of total readership those interested in information technology. A similar targeting process can be achieved by careful positioning within magazines according to their editorial features. A further benefit arises from these self-selecting readers being mentally 'tuned in' to information technology developments, and thus more likely to be receptive to promotional messages about products and services in this area.

These same publications also provide Public Relations opportunities, discussed in Part 3C. To take advantage of these PR opportunities calls for the same in-depth knowledge of each publication's format and editorial.

MAGAZINES

Magazines, as newspapers, can deliver a detailed promotional message. Actual delivery varies widely, for magazines are published in a wide variety of formats and differ in page size, number of pages, printing quality, colour availability and advertising facilities. Space is usually sold by the page and fractions thereof, and a variety of special positions, eg, facing editorial matter or inside front cover, may be available.

The promotional message often benefits from an important attribute in favour of magazines: the readers' state of mind when the message is delivered. This is frequently linked with another favourable aspect, in that magazine audiences are usually more distinctly defined than with the broad coverage of newspapers. These two points together bring considerable benefits, since the advertiser reaches a clearly defined group of prospects when they are likely to be receptive to his message.

Effectiveness is increased by the fact that most magazines are referred to several times, thus increasing the target market's opportunities to see any advertisement.

Possible drawbacks of this media group include timing, since magazines cannot deliver messages on a given day as can newspapers. The physical life of magazines is far longer, and the promotional message may be delivered at any time during this period. Furthermore, long copy dates may restrict use of magazines by advertisers seeking to make swift announcements, or whose message content is subject to unexpected alterations. Developments in print technology have had their effect here – some magazines which formerly went to press months before the cover date now have copy-handling periods of ten working days or less, thus directly increasing their flexibility.

The comments so far made are generalisations, and it is unrealistic to view all magazines as one homogenous medium. They can be grouped under three broad headings, each of which sub-divides: special interest publications, controlled circulation distribution and general magazines.

SPECIAL INTEREST MAGAZINES

These publications, as the name implies, appeal to groups having a special interest in common, but they can be sub-divided into different categories according to the nature of that interest, which may be a hobby, sport or other activity or – more relevant to business advertisers – by occupation (industrial, commercial or professional).

Some media commentators divide such publications into four specialist categories:

- *Business press* – this group covers publications devoted to matters of general interest to business executives, and includes magazines dealing with economic trends, finance, general management, and the business implications of technological developments or of political and world affairs. They can offer high quality contact with opinion formers and senior managers. Depending on circulation size, such publications may overlap with general magazines, discussed below;
- *Professional magazines* – these publications reach readers whose occupations call for special qualifications. The accounting, legal and medical press come under this heading, as do the journals of many Institutes and Associations. Advertisers use them for direct selling and also, because many readers are in higher managerial positions, for reaching those who influence purchasing decisions;
- *Industrial and technical periodicals* – these deal with practical aspects of manufacturing and process industries such as agriculture, building, chemicals, electrical and electronics, engineering, or plastics. There may be some overlap with professional magazines, in that many readers hold specialist qualifications. Many such publications extend their editorial coverage to include general business matters. They offer access to readers with purchasing influence at many different management levels within these specialist markets;
- *Trade journals* – these merit separate attention because business advertisers use them when their market is a 'reseller' one, and they wish to contact retailers in their vital role as intermediaries with the public. Trade press advertisements generally feature details of forthcoming consumer advertising, display material available, trade margins, merchandising incentives, and the profit to be gained – rather than urging readers to buy for their own use (a few advertisers, selling such things as shop fittings, use the trade press to sell to retailers direct rather than as intermediaries, but the bulk of trade press advertising is of the reseller variety).

Analysis of these four categories should recognize the difference between 'vertical' and 'horizontal' media (and markets). The former cover a single trade or industry at all management levels from top to bottom, whereas horizontal media cover readers occupying similar positions spread across a wide range of industries: accountants, for example. The circulation of some horizontal 'special interest' magazines has increased to such an extent that they are included within the National Readership Surveys described below, and could thus be considered under the heading of general magazines. As already pointed out, there are no clear dividing lines between media groups. Business advertisers with 'horizontal' markets can, depending on the number of buyers, always consider mass media discussed below, such as the general press or even TV, evaluating them by coverage of the A, B, and C1 socio-economic groupings.

Despite differences in the way the various special interest media groups are used, they share certain common considerations, relating to the number and type of readers. National newspapers and magazines can generally be evaluated by readership data as well as by circulation figures, but it is often impossible to make a similar statistical evaluation of some specialist publications. Circulation figures may be available, but not always. Furthermore, where circulation is known, this frequently reveals that the publication does not fully cover the market in question.

A counter argument to incomplete coverage is that the readers the media *do* reach are opinion-formers, enthusiasts and heavy users of products or services, and that those who do not buy the publication cannot have the same degree of commitment. This, however, only highlights another point sometimes made against these publications: that, more often then not, all that is known about coverage is what can be deduced from the magazine's title and contents, since no readership data may be available. There are a number of specialist readership surveys, described in Chapter 9, but such data is by no means universally available.

Many specialist publications reach only a proportion of the total market, and little is known about that relatively small proportion. This somewhat harsh statement summarises the problem often faced when attempting to evaluate these media. Instead of hard data about readership, advertisers must rely on personal knowledge of what is read and respected in their customers' industries. When several publications compete for the same market, as is frequently the case, in-depth study of actual copies is all the more important (see *Rule-of-thumb research*, page 101).

RESEARCH DATA

AUDIT BUREAU OF CIRCULATIONS
(13 Wimpole Street, London W1M 7AB)

ABC's function is the certification of circulation data by standard audit procedures. The Bureau protects advertisers and agencies from false claims, and at the same time furnishes media-owners with a certifying document accepted as authentic by all who purchase space in member publications.

CIRCULATION AUDITS

To ensure audits are conducted uniformly, the Bureau sends all publisher members, in advance of each audit period, forms for completion by an approved independent auditor (who is generally also the financial auditor to the publishing company).

The Bureau checks the completed *Publisher's Return Form* and, subject to its being correct, issues an *ABC Certificate* covering the period audited and publishes the results. Net sales are the only audit category: these are *bona fide* copies bought by individuals either from the retail point or by direct subscription.

In some cases, a *Publisher's Statement* or a *Media Data Form* may give further information:

PUBLISHERS' STATEMENTS

All *Publisher's Return Forms*, through which the ABC audits paid-for sales, have provision for a *Publisher's Statement*, in which the publisher can give other information not included on the *Certificate of Audited Sales*. This statement is automatically transferred to the *ABC Certificate*, but is not subject to audit and the Bureau accepts no responsibility for its content.

MEDIA DATA FORMS

The ABC operates an additional service for business and professional journals. Certificates of Net Circulation give a *quantitative* analysis. To show the *quality* of this circulation a publisher may, after certification has been granted, complete a *Media Data Form*. Entry to the scheme is voluntary. The contents are not independently audited but are subject to ABC inspection and verification. The completed MDF is checked by the Bureau and given the stamp of approval prior to reproduction. An MDF is constructed in four parts:

- *Part I* contains details of the publishing company, its staff, its advertisement rates, the market served by the journal and brief details of any research;
- *Part II* is a reproduction of the latest ABC Certificate of Net Circulation;
- *Part III* gives a geographical breakdown of a normal issue within the ABC average together with brief details of the analyses available;
- *Part IV* reports on editorial policy, analyses an issue within the audit period and contains any optional statement by the publisher giving information which may assist the buyer of space.

Although the *Media Data Form* is issued as a standard four-page document, publishers may extend any or all sections at will. Eight, ten and 12-page MDF's are frequently produced and have proved most successful.

Entry to the MDF scheme is optional and the data provided is of varying usefulness. Where data forms are issued, however, advertisers should be grateful for such additional information as is provided.

RULE-OF-THUMB RESEARCH

In the absence of any formal data (and even when statistics *are* available), a practical approach is, as always, to check copies of the actual publication. Useful things to look for, in addition to relevant editorial, are practical signals of readership such as lively correspondence columns, and pages of 'Situations Vacant' advertisements (from which employers *know* by direct response whether the medium reaches the market).

CONTROLLED CIRCULATION DISTRIBUTION

Incomplete coverage of, and lack of readership information about, some specialist markets has led to the publication of controlled circulation magazines sent to individuals in certain defined categories. The publication is not sold but distributed free of charge through the post, in the same way as subscription copies.

Conventional publishers have two income sources: sale of copies and sale of advertising space. Controlled circulation media-owners forego cover revenue in the belief that they can make greater profit through increased advertisement revenue, by the promise of 100 per cent coverage of advertisers' target markets (the same principle applies to free newspapers and magazines, discussed below).

The benefits of controlled circulation stem from the distribution method, which overcomes the two main drawbacks of conventional publications: incomplete coverage and lack of readership data. Controlled circulation journals cover the market completely, by definition, and readership information is available simply through analysis of the mailing list to which the journal is sent. Furthermore, as copies are sent only to those who request them, recipients presumably do *read* them. Thus, in theory, the medium is near perfect. Any medium has its drawbacks, however, and those of controlled circulation arise from the validity of the journal's mailing list.

Controlled circulation gives full market coverage only if the advertiser's target market matches the publication's market. Should the journal's definition be wider or narrower, this necessarily means either waste circulation or incomplete coverage. Furthermore, there is the question of how the mailing list was compiled. Defining a market is one thing, but obtaining a list of all those meeting these criteria is another. This problem is further complicated by the normal difficulty of keeping any mailing list up-to-date.

FREE CIRCULATION RESEARCH

Two main types of free circulation are recognized by the Audit Bureau of Circulations: controlled circulation and society/association free circulation.

CONTROLLED CIRCULATION

This category consists of single copies sent free and post-free to individuals who precisely fit the 'term of control', which must be published in each issue of the journal. This term of control defines the industrial, commercial or professional classification covered by the journal together with the job qualification the reader must have in order to qualify for receipt. Controlled circulation sub-divides into three categories:

- *Individually requested* – each copy in this category must be backed by a signed request card dated no more than three years before the date on which the copy is despatched. The recipient must receive every issue addressed to him by name;
- *Company requested* – this applies when the request document is signed by a senior official of a qualifying company, designating named executives to receive the journal. Again each recipient must individually receive every issue, and the request document signature must be within the three-year limit;
- *Non-requested* – this term covers all other controlled-circulation copies, ie where no valid requesting document is on file. Recipients need not receive every issue nor is it necessary to address each copy to an individual by name. However, where the individual name is not known, the address must bear the job function of the recipient. Non-requested copies also include copies shown under the two previous headings, but where the request document has gone out of date.

SOCIETY/ASSOCIATION FREE CIRCULATION

A second type of free circulation recognized by ABC relates to societies or associations. No term of control is necessary, as this is implied by the relevant membership criteria. As with controlled circulation journals, this type of free circulation sub-divides into three categories:

- *Non-optional circulation* is where the journal is sent to all members without any additional payment.
- *Unpaid optional circulation* is where, without extra cost, a section only of the membership receives the journal. The question to ask, under such circumstances, clearly concerns the criteria by which this selection is made.
- *Paid optional circulation* is where members pay a sum additional to their normal subscription in order to receive the journal.

HYBRID CIRCULATION

Some mainly unpaid publications are subject to a double audit, in that free circulation is audited as just described, but copies are also available for purchase by individuals who do not meet the term of control or are not members of the society or association. Purchased copies are audited in the usual way.

OTHER FREE MAGAZINES

Another distribution variation is for magazines to be given away free. Verified Free Distributions Ltd, an ABC subsidiary, not only audits free local newspapers and magazines as described below, but also covers *courtesy publications* available for pick-up at hotels, airlines, clubs etc. This is known as a bulk verification service and has a different VFD certificate.

PRODUCT INFORMATION CARDS

A number of trade, industrial and technical journals produce bound-in pages of reply-paid postcards or alternatively mail these separately as packs of cards to their controlled circulation. They carry no editorial and are simply vehicles for brief advertising messages. Alone or in support of display advertising, they can provide direct enquiries at relatively low cost.

DIRECTORIES

Not all directories are of the 'delivered to your home free' variety: numerous annuals and buyers' guides or technical indices aim at business rather than consumer markets. Some may be in microfiche or on-line, rather than the usual printed format. Whilst some are highly reputable, others present a problem in that their publishers provide no audited media data.

In the absence of 'hard information' the approach, as always, must be *rule-of-thumb* research, making a careful analysis of each publication. Do the publishers offer basic free editorial entries to *all* companies supplying the goods and services they claim to cover? Do they actively canvass suppliers to obtain these free entries? If not, how can such directories really fulfil their role as universal works of reference?

Further details about such reference publications are contained in British Rate & Data's guide to *Directories and Annuals*, described on page 85.

FURTHER RESEARCH DATA

SPECIALIST SURVEYS

Those databases devoted to specific business-to-business areas are detailed in the next Chapter. Such surveys often extend beyond readership to cover other media, such as TV and video. More general information about the business press is available from *British Business Press*, described below.

BRITISH BUSINESS PRESS
(Imperial House, 15–19 Kingsway, London WC2B 6UN)

BBP is the marketing bureau set up by leading UK publishers of business, trade, technical and professional journals under the auspices of the *Periodical Publishers Association* described on page 106 – its aim is to highlight the professionalism and effectiveness of the business press to advertisers and agencies, to the business community at large and to educators of the next generation of marketing management. It publishes a series of free booklets on business-to-business advertising, including:

- *How British Business Advertises* – research summary;
- *A Commonsense Approach to your Communications Budget* – executive guidelines, with checklist for action;
- *Better Media Planning* – executive guidelines, with checklist for action;
- *Better Business Advertising to the Boardroom* – Research Summary Business Advertising Planner – 96-page review of 250 leading business magazines, with contact names (see page 112).

Copies can be obtained from the British Business Press, Booklets Department, PO Box 362, Bristol BS99 7GF.

GENERAL MAGAZINES

This broad category divides into numerous sub-groups, but overall such publications appeal to the broad mass of men or women or both. They increasingly segment by lifestyle, however, and there is scope for finer audience selection, as their readerships tend to have more clearly defined characteristics than newspapers' audiences. The reader characteristics of most general magazines are included in the National Readership Surveys described on page 105. Total readership can accordingly be sub-divided into socio-economic groupings and other demographic criteria, which makes precise audience selection much easier. This finer degree of selection, coupled with the criterion of a receptive audience, can make general magazines a powerful medium for advertisers with horizontal business markets as much as for manufacturers of consumer products. Some general interest magazines offer split-run, regional and test-town facilities as well as national advertising.

Data about general magazines' circulation and readership is provided by ABC and TGI, already described. This information is supplemented by other databases.

JOINT INDUSTRY COMMITTEE FOR NATIONAL READERSHIP SURVEYS
(44 Belgrave Square, London SW1X 8QS)

The National Readership Survey publishes the results of 28,500 interviews a year. The research, currently undertaken on behalf of JICNARS by Research Services Ltd, covers more than 200 publications, including a number of national magazines as well as National and Sunday newspapers.

NRS subscribers receive Volume 1 (based on fieldwork for the period July to the following June) and Volume 2 (based on the calendar year's fieldwork). Both volumes contain the following information:

- Average issue readership analysed by sex, age, social grade and area;
- Profile tables showing readership composition;
- Tables showing ITV and Channel 4 viewing, Independent Local Radio listening, and cinema-going;
- Readership among special interest groups;
- Group readership figures;
- Frequency of reading.

Volume 3 contains duplication tables showing the extent to which readers of one publication also read others, and subscribers also receive various NRS bulletins containing interim, advance or additional information.

Although the published reports contain several hundred tabulations, the amount of data stored on tapes is very much larger, and there are facilities for extracting additional information required by subscribers. (Special computer runs, to provide additional tabulations not contained in the main reports, are possible with most databases.)

MAGAZINE PAGE EXPOSURE CONSORTIUM
(E W Whitley, Readers Digest, 25 Berkeley Square, London W1X 6AB)

MPX is a new media measurement sponsored by a consortium of major magazine publishers: it measures the number of times the average page in a magazine is read or looked at by the average reader.

The research adds a new dimension to media evaluation and campaign planning, since the National Readership Surveys treat all readers equally, whereas readers of some publications will see an advertisement more than once.

The research used the NRS questionnaire and interview methodology, and then asked three additional questions to establish:

- The number of days a title is read in the publication interval;
- Number of issues seen when the publication was last read;
- Proportion of pages read.

MPX scores are the product of these three components, and data is available, in the usual demographic groupings, for 19 different magazine groupings. Some have business-to-business relevance, including:

- *Upmarket weeklies* – covering *Investors Chronicle, Financial Weekly, Economist,*

Punch, Time Out, The Field, The New Scientist, The New Statesman, New Society, Country Life, The Spectator, and The Listener;
- Quality Supplements – covering The Observer Magazine, The Sunday Times Magazine, and Telegraph Magazine.

PERIODICAL PUBLISHERS ASSOCIATION
(Imperial House, 15–19 Kingsway, London WC2B 6UN)

The PPA's aims include promotion 'to help secure an increasing share of advertising budgets, nationally and internationally, by promoting to advertisers and agencies the collective claims of periodicals'. To this end, the PPA undertook research which demonstrates how magazine advertising can enhance awareness of a simultaneous TV campaign.

Entitled *'Multiplying the Media Effect'*, it contains seven detailed case studies showing how television and magazines together produced more effective communication than either medium could achieve alone.

NEWSPAPERS

Newspapers can deliver detailed messages at short notice and on a given day to a media audience of known size and composition, as circulation and readership figures are generally available. Space is usually sold by the single-column centimetre (scc), and in multiples thereof. Bookings can be either ROP (run-of-paper rate, at which companies have no control over where their advertisements appear) or advertisers can pay extra for any of a wide variety of special positions. Classified and semi-display advertising is also available. There are two main categories: national and regional.

NATIONAL NEWSPAPERS

The advantages of national newspapers – in addition to the benefits just mentioned – are best summarised by the two parts of the name: 'national' and 'news'papers. Advertising appears nationally (although it is increasingly possible to advertise on a regional basis) and the promotional message benefits from an atmosphere of urgency and immediacy. Colour is increasingly available, either in the normal run of printing or as separate supplements.

Different newspapers appeal to different types of readership, but they can be grouped into two broad categories – 'broadsheet' and 'tabloid'. The former are read more by the A, B and C1 socio-economic grades, who are defined as 'Managerial, administrative and professional', at higher, intermediate and junior or supervisory levels. Business advertisers wishing to reach large numbers of up-market potential purchasers spread across a wide range of industries are thus likely to use these broadsheet media rather than the popular 'tabloid' press, the majority of whose readers are in the C2, D and E socio-economic grades.

Sunday newspapers have the additional benefit of being read in a more relaxed state of mind. Sunday is not a working day but this is rarely a hindrance, for business products are seldom purchased on impulse and Sunday's leisure environment facilitates writing for further information. In addition, some Sunday newspapers have a longer life, being kept and re-read later in the week, or even retained for reference. As with dailies, there are tabloid and broadsheet Sundays, and an in-depth knowledge of each newspaper is again essential. Some, for example, divide into distinct sections, one perhaps devoted to business matters. The various colour supplements often have a 'lifestyle' emphasis, and so can be considered under the twin headings of newspapers and magazines, as discussed above.

The national press has always been subject to circulation and readership battles, but the medium has recently been revitalised by changes in ownership, the introduction of new titles, supplements and sub-sections, by increasing segmentation of the marketplace, by changes in format and presentation, and by circulation wars between competing publishers. Nevertheless, the basic points made earlier still apply.

Recent developments in printing technology have radically changed the press medium, particularly national newspapers. Journalists' editorial was formerly typeset and proof-read by others; copies printed in Fleet Street were then bulk transported by rail (or by other special arrangements). The move to London's Docklands revolutionised these practices. 'Direct input', which enables journalists to typeset and check their own material, resulted in considerable cost reductions. Further savings were achieved by vacating high-cost old-technology premises in Fleet Street, and siting new-technology facilities in the low-cost Docklands area. Further economies resulted from sending heavy bulk supplies of newspapers by road rather than rail – or even achieving a double saving in both production and distribution costs by printing at provincial centres with spare capacity, having sent the 'London-set' material there electronically. This also speeded distribution, thus saving time as well as money. The same technology is used by some media-owners (eg, *The Financial Times*) to publish international editions.

These developments drastically reduced the 'entrance fee' for new media, and had an equally dramatic effect on existing publications, as regards colour availability and the print quality of advertising messages.

London is not truly national but is too large to be classed as local, so London's evening paper, *The Evening Standard*, is in a category of its own. Readership figures are provided by the National Readership Surveys, however, so it is best considered under that heading – or at least as semi-national. As the area contains a high concentration of commercial firms, the paper carries a considerable amount of business advertising aimed at this valuable target group.

NATIONAL NEWSPAPER RESEARCH DATA

Information about the circulation and readership of national newspapers is readily available, through ABC, JICNARS and TGI, already described. In addition, MPX scores are available for some supplements.

REGIONAL NEWSPAPERS

This media group sub-divides into two main categories – paid-for and free. The papers frequently carry considerable amounts of local traders' advertising, but are also used by those with national distribution to boost sales in selected areas, to benefit from local interest, to deliver regionalized messages, and to tie in with local dealers. As before, the advertising message can be quickly spread on a selected day, and detailed information can be included. Colour is increasingly available, and the changes in print technology are as important for regional as for national press.

A factor that sometimes deters advertisers from using local media, paid-for or free, is lack of readership information on the lines of JICNARS' provision. Another factor is that, when co-operative dealer promotions are mounted in local media, this involves the advertiser in contacting his stockists to seek their co-operation, and then administering the joint campaign. Even if local press campaigns are mounted on a solo basis, they still call for considerable work in selecting suitable publications, placing individual orders, sending individual advertising material and correcting individual proofs, and then paying individual invoices. The sheer physical labour becomes increasingly burdensome the larger the number of publications included in the schedule. The services of the Association of Free Newspapers, described on page 109, are important in this respect.

Until recently, parallel services for paid-for papers were provided by the now defunct Regional Newspaper Advertising Bureau. The need for these central services continues, however, and it remains to be seen if the gap left by RNAB's demise will be filled by some other co-operative network.

PAID-FOR REGIONAL NEWSPAPERS

Regional morning newspapers are usually up-market in approach, and consequently have lower coverage. Regional evenings, on the other hand, usually have more of a mass appeal and therefore larger circulations. The few regional Sunday newspapers combine the benefits of local interest with the advantages of Sunday publications described above. Finally, there are local weeklies – for which circulation figures (usually small) are not always ABC audited, and sometimes not even available. Local weeklies are likely to have a longer life, being kept a full week for reference.

The circulation of paid-for regional newspapers is audited by the ABC described on page 132.

Many publishers of paid-for newspapers are also involved with the free publications discussed below.

FREE PUBLICATIONS

Some newspapers – and magazines or directories – are issued free, either distributed door-to-door or given away at central points such as stations where they are handed to people on their way to work. This type of free publication differs from the controlled circulation publications described above, which are distributed through the post. Both types of free publication share a point of common principle, however: they have forgone cover revenue in the belief that they will more than recoup this through increased advertisement revenue, obtained by the promise of complete market coverage.

Free newspapers have been published in England for more than 100 years, but more recently there has been an upsurge. The papers themselves range from some that contain nothing but advertising to those with 30 per cent editorial. New developments include publishers of paid-for journals converting them to free distribution, or launching new titles and offering advantageous combined rates for advertisers using both media.

FREE NEWSPAPER RESEARCH DATA

The early days of free newspapers were sometimes described as a dumping operation, and apocryphal stories tell of schoolboys throwing them away by the bundle. A major step to official recognition was taken when the Audit Bureau of Circulations launched its 'Verified Free Distributions' subsidiary to certify the distribution of free publications.

VERIFIED FREE DISTRIBUTIONS LTD
(13 Wimpole Street, London W1M 7AB)

VFD is the independent certifying authority for all publications whose distribution is not through regular news trade channels or by single addressed copies mailed through the Post Office.

Each applicant publication's records and distribution system are scrutinised by a VFD Inspector to determine eligibility to join the system. The check confirms good record-keeping and distribution control, including agreed standards of regular and systematic back-checking on delivered copies. The publisher maintains issue-by-issue records on VFD forms, which are then audited by an approved independent firm of chartered accountants. If the results are approved, a VFD *Certificate of Average Net Distribution* is issued. This information, in addition to a description and map of the distribution area, forms the basis of the VFD certificate.

VFD operates an optional additional *Three Star* certification based on agreed levels of interviews with recipients of free delivered publications, either by telephone or face-to-face, confirming the level of regular receipt.

The introduction of VFD answered the question of whether free newspapers were properly distributed. The next question was 'Do people read free publications?'

THE ASSOCIATION OF FREE NEWSPAPERS
(Ladybellegate House, Longsmith Street, Gloucester GL1 2HT)

AFN mounted three major pieces of research to 'explode the myths of free distribution'. These U & A (Usage & Attitude) surveys revealed both high readership and high average reading time, and favourable reader attributes. Readership data on free newspapers is also included in the National Readership Surveys and in the Target Group Index, already described.

AFN also offers a range of services to those wishing to use this media group:

- *Research and Data* – AFN can tell advertisers which individual titles circulate in areas of interest, and provide valuable information about these areas as well as relevant titles' coverage;
- *Single Order Service* – the Association provides facilities through which advertisers can cover a number of publications with a single order, advertisement proof and invoice, making it far easier from an administrative point of view to justify the use of local media;

- *Dealer Service* – should a manufacturer offer his dealers, agents or distributors a co-operative scheme (perhaps providing advertising material and sharing costs) AFN can assist in obtaining their co-operation. Given details of the joint promotion and the location of dealers, the Association then circulates member newspapers in whichever towns distributors are located. Representatives of these newspapers then make sales calls, thus supplementing the company's own efforts to secure maximum dealer participation in the sales drive.

These services may perhaps be extended to cover paid-for publications as before, bearing in mind the potential advertiser's practical needs for them.

THE PRESS MEDIUM OVERALL

Before turning to other media, it is important to see the press medium in context. What was formerly a relatively static marketplace has become fast-moving and dynamic. Quite apart from changes in printing technology, publishers compete fiercely for the same markets, adapt existing publications, and launch new titles. New titles may appear which do not perhaps correspond to the broad categories listed. In the absence of formal data about any new press or other media, the approach must, as always, be a practical one, examining the new publication in detail, and considering it in the light of the criteria discussed in Chapter 6.

CHAPTER NINE

Specialist Readership Surveys

In addition to the general databases already described, a number of specialist readership surveys are relevant to business-to-business promotional planning. Some extend their coverage beyond readership figures, to include usage (read regularly, read half or more etc) and attitudes (best source of new ideas, usefulness of advertising etc) as well as other media (direct mail, exhibitions, seminars, television, etc).

Although undertaken primarily for advertising reasons, they also serve other purposes. These specialist surveys can provide valuable desk research data about target markets. Some also offer a field research opportunity, through an 'omnibus' facility which permits subscribing companies to include their own specific questions within the questionnaire – for example about awareness and opinions of products and services, and advertising recall. The data relating to such questions remains confidential, and is not released to other subscribers. The surveys also have direct public relations relevance, through the information they provide about those who will read news releases.

Although the published reports contain many tabulations, the amount of data stored on tapes is very much larger, and there are often facilities for extracting additional information (at a fee appropriate to the cost of providing the tabulations required). Some media-owners commission these tabulations direct, as part of their own media research provision, to provide additional information which they hope will make potential advertisers view their media more favourably.

A problem that arises with some specialist surveys is that, unlike the Joint Industry Committee surveys mentioned earlier, the research is not always undertaken on a regular basis. Some indeed have been 'once off' exercises – mounted and published, but never repeated. Some such surveys, being out of print as well as out-of-date, have been omitted from this review.

When media-owners commission their own research, promotional planners sometimes suspect such research of being biased in favour of the medium sponsoring it. In this respect it is relevant that the Institute of Practitioners in Advertising, through its Research Committee, provides a service for member agencies in reporting on such surveys in an *Appraisals Bulletin*. The IPA also welcomes advance consultation in regard to any surveys proposed by media-owners.

Specialist surveys are clearly not of general interest. Readers are therefore advised to make a quick visual check of subject headings, rather than to read through this chapter in the usual way, to see if there are databases specific to their business area. Those fortunate enough to find relevant headings should then return to those sources for more detailed study later.

Readers should also check the *Business Advertising Planner – Media Guide and*

EXISTING MEDIA – THE ADVERTISING ROUTE

Research Index Planner 1988/1989, available from British Business Press (see page 104). This is an executive guide to better business marketing and advertising, with notes on strategic planning, and details of more than 250 business magazines and research in 23 major business categories. Within each category, relevant publications are listed together with an outline of editorial policy, a readership profile, circulation, type area, advertising page rate, and services. (Inserts/Insets, Product Information Cards, Reader Enquiry Service, Recruitment Advertising, and Research available). The 23 major business categories are:

- Advertising/Marketing/Conferences
- Audio Visual/Radio and TV
- Business Services/Property/Architecture
- Business Management/Equipment Personnel
- Chemicals
- Computers
- Electrical Industry/Appliances
- Electronics
- Energy/Fuels
- Engineering
- Factories
- Farming
- Food Processing
- Freight
- Materials Industries
- Metal Industries
- Packaging
- Printing
- Public Works/Construction/Ports
- Retailing
- Services
- Shipping and Marine
- Transport/Road/Rail/Air

A research index lists research reports freely available from individual publishers:

- British Baker
- Building
- Cabinet Maker & Retail Furnisher
- Caterer & Hotelkeeper
- Chartered Quantity Surveyor
- Chemist & Druggist
- Commercial Motor & Motor Transport
- Computer Weekly
- Community Care
- Contract Journal
- Electrical Products
- Electronics Weekly
- Eureka
- Farmers Weekly
- Farmers Weekly/Crops/Big Farm Weekly/Power Farming
- Flight International
- Gas Marketing
- The Grocer
- Hardware Trade Journal
- Health & Safety At Work
- Housewares
- International Freighting Weekl
- Laboratory News
- Lloyd's List
- Lloyd's Loading List
- Motor Trader
- Motor Transport & Commercial Motor
- Office Equipment News
- Off Licence News
- Packaging News
- Packaging Week
- Printing World
- Speciality Chemicals
- Sports Retailing
- Super Marketing
- Surveyor
- Timber Trades Journal & Wood Processing
- Works Management

The Planner also includes an enquiry form, through which readers can request the media packs of those magazines of interest.

SPECIALIST READERSHIP SURVEYS

These include the following:

AGRIDATA READERSHIP AND MEDIA SURVEY
(Taylor Nelson Agriculture, Taylor Nelson House, 44–46 Upper High Street, Epsom, Surrey KT17 4QS)

Agridata is a media survey with four research samples comprising arable, cattle, sheep, and pig farmers. The survey covers all main agricultural journals and gives details of:

- Readership figures;
- An analysis of these figures by farm type, size and region;
- Expenditure on all major farm inputs;
- How many livestock are owned;
- How many hectares are farmed.

Agridata also covers regional newspapers, television viewing, attendance at agricultural shows and marketplaces, and use of on-farm computers and computer bureaux for farm business, television information systems such as Teletext, and video recorders.

Attitudinal questions test thoroughness of reading (how much of journal is read, and how many times picked up) as well as preference ('most overall value', 'most interesting to read' and 'best journal' on a range of editorial topics).

Results are published twice a year, with the previous 12 months' readership and viewing figures shown.

The survey also has an 'omnibus' facility, offering Taylor Nelson clients the opportunity to add questions of their own choosing, which are confidential to them.

See also: FARMING, page 121.

ARCHITECTS SURVEY
(InDaL (Industrial Data Limited), Evelyn House, 62 Oxford Street, London W1N 9LD)

The *National Architects Survey* is a syndicated research survey amongst practising architects in Great Britain. It is conducted at least once, and usually twice, a year.

The sample of architects is selected on a random basis from the ARCUK *Register of Architects*, a comprehensive list of all qualified architects, including the self-employed and those in both private practice and the public sector. The survey divides into three sections, any combination of which can be purchased:

- *Readership Data* – readership and usefulness of weekly and monthly architectural publications;
- *Reference Sources* – availability and usefulness of published reference sources such as *Barbour Index* and *RIBA Product Selector;*
- *Omnibus Facility* – subscribers can purchase question space to investigate matters of interest to them. All such questions are confidential to the company concerned.

See also: BUILDING CENTRE READERSHIP SURVEY, page 114.

ASIAN BUSINESSMAN READERSHIP SURVEY
(Research Services Ltd, Station House, Harrow Road, Wembley HA9 6DE)

Conducted in 1985 this survey covered nine countries in the Far East, using 16 language versions of the questionnaire. There was an initial telephone stage to determine company eligibility and individuals' names in selected job titles/functions. The questionnaires were mailed out to identified businessmen and an overall response rate of 58 per cent was achieved. A second ABRS is now being conducted, to be released in Spring 1989.

BANKING

See EUROPEAN BUSINESSMAN READERSHIP SURVEY, page 120; FINANCE, below.

BUILDING CENTRE READERSHIP SURVEY
(The Centre for Construction Market Information, 26 Store Street, London WC1E 7BT)

The aim of this *Readership Survey of Construction Industry Management and Professional Practice* is to provide information on readership of magazines, use of product cards, reference sources and new technology by managers and professionals in the UK construction industry. Four categories of managers and professionals were surveyed:

- Architects
- Quantity Surveyors
- Building Surveyors
- Chartered Institute of Building Members

The main report contains the following tables:

Magazines (separate figures are given for weekly and monthly magazines)

- Readership
- Reading Frequency
- Quality of Readership
- How Normally Read/Copy Disposal

National newspapers:

- Readership

Product cards:

- Awareness and Frequency of Use
- Number of Cards Used/usefulness

Reference sources:

- Availability
- Use of
- Usefulness/Number Using
- Library

SPECIALIST READERSHIP SURVEYS

The survey also covers the availability of new technology, and a further section covers specification influences.

The Centre for Construction Market Information is a specialist organization which provides a wide range of other market research services.

See also: CONSTRUCTION INDUSTRY READERSHIP SURVEY, page 116.

BUSINESS

See ASIAN BUSINESSMAN READERSHIP SURVEY, page 114; BRITISH BUSINESS PRESS, page 104.
And the following sources:

BUSINESSMAN READERSHIP SURVEY
CAPTAINS OF INDUSTRY
EUROPEAN BUSINESSMAN READERSHIP SURVEY
EUROPEAN INSTITUTIONAL INVESTORS RESEARCH
INTERNATIONAL FINANCIAL MANAGERS SURVEY
INVESTMENT INTERMEDIARIES
MANAGING DIRECTORS READERSHIP SURVEY
PAN EUROPEAN SURVEY

BUSINESSMAN READERSHIP SURVEY
(Research Services Limited, Station House, Harrow Road, Wembley HA9 6DE)

The 1988 survey is the ninth in a series conducted on behalf of the Business Media Research Committee (BMRC) which represents most UK quality national newspapers and business magazines.

The definition of a businessman is '*a man or woman whose occupation implies the exercise of significant managerial, executive, technical or advisory functions and who works in an organization eligible on grounds of size.*' This overall description covers some 80-plus occupational groups. Eligibility depends also on satisfying a number of additional criteria: one is '*that with the exception of a small number of technically qualified C1s . . . the informant would be classified as A or B social grade.*' There is thus comparability with National Readership Survey data.

The survey covers more than 150 titles (including all national newspapers and a wide selection of business management, industrial and specialist, technical as well as general interest publications), and is designed to generate the same readership information as the NRS:

- Average issue readership;
- Reading frequency – past year reading, reading frequency, recency of reading, and yesterday reading.

Data covers readership by age, social grade, highest educational qualification and survey region. Other main sections are devoted to Income, Status, Occupation, Industry, Responsibility, Financial Investments, Travel, Car Ownership/Hire Care Usage/Credit Cards held, ITV Viewing, Duplication Tables, Cumulative Readership and Source of Copy.

CAPTAINS OF INDUSTRY
(MORI, 32 Old Queen Street, London SW1)

The 1987 report is the fifth in a series of surveys among Chairmen, Managing Directors and other main Board Directors of Britain's 500 major companies, through MORI (Market & Opinion Research International). The purpose of the study was to investigate the attitude of 'Captains of Industry' towards industry and commerce, current problems facing companies, prospects for the economy, the role of government in industry, the criteria on which companies and organizations are judged, knowledge of and attitudes towards a range of particular industries and companies, and – most relevant to this book – sources of information and readership of newspapers/magazines. In this last respect the survey covers, for national and Sunday newspapers and for selected magazines:

- Average issue readership;
- Regular readership;
- Usefulness for company information;
- Sources of information, and most useful in work.

COMPUTER READERSHIP SURVEY
and
COMPUTER INDUSTRY SURVEY
(The Codex Partnership, 10 Barley Mow Passage, London W4 4BR)

These surveys cover Data Processing Managers from government departments, local authorities, banks and other industrial categories, throughout the UK.

The Readership Survey covers 51 computer titles and 22 non-computer related titles, including national daily and Sunday newspapers, and gives information on Data Processing Managers' reading habits, which titles they prefer and how often they are read.

The Industry Survey includes further media information, including views on the value of computer exhibitions, and how much television Data Processing Managers watch.

In both surveys company information is available by industrial classification, departmental size, attitudes to industrial innovation and staff recruitment, budget size, types of equipment used, etc, all cross-referenced against media titles.

CONSTRUCTION INDUSTRY READERSHIP SURVEY
(Mass Observation (UK) Limited, Clifton House, 83–89 Uxbridge Road, London W5 5DA)

This survey, prepared in 1986 for Morgan-Grampian (Construction Press) Ltd, presents the results of a readership survey among heads of plant hiring/buying in the construction industry: it continues a series of earlier surveys. The objective is to measure the readership of eight construction and civil engineering publications, and seven quality national newspapers, among heads of plant hiring/buying in the industry sectors which collectively comprise the construction industry – plant hire companies, civil engineering contractors, local authorities, extraction companies and public utilities. A further objective is to estimate the number of relevant people employed in each industry sector.

The report contains the following readership tables:

- Average Issue Readership
- Read in Last Year
- Frequency of Readership
- Readership in Combination

It also gives data on editorial preferences – which publications were best for news, for technical features, and for information on plant and equipment.

Further tables cover membership of the Institute of Civil Engineers, and planned increase or decrease in expenditure on plant purchase or hire.

See also: BUILDING CENTRE READERSHIP SURVEY, page 114.

DATA PROCESSING

See COMPUTER READERSHIP SURVEY and COMPUTER INDUSTRY SURVEY, (page 116), and EUROPEAN BUSINESSMAN READERSHIP SURVEY (page 120).

DESIGN ENGINEERING
(Mass-Observation (UK) Limited, Clifton House, 83–89 Uxbridge Road, London W5 5TA)

The 1988 Readership Profile Survey was prepared for Morgan-Grampian (Publishers) Ltd. The main objectives of the research were:

1. To gauge receipt and readership of a selection of engineering trade magazines.
2. To investigate readers' attitudes towards various aspects of Design Engineering, including:
    i) Frequency and depth of readership
    ii) Action taken on receipt of issue
    iii) Pass-on readership
    iv) Regular sections of Design Engineering
       – how often they are read
       – how useful they are
    v) The use of abbreviations and technical information
    vi) Coverage of various topics
3. To determine readers' involvement in the specification and purchase of various products, in terms of:
    i) Direct involvement in the specification/purchase of various products and services.
    ii) Products/Services specified/purchased
    iii) Action taken when interested in a product or service seen in Design Engineering
4. To examine readers' present job function in terms of the current discipline in which they are employed, and whom they liaise with during work projects.

5. To establish the job function, age, company size and type of organization of the respondent.

See also: ENGINEERING INDUSTRIES READERSHIP SURVEY, page 119.

DOCTORS

See HOSPITAL MEDIA SURVEY, page 122; MEDICAL ADVERTISING – JICMARS, page 123.

ELECTRONICS READERSHIP SURVEY
(NOP Market Research Limited, Tower House, Southampton Street, London WC2E 7HN)

This survey was undertaken in 1985 for JIC-ERS (The Joint Industry Committee for Electronics Readerships Surveys) and examines readership of professional electronics publications and national newspapers. The industry splits into three sections:

- Electronics Original Equipment Manufacturers
- Intensive User Industries
- Electronics Consultants

This is the first comprehensive survey of the electronics industry, and contains the following tables:

- Average Issue Readership
- Duplication of Readership
- Total Readership
- Frequency of Readership
- Cumulative Readership
- Usefulness in Job
- News Content
- Technical Features
- New Product Information
- Job Opportunities
- Useful Sources of Information
- Way In Which Copy Is Received
- Further Information Sources.

ELECTRONICS TIMES
(Mass Observation (UK) Limited, Clifton House, 83–89 Uxbridge Road, London W5 5TA)

This 1988 Reader Profile Survey was conducted for Electronics Times. The objectives of the research were:

- To obtain overall ratings of ET compared with its competitive weeklies, Electronics Weekly and Electronic Express;
- To examine usage of and attitude towards the regular sections and special features;

- To gauge attitudes towards specific aspects of the magazine, eg signposting, ease of reading;
- To find out how often the magazine is read, and in what degree of detail.

ENGINEERING INDUSTRIES READERSHIP SURVEY
(Mass Observation (UK) Limited, Clifton House, 83–89 Uxbridge Road, London W5 5TA)

The 1986 survey is the fifth in a series prepared for Morgan-Grampian (Publishers) Ltd. The main objective is to measure the readership of thirty engineering and purchasing publications, and seven quality national newspapers, amongst the main engineering functions and the purchasing function in companies employing 50 or more people in the engineering industries. A secondary objective is to estimate the number of people employed in each job function measured.

The establishment universe consists of firms in Standard Industrial Classification Division 3 (Engineering, Metals and Vehicles), within the following classes which constitute this division:

- 31 Metal goods not elsewhere specified
- 32 Mechanical engineering
- 33 Office machinery and electronic data processing equipment
- 34 Electrical and electronics engineering
- 35 Motor vehicles and parts
- 36 Other transport equipment
- 37 Instrument engineering

The job function universe comprises:

- Technical director
- Design engineering
- Production engineering
- Works/maintenance engineering
- Purchasing

The survey tables give average issue and cumulative readership tables, together with separately tabulated readerships for three publications which do not fall either into the horizontal or vertical job function category, and readership combination tables.

See also: DESIGN ENGINEERING, page 117.

EUROFOOD READERSHIP SURVEY
(Morgan-Grampian plc, 30 Calderwood Street, Woolwich, London SE18 6QH)

The 1988 survey was conducted by Mass Observation (UK) Ltd. The objectives of the research were:

1. To measure readership of the major business publications that serve the food industry, among those readers responsible for specifying or purchasing in four target markets:

- Food processing machinery/equipment
- Food ingredients/additives
- Food packaging machinery/equipment
- Food packaging materials

2. To establish respondents' opinions as to the usefulness and authority of the above publications.

Tabulations include:

- Average Issue Readership
- Frequency of Reading
- Most Useful Publication
- Most Authoritative Publication
- Profile of Respondents

EUROPEAN BUSINESSMAN READERSHIP SURVEY
(Research Services Limited, Station House, Harrow Road, Wembley HA9 6DE)

This survey, produced for a number of leading financial and business publications, studied senior executives in medium and large sized companies in some 16 European countries. There are three size ranges of organization:

- 250–499 employees
- 500–999 employees
- 1000 or more employees

The executives' universe is defined in a different way for each size range in industrial and commercial companies but, overall, covered the heads of the following job functions: Advertising Publicity Public Relations, Chief Executive, Computing DP, Corporate Planning, Deputy Chief Executive, Export Sales, Finance, Home Sales, Marketing, Marketing and Advertising, Personnel, Personnel Training, Production Technical Services, Purchasing, Research and Development.

The job functions within banks and insurance companies necessarily differ from those in other companies. The list of eligible functions varied according to company size but overall covered the following:

- Banks: *Chief Executive, Corporate Finance Services, Foreign Exchange, Investment/Fund Management, Management Services (including Data Processing), Marketing, Publicity Advertising/Public Relations, Syndicated Loans/Eurobonds.*
- Insurance: *Chief Accountant/Head of Finance, Chief Actuary, Chief Executive, Computing/Data Processing, General Manager, Investment/Fund Management, Marketing Manager, Publicity/Advertising/Public Relations.*

The survey investigates the reading behaviour of senior executives, and covers 13 international English language publications and more than 200 business-orientated national publications. It provides a profile of executives in terms of age, salary, and frequency of air travel. The main tables are devoted to country of residence, industry, responsibility, and air travel and company size. Supplementary analysis covers essential business reading, cumulative coverages, schedule analysis guide, cost ranking, and guide to publications.

SPECIALIST READERSHIP SURVEYS

EUROPEAN INSTITUTIONAL INVESTORS RESEARCH
(Research Services Limited, Station House, Harrow Road, Wembley HA9 6DE)

This report presents the results of a readership survey of institutional investors in European financial institutions. The 1986 survey updates earlier research, and is sponsored by the Financial Times and The International Herald Tribune.

The universe is defined as individuals with specified job titles working for European financial institutions which manage portfolios containing US securities. Eligible job titles were: Analyst, Investment Head, Overall Investment Head, Portfolio Manager. The survey covered 13 countries.

Questions in the survey covered average issue readership, frequency of reading of publications, and which were considered 'essential business reading'. Respondents were also asked to classify themselves in terms of the interests in which their companies were primarily engaged.

FARMING
See AGRIDATA, pagge 113.

FARMEDIA
(Produce Studies Ltd, Northcroft House, West Street, Newbury, Berkshire RG13 1HD)

Farmedia is a readership survey of agricultural media, principally the agricultural press, in Great Britain. It is conducted regularly (usually annually, sometimes more frequently) among a nationally-balanced sample of farms in Great Britain.

Farmedia provides conventional readership analysis (total penetration of each publication on farms, average issue readerships, etc) with appropriate profiles (by region, type of farm, farm size, etc). It also estimates the number of readers with decision-taking responsibilities for different activities on the farm (eg livestock, cropping, purchase of machinery etc). Further features are:

- It provides estimates of the opportunities to see an 'average' (run-of-press) advertisement. Each publication is accorded a *'MOTSA'* (minimum opportunities to see an advertisement) value;
- It examines important features of readership, such as the amount of time spent reading, number of reading occasions and pass-on readership etc;
- It presents data on a publication-by-publication basis. Thus, although it covers more than twenty titles, an advertiser interested in only a small number need subscribe only for those profiles of interest.

FARMEDIA is produced by Produce Studies Ltd, a specialist agricultural marketing research company.

FINANCE
See EUROPEAN BUSINESSMAN READERSHIP SURVEY, page 120; EUROPEAN INSTITUTIONAL INVESTORS RESEARCH, above; INTERNATIONAL FINANCIAL MANAGERS SURVEY, page 122; INVESTMENT INTERMEDIARIES READERSHIP SURVEY, page 122.

FOOD INDUSTRY
See EUROFOOD READERSHIP SURVEY, above.

HOSPITAL MEDIA SURVEY
(Taylor Nelson Media, Taylor Nelson House, 44–46 Upper High Street, Epsom, Surrey KT17 4QS)

This readership survey of hospital doctors covers readership of specialist medical publications. The main tabulations are:

- Average Issue Readership
- Regular Issue Readership
- Amount Read
- Time Spent Reading

Data is presented by medical specialism and grade, and data on prescribing habits is also reported.

INSURANCE INDUSTRY
See EUROPEAN BUSINESSMAN READERSHIP SURVEY, page 120; INVESTMENT INTERMEDIARIES, below.

INTERNATIONAL FINANCIAL MANAGERS SURVEY
(Research Services Limited, Station House, Harrow Road, Wembley HA9 6DE)

The report presents the findings of a readership survey of senior financial managers in Europe's largest companies, carried out on behalf of Business Week, The Economist, Euromoney, The Financial Times, Institutional Investor International and The Wall Street Journal/Europe. The 1985 survey updates earlier research, and covers more than 40 national and international publications dealing with finance.

The study universe includes the international financial managers of industrial, trading, transport, insurance and advertising companies that had a minimum turnover in 1982 of US$150 million. For this survey, the catering industry was included for the first time. The companies surveyed were in 13 countries.

The tables cover Average Issue Readership, Essential Business Reading, Rank Order, Percentage of Export Business and Company Ownership; and Area of Responsibility and Job Title.

INVESTMENT INTERMEDIARIES READERSHIP SURVEY
(Taylor Nelson Media, Taylor Nelson House, 44–66 Upper High Street, Epsom, Surrey KT17 4QS)

This is a new Joint Industry Committee survey, covering readership of quality daily and Sunday newspapers, weekly and monthly financial titles, by independent financial intermediaries (either employed by members of the

Financial Investment Managers & Brokers Regulatory Association, or FIMBRA members in their own right). All readers spend at least two thirds of their time advising clients on packaged investment products.

The main tabulations are average issue readership and frequency of reading by size of establishment, number of life specialists etc. For key publications, data is presented for amount read, number of times looked at, time spent reading, and perceived usefulness.

The survey is sponsored by the publishers of the four weeklies: Financial Adviser, Investment Adviser, Money Week, and Money Marketing, together with several advertising agencies. The intention is that this will become a regular annual survey.

MANAGING DIRECTORS READERSHIP SURVEY
(NOP Market Research Limited, Tower House, Southampton Street, London WC2E 7HN)

This survey, undertaken in 1986 for Morgan-Grampian (Professional) Press Limited, is the seventh in a series carried out among Managing Directors, to provide information about their reading habits and business activities. The survey covered selected business management publications and national newspapers, and contains the following tabulations:

- Average Issue Readership
- Read At All
- Frequency of Readership
- Cumulative Readership
- Combination Tables
- Television Analysis (Light, Medium and Heavy Viewing).

There are further tabulations for

- Travel
- Company Cars
- Computing and Communications Equipment
- Property
- Financial
- Membership of Professional Institutes/Associations
- Income and Age

MEDICAL ADVERTISING – JICMARS
Joint Industry Committee of Medical Advertisers for Readership Surveys, (9 Nelson Road, London N8)

This annual survey is sponsored by JICMARS, which comprises representatives of the Medical Press, Pharmaceutical Advertisers and Advertising Agencies.

The universe is defined as all doctors in General Practice, and the sample drawn from the Medical Mailing List, with fieldwork undertaken by Research Surveys of Great Britain. The questionnaire is designed to obtain information on:

- Total number of General Practitioners claiming to read or look at each publication;
- Claimed frequency of reading;
- Readership within the publication interval, used to derive 'average issue readership' data;
- Measures on 'quality of reading';
- Validation checks involving spread traffic-checks for four randomly selected publications

Since 1983, experimental questions on listenership/viewership of audio and video cassette publications have been included: these appear to have worked satisfactorily.

Further questions cover exposure to the following media, and provide additional breakdowns:

- Pharmaceutical Company Representatives
- Pharmaceutical Company Direct Mail
- Pharmaceutical Company Sponsored Meetings

There is also data about 'Total Face to Face Exposure' – this measure combines the number of representatives seen and the number of meetings attended by each respondent.

Response data is available in terms of area, date qualified, medical qualification ('UK and Eire' or 'Other'), sex, list size (approximate number of patients), and 'innovators' (usage of new or relatively new products), UK and Eire.

PAN EUROPEAN SURVEY
(Research Services Limited, Station House, Harrow Road, Wembley HA9 6DE)

Pan European Survey 4 is sponsored by Business Week, The Economist, The Financial Times, International Herald Tribune, and Scientific American (and purchased by a number of other publications): it updates three earlier studies. The PES is a media and marketing research study of high status professional and executive men in 13 European countries. Economically active men aged 25 and over are eligible if they have achieved high status through their educational or professional qualifications, or their level of income.

The purpose is to provide accurate and up-to-date information on the readership of national and international dailies, and of up-market business, general and women's magazines. The survey is also a source of data on the ownership and use of many products and services, and on the occupational and demographic characteristics of men of high status.

PLANT HIRING/BUYING
See CONSTRUCTION INDUSTRY READERSHIP SURVEY, page 116.

SURVEYORS
See BUILDING CENTRE READERSHIP SURVEY, page 114.

TRANSPORT WEEK
(Morgan-Grampian plc, 30 Calderwood Street, Woolwich, London SE18 6QH)

This 1988 Reader Usage Survey was prepared by Morgan-Grampian from data produced by PAS Business Surveys. The aim of the survey was to examine the following:

- Transport Week's readership;
- Readers' attitudes towards the editorial of the magazine;
- Reader's opinions of the magazine's format and job usefulness;
- Duplication of readership amongst other Transport Industry Publications;
- Demographic profile of respondents;
- Nature of respondent's organization.

TRAVEL AGENTS READERSHIP SURVEY (TARS)
(Travel and Tourism Research Limited, 39c Highbury Place, London N5 1QP)

The 1988 survey updates an earlier study, with research among ABTA travel agents nationwide. The questionnaire covers the main travel media, and obtains information on:

- Average issue readership;
- Reading frequency;
- Duplicate readership;
- Depth of readership;
- Opinions of publications (useful, interesting, reliable, etc).

There is also an omnibus facility, making it possible for clients to include additional confidential questions.

Travel and Tourism Research is a specialist market research company which offers a range of other research services to the travel industry, including regularly published multi-client studies examining the image of airlines, tour operators and car rental companies.

TRAVELMETER
(Research Services Ltd, Station House, Harrow Road, Wembley HA9 6DE)

This survey is specifically designed to measure the size and scope of the air travel market in Europe. Almost 95,000 households were contacted between May 1986 and April 1987. A sample of 4,621 air travellers was achieved representing 25.1 million adults who had flown in the 12 month period in the seven survey countries of Belgium, France, Germany, Great Britain, Italy, Netherlands, and Switzerland. Holiday and business travel characteristics were covered as well as readership of in-flight magazines, opinion of airlines, and demographic data.

CHAPTER TEN

Exhibitions

According to the British Business Press survey, exhibitions rank third in importance for business advertisers, if measured in percentage of promotional expenditure terms – first was business press, and second was brochures and catalogues. By this book's functional definitions, however, exhibitions are the second largest *advertising* medium, in that printed materials are classed as 'created media' as there is no contractual relationship with the owner of an existing medium. Whether second or third, exhibitions are clearly an important medium for business advertisers. According to the new Exhibition Industry Federation described below, there are more than 45 exhibition venues in the UK, at which some 640 exhibitions are held annually, and expenditure on exhibitions is increasing: the Federation estimates that exhibitions' share of UK businesses' media spending doubled between 1980 and 1986.

TYPES OF EXHIBITION

Exhibitions range from those of general interest to those appealing to special interest groups – it is the latter with which business advertisers are most concerned, since they offer the benefit of a selected audience, implied by the exhibition's subject matter. Some exhibitions may, however, be 'hybrid', with restricted entrance for the first few days, after which they open to the public. In the course of time, some exhibitions may move along the scale: specialist exhibitions sometimes arouse such general interest that public attendance gradually outnumbers special interest visitors (and thus dilutes the specific targeting sought).

Geographical variations can cut across this general and special interest scale, since exhibitions may be local, regional, national or even international in their coverage.

THE ADVANTAGES OF THE EXHIBITION MEDIUM

The benefits of this medium are almost self-evident. Exhibitions offer demonstration combined with personal contact. Sales staff meet potential customers on neutral ground, where they can demonstrate the product (a major advantage when it is too bulky to take round) and can do so under ideal conditions, in settings specially designed for the purpose. It is important, therefore, when briefing a Stand Designer, to ensure he is fully aware of *functional* requirements. Prospective buyers can inspect the product, try it for themselves and ask questions. The exhibitor can answer queries, distribute samples or literature, obtain names and addresses to follow up for future action, or take orders on the spot. It is vital to have a professional system for recording visitors to the stand, to ensure efficient follow through. The names recorded on stand enquiry cards can then be incorporated in database marketing systems, as discussed in the next chapter.

Many special interest exhibitions, as well as selecting suitable audiences, also represent the one occasion in the year to contact virtually *all* prospective customers, since the opportunity to view and compare all current models ensures a consistently high attendance. In some cases, tradition has resulted in a positive cycle – all prospective customers attend the exhibition because they know all important firms will be there, which is the very reason why all major firms take stand space.

Exhibitions also provide opportunity for Sales Directors and other senior staff to greet those they cannot call on regularly themselves, and express appreciation of support given during the year. When this appreciation is coupled with hospitality, the facility is sometimes abused by buyers making the rounds of the exhibits, which are reduced to the role of free bars. Accordingly, the main advantages of exhibitions – demonstration and personal contact – should always be kept to the fore.

A further benefit arises from the descriptive entry each exhibitor receives in the catalogue, which many visitors keep for reference. There is also the possibility, for a fortunate few, of valuable editorial publicity: most exhibitions merit considerable media coverage, and those with revolutionary products, striking displays, or whose stands are visited by the VIP who opens the exhibition, may be the subject of many editorial or photographic features. There are other PR opportunities for those not so fortunate: most exhibition organizers provide a press office, through which to distribute information packs about the firm and its products.

THE DRAWBACKS OF THE MEDIUM

Apart from possible lack of audience data, discussed below, the main drawback to exhibitions is their high cost. They are often more expensive than at first expected, for the cost of designing and constructing the stand can far exceed site costs, particularly when exhibitors compete for attention with lavish displays. Another problem may be getting a good stand location, since premium positions are in heavy demand (as well as expensive). If a stand is not located where most visitors will see it (and even when it *is* well sited), further expenses are usually incurred in ensuring – through press advertisements, direct mail invitations, and perhaps an incentive offer – that exhibition visitors know where to find the stand, and are motivated to visit it.

In addition, there are numerous running costs: catalogue advertisements, electricity, hospitality expenses, insurance, literature, samples, telephone installation and calls, and temporary 'hospitality and reception' staff. There are also the hidden costs of company staff, who must be present to deal with those questions temporary staff cannot answer; there may also be hotel, travel and other expenses.

The longer the exhibition's duration, the higher the costs of stand construction, staff and running costs. Frequently, too, exhibitions occupy more top management time, before and during the exhibition, than is customary with other media.

There can also be practical problems, and the contract's small print should be checked carefully: regulations may restrict what exhibitors are allowed to do on their stands. The practicalities of exhibiting should equally be considered – if the product is a bulky or heavy one, is it perhaps too big to get through the exhibition hall's doors, and are there any load-bearing restrictions?

Finally, most exhibitions permit only a once-a-year market stimulus. Where repetition/continuity is achieved by participation in a series of exhibitions, expenses rise proportionately.

EXHIBITION REVIEW

After participation in any exhibition, the advertiser should, as with all media, evaluate results. A post exhibition de-briefing should be held before memories fade, and a Stand Manager's Report prepared, summarising the outcome, and indicating practical steps to be taken for the future.

OTHER FORMS OF DEMONSTRATION

Formal exhibitions are not the only medium to offer facilities for demonstration and personal contact. As always, if existing media are not suitable, companies may have to create their own: accordingly some firms mount private exhibitions, either on their own premises or by using portable displays which they erect in premises hired for the occasion. This type of exhibition can often be combined with an invited audience film or video show. Exhibition Industry Federation figures show more than £100 million spent on private events such as conferences, product launches and in-house meetings. Some firms, in preference to portable exhibition stands, construct mobile displays in special trailers, buses or railway carriages which they then send round the country.

The ultimate in personal contact and demonstration is, of course, achieved with salesmanship. Rather than use conventional media, sales representatives may demonstrate the product. Even here, however, the range of media includes activities which can assist such marketing operations. Created media such as display cases and back-projection film or video units that assist representatives in their selling task, are further examples which show that personal selling by representatives and indirect selling through promotion are not separate activities but overlap considerably.

EXHIBITION AUDIENCE RESEARCH

Unfortunately, not all exhibition organizers provide the ABC audited data described later. A drawback which the medium shares with the special interest press is that in some cases all that is known about the exhibition's coverage is what can be deduced by common sense from its title. When evaluating possible exhibitions in the absence of hard data, useful practical signals of relevance include a statement by the organizers about the exhibition's aims and content, and whether it is being mounted in association with any sponsors: many specialist exhibitions complement a professional body's conference, which may attract high attendances. Whether or not this is the case, potential exhibitors should obtain details of the promotional campaign the organizers propose mounting to attract visitors. It is also worth checking the organizers' track record, and whether or not they are members of the relevant professional body, The Association of Exhibition Organizers.

The audience data situation is undergoing considerable change, however, as an Exhibition Industry Federation, described on page 131, was formed recently. One of its major aims is to gather reliable quantitative and qualitative statistics concerning the British exhibition industry. To achieve this, a *Certified Clearinghouse for Data on Exhibitions* (CCDE), an independent organization, has been established to collect and collate the figures. The CCDE, which has developed an open audit specification (a low cost method of providing certified data on shows), will provide statistics on the number of visitors and exhibitors at each event. Furthermore, the Polytechnic of North London has been commissioned to survey all exhibition expenditure in the UK by both exhibitors and visitors.

FURTHER INFORMATION SOURCES

THE AUDIT BUREAU OF CIRCULATIONS
(13 Wimpole Street, London W1M 7AB)

The ABC administers through its Exhibition Data Division a system to audit exhibition attendances both as to quantity and quality. The ABC-verified document is named the *Exhibition Data Form*.

The EDF is constructed in four parts:

Part I contains general information about the exhibition, the organizers and sponsors, what items were exhibited and the target audience. Last, it details the certified attendances both paid (registered and unregistered) and free (registered only).
Part II is devoted to analyses of the registered attendance. It is mandatory to analyse geographically, by job function/qualification and by industrial, commercial or professional classification. Other analyses are at the organizer's discretion, but must be based on a full count of all visitor registration cards.
Part III gives details of the stand space sold and of the exhibitors together with research information.
Part IV contains optional statements by the organizer and details of any conference or symposium held in conjunction with the exhibition.

Any part of the EDF can be extended to allow fuller information to be given.

The audience, stand space and exhibitors' statistics must be certified by a nominated independent auditor, normally the financial auditor to the organizer. All information contained in the EDF is further subject to ABC inspection and verification.

DEPARTMENT OF TRADE AND INDUSTRY –
Fairs and Promotions Branch
(52 Horseferry Road, London SW1P 2AG)

The DTI produces each year a comprehensive listing in booklet form of exhibitions of international interest held within the UK.

EXHIBITIONS

BRITISH TOURIST AUTHORITY
(Thames Tower, Black's Road, Hammersmith, London W6 9EL)

The BTA produces an annual *Trade Fairs and Exhibitions Calendar* and *International Conference Calendar*, listing major events at British venues, and a range of literature featuring specialist meeting facilities throughout Britain.

The BTA's *Marketing Britain's Exhibitions Overseas* advisory guide is aimed at newcomers to the business wishing to promote their British events overseas for the first time.

CONFERENCES & EXHIBITIONS DIARY
(Themetree Ltd, 2 Prebendal Court, Oxford Road, Aylesbury, Bucks HP19 3EY)

This Diary is published quarterly and is categorised into 42 comprehensive sections. Within each, events are listed in date order, with title, venue and location, and the address and telephone number of the organizers.

EXHIBITION BULLETIN
(The London Bureau, 266–272 Kirkdale, Sydenham, London SE26 4RZ)

This monthly publication is a comprehensive guide to UK and worldwide exhibitions, giving information about some 2,000 events spanning thirty months, covering dates, venues, organizers and technical services. It contains a world classified industrial and trade index of fairs and exhibitions.

EXHIBITION AND CONFERENCE FACTFINDER
(Batiste Publications Ltd, Pembroke House, Campsbourne Road, Hornsey, London N8 7PE)

This monthly publication gives comprehensive details of Britain's major venues, events, services and suppliers, together with news, opinions and reviews, to a target circulation of management, advertising and marketing executives.

EXHIBITION INDUSTRY FEDERATION
(Sheen Lane House, 254 Upper Richmond Road West, London SW14 8AG)

The activities of this new Federation are best illustrated by a quotation from its own literature:

'The Exhibition Industry Federation has been formed to encourage a collective effort to boost the UK exhibition business by:

    Association of Exhibition Organizers
    British Exhibition Contractors Association
    British Exhibition Venue Association
    National Association of Exhibition Hall Owners

The objectives of the Federation are:

- To increase existing trade by enhancing the reputation of present events;
- To help develop trade from overseas;

EXISTING MEDIA – THE ADVERTISING ROUTE

- To stimulate new business, extending the range of exhibitors and exhibition visitors;
- To encourage new events and new techniques by generating interest among new groups of communicators – industry, government, public bodies;
- To undertake market research to show:
  i) the size and strength of the industry, its wealth and job creation potential
  ii) to promote the effectiveness of the exhibition media
  iii) to identify and indicate new trends and sales opportunities
  (iv) to help ensure that the exhibition industry maximises its share of expending promotional spend;
- To raise the image of the industry through corporate public relations activity to attract new business interest from home and abroad, liaising with central and local government.'

One of the new Federation's initial tasks will be to provide a factsheet, providing all available statistics on the Industry. This will also give details of British Exhibition Venue Association (BEVA) and National Association of Exhibition Hall Owners (NAEH) member venues offering more than 2,000 square metres of exhibition space, plus useful addresses and telephone numbers.

INCORPORATED SOCIETY OF BRITISH ADVERTISERS
(44 Hertford Street, London W1Y 8AE)

ISBA promotes and protects members' interests through relevant Committees, one of which is devoted to Exhibitions. The Society's publications include a *Guide to Exhibitors*, to assist advertisers in the planning and organization of exhibitions in the UK and overseas. The Society also undertakes an Annual Exhibitions Expenditure Survey. This covers total expenditure by UK exhibitors on:

- Trade and Consumer Exhibitions in the UK;
- Exhibitions, by Venue – figures are given for total spend and percentage share;
- Private Exhibitions (including In-Store and In-Hotel events);
- Overseas Exhibition Expenditure by UK Companies;
- Media Rate Increases (£M and percentage share);
- Comments on the future (expected increases, decreases or savings, together with reasons).

PR-TEL
(52 Poland Street, London W1V 3DF)

The PR-TEL service, described more fully on page 132, provides a constantly updated diary of forthcoming UK exhibitions. Exhibition title, venue, organizers and contact telephone number are provided.

VENUES

Some exhibition venues produce their own calendar of events, as do Venues Associations.

CHAPTER ELEVEN

Direct Mail

Direct Mail, which ranks next to Exhibitions in importance according to British Business Press's survey, can serve many business-to-business functions: customer, dealer, employee, sales force and shareholder information, direct selling, and sales lead generation. It can be used for merchandising, public relations and sales promotion purposes, and is also being developed for direct and database marketing, discussed below.

THE ADVANTAGES OF DIRECT MAIL

A direct advantage of postal delivery of promotional messages is selectivity, since activity can be directed at defined target groups. Furthermore, direct mail ensures complete coverage and the absence of wastage, since the mailing covers and is restricted to the selected categories. All depends on the mailing list's accuracy: there are numerous list sources, but fundamentally only two types – your own and other people's.

In many cases a company can build a list from internal sources – representatives' reports, for example, publishers' reply cards, customer enquiries, and response data from previous promotional activities.

Where internal records are impracticable, external sources can be consulted. Published directories provide valuable lists of prospects, subject to two drawbacks. One is that when there are several such reference sources (as is usually the case) it is essential to cross-check them, for to mail the same individual more than once is wasteful of resources, and annoying to the recipient.

Removal of duplicate names (sometimes called 'merge and purge') is straightforward in comparison with the problem of sources showing different occupants of the same position. The discrepancy probably arises from the directories going to press at different times, with staff changes taking place in the interim. Even 'merge and purge' is not as simple as it seems, since computers will eliminate only identical entries and cannot distinguish between variations. Database marketing systems, however, increasingly provide more sophisticated ways of eliminating duplication.

Staff changes highlight the second drawback of published sources – keeping any list up-to-date. This involves the considerable chore of deleting 'dead' returns from previous mailings, as well as checking relevant publications regularly for news of staff changes, and details of new businesses set up (or old ones closed down). For these reasons, many firms rely on direct mail houses, specialist agencies or list brokers for comprehensive and up-to-date mailing lists. An increasing number now specialise in business-to-business listings, and other organizations publish directories of lists and sources.

The direct mail medium brings other advantages, such as personalisation. Direct mail letters can be bulk prepared and each recipient's name and address then 'matched in', with the sender's signature realistically reproduced, to give the effect of a personal letter. Many direct mail letters are in fact individually typed (on automatic machines) and personally signed for greater authenticity.

Direct mail's flexibility permits sending different messages to different target groups. 1992 may see the removal of barriers to European trade, but the single trading area will still comprise different countries – through direct mail, prospects can be addressed in their own language. A further benefit in this respect is that distance is no object, whereas a representative's visit would be most costly.

Flexibility is a major benefit even within the UK market, and becomes even more important as direct mail becomes computer-based. Mailing lists are increasingly segmented, and sophisticated retrieval systems can send relevant letters to buyers of different products, or adopt other variations – different letters to those who have bought within the last month or stated multiples thereof. The computer can even signal those who have not responded within, for example, the last year, thus making it possible to clean the list by removing 'dead' addresses.

Direct mail's flexibility also permits advertisers to turn the tap on and off with ease. This could be important if, for example, production restraints or sales force capacity call for a limited number of enquiries, or for controlled flow over time.

The advertiser can, if expedient, test different promotional messages, creative formats, mailing lists or other campaign aspects, before the main mailing. Pre-testing – a difficult task with other media – is relatively simple with direct mail.

Timing is another advantage, since promotion is not restricted by any media-owner's publication dates: the advertiser can select the most suitable dates and frequency for delivery of promotional messages. For business-to-business purposes, it is advisable to avoid Mondays or Fridays, when enthusiasm for business is not always at its highest!

A further advantage is that reply-paid cards or envelopes can stimulate customer response. Reply-paid folders or freepost coupons in press advertisements take up costly space and can be unattractive. Such press advertising cannot be so selective and prospective customers must still write in their names and addresses. With direct mail, on the other hand, recipients' particulars can be entered beforehand, so the only action necessary is to post the card. Such direct response can provide valuable sales leads and also makes campaign control and evaluation that much easier.

Direct mail can also serve to distribute leaflets, videos, booklets or even samples. In short, there is no restriction on the information to be disseminated: some direct mail shots amount to reference books, kept by recipients as useful sources of information. Other mailings feature eye-catching attention devices.

Direct mail's attention factor is somewhat controversial. Many claim that business executives receive so much direct mail they throw mailings straight into the waste-paper basket. Some individuals doubtless do receive many mailings, but this is perhaps a creative rather than a media problem. A direct mail letter thrown away is proof that the mailing DID receive attention – if only to detect that it was a mail shot! Attention *was* given, and the creative problem is devising a mailing shot to retain that attention. I do not accept the generalisation that 90 per cent of direct mail is wasted: 100 per cent of bad direct mail is thrown away, and good material carefully studied – the recipient may not even consider it a direct mail shot.

Direct mail houses can help here, and their services come under four broad headings:

- Provision of mailing lists;
- Physical handling of the mailing;
- Creative advice on the campaign to be mounted;
- Technical advice on postal rules and regulations, postage rates and rebates and so on.

Also highly relevant in this context are the various direct mail organizations listed later.

THE DISADVANTAGES OF DIRECT MAIL

Two possible drawbacks – availability of suitable mailing lists, and the attention factor – have hopefully been overcome. The main drawback to direct mail is cost. Though often low in total outlay, direct mail can be expensive on a cost-per-contact basis. A well-planned campaign can, however, give a low cost per enquiry, or even per sale.

As always, the promotional task is to assess benefits against drawbacks. In this respect, this formerly static medium has recently undergone major technological changes: the computerisation of mailing lists, and new printing methods. These developments are of great importance, bearing in mind the rapid increase in direct marketing, in which direct mail plays so vital a role.

DIRECT AND DATABASE MARKETING

Direct marketing has been described as:

> 'Any activity which creates and profitably exploits a direct relationship between seller and prospect.'

The two consequences of direct marketing are:

- The need for measurement of results;
- The recording of names and addresses.

This has led to the development of database marketing, a concept rooted in the old philosophy of getting closer to customers. An organization which identifies its prospects, understands their needs, meets these needs, and treats these customers well, can forge ahead of competitors. Database marketing, a sophisticated new means of serving this old philosophy, is outlined within this chapter since it is through direct mail that direct marketing is most frequently implemented. The principles apply, however, to other forms of marketing, and the database approach is used with equal effect to increase salesforce effectiveness or for telemarketing, and results fed back into the same database.

A mailing list should be more than a collection of names and addresses: it should be a complete database of the target market. As the word 'database' suggests, the information is usually stored for use on a computer. The database should be planned so that:

- Customer records contain purchasing history as well as company name, address(es) and telephone numbers;
- The records contain individual and decision-making unit names, as well as company details;
- Different sections of the list are readily identifiable (eg industry type, size of company, purchasing patterns, or other criteria);
- The database records promotional history – what activities have taken place, which customers were targeted, who responded, and how;
- It is regularly up-dated – lapsed customers identified and removed, and new details (enquiry/purchase history, or address changes etc) entered as soon as available;
- The information is available on line during each transaction, thus improving the ability to meet customer needs;
- Mailing lists acquired from other sources can be 'merged and purged' against names already on the database;
- Addresses are postcoded, for ease and efficiency of mailing.

With conventional marketing, market segmentation is often achieved by de-segregating large market groups into smaller target categories, whereas database marketing achieves accurate segmentation the very opposite way – by aggregating individual customer records.

The final stage of promotional planning, the evaluation of results, is particularly applicable to database marketing. Promotional activity can result in enquiries which serve as sales leads, and permit a tracking system far more sophisticated than the simple recording of conversions into orders. The database should record not only goods sold but also analyse purchases in 'R, F and V' terms, so the market can be segmented in terms of *Recency, Frequency* and *Value*, as well as industrial or job classifications or other criteria. Results, fed back into the database, then serve as an integral part of a marketing information system.

An effective database makes it possible to maximise customer potential, and:

- Select customers whose records indicate they are ripe for possible repeat orders;
- Select those whose purchase patterns suggest they are prospects for other products/services from the range;
- Assist with call and journey planning;
- Produce pre-call briefing documents for sales representatives;
- Standardise post-call reporting;
- Select specific market segments for promotional activity;
- Apply regional or timing controls to mailing activities.

Additionally, such database information can be a guide for targeting 'cold' mailings to potential customers with whom there has been no previous contact. Such new lists should of course be merged and purged against those names already on record, the response to such mailings evaluated, and the database adjusted accordingly.

Database marketing can also serve as an effective tool for moving potential customers up a five-rung 'ladder of loyalty', leading them through five market stages:

1. *Suspects* – potential customers who have not yet indicated interest in the product or service;
2. *Prospects* – those who have indicated interest, but not yet purchased;
3. *Customers* – those who have purchased;
4. *Loyal Customers* – those who buy regularly;
5. *Advocates* – those beyond passive brand loyalty, who actively recommend the product to others.

Database marketing is not just a means of communicating with customers, but rather a new way of defining supplier/customer relationships. It is equally a new way of doing business that provides marketing and management information: the database could eventually replace conventional market research, through promotional campaigns designed to provide any necessary information. By providing data for mapping market trends, database marketing helps ensure opportunities and threats are swiftly identified, and speeds the process of capturing the market opportunities and neutralizing the threats. The system can also provide management ratios, such as promotional activities to sales calls, calls to proposals submitted, proposals accepted, and average order value.

The database approach thus serves as a basis for management and marketing planning, sales force control and telemarketing, just as much as does direct mail. It can further be used to co-ordinate these separate activities, so all interlock to maximum effect. In the multi-structure organizations discussed earlier, which sell many products through a variety of channels, database marketing can ensure all approaches to customers are consistent and co-ordinated. It is equally applicable to other contacts with, for example, shareholders, dealer/agent networks, or employees.

SOURCES OF INFORMATION

BENN'S DIRECT MARKETING SERVICES DIRECTORY
(Benn Business Information Services, PO Box 20, Sovereign Way, Tonbridge, Kent TN9 1RQ)

This new publication, published twice a year, provides full details of both business-to-business and consumer lists, and services ranging from computer bureaux to mailing houses to sales promotion companies, while editorial features provide expert opinions on a range of topical subjects. The BDMS Listline telephone enquiry service provides the latest information on all classified lists in the directory.

BRAD DIRECT MARKETING LISTS, RATES & DATA
(Maclean Hunter House, Chalk Lane, Cockfosters Road, Barnet, Herts EN4 0BU)

It is intended that this new publication should do for direct marketing what BRAD (see page 85) does for advertising. Published twice a year, it contains details of business (and consumer) mailing lists available for hire in the UK, plus direct marketing service companies – from specialist advertising agencies to mailing houses and telephone marketing companies. Each edition also contains editorial comments on the future of direct marketing, plus interviews with leading figures in the business.

BRITISH DIRECT MARKETING ASSOCIATION
(Grosvenor Gardens House, 35 Grosvenor Gardens, London SW1W 0BS)

The BDMA represents companies involved in the broader sphere of direct marketing, as well as in direct mail advertising specifically.

Its objectives include: improving the understanding of direct marketing techniques – including direct mail – and encouraging its growth; gaining increased public acceptance of the benefits of direct marketing; and representing the interests of the industry with government and other authorities.

The BDMA organizes conferences, seminars and working lunches on a range of direct marketing topics, and offers a legal and commercial advisory service to members.

BRITISH LIST BROKERS ASSOCIATION
(Premier House, 150 Southampton Row, London WC1B 5AL)

The BLBA is the professional association of the main UK list brokers, and members comply with the Association's Code of Practice. A list of BLBA members and further details are available from the Association's Secretary.

DIRECT MAIL PRODUCERS ASSOCIATION
(34 Grand Avenue, London N10 3BP)

The DMPA is the professional association for some 120 direct mail agencies. While individual member agencies may have particular specialisms, the Association's total membership covers the complete range of direct mail services and facilities.

Agencies are admitted to DMPA membership only after careful scrutiny, and all members subscribe to the Code of Advertising Practice, the Code of Sales Promotion Practice, the Mailing Preference Service, and the Association's own Code of Practice.

The DMPA office is available to answer enquiries and to advise on the member agencies best suited to particular needs.

DIRECT MAIL SALES BUREAU
(14 Floral Street, Covent Garden, London WC2E 9RR)

The DMSB was set up jointly by the direct mail industry and the Post Office: its brief is to explore new markets for direct mail and, in particular, to encourage advertisers and their agencies to use the medium by helping them with their campaigns. The Bureau has produced a comprehensive *Planner's Guide to Direct Mail*, and its team of experts can provide advice on targeting, planning and evaluating direct mail campaigns.

DIRECT MAIL SERVICES STANDARDS BOARD
(26 Eccleston Street, London SW1W 9PY)

The purpose of the DMSSB is to maintain and enhance professional and ethical standards among the suppliers of direct mail services, and to confer recognition on suppliers who meet those standards.

The Board provides advice for advertisers in selecting, from among its 160 recognized agencies, those offering services appropriate to particular cases.

INCORPORATED SOCIETY OF BRITISH ADVERTISERS
(44 Hertford Street, London W1Y 8AE)

ISBA has published a *Guide to Direct Mail*, which emphasises the essential points an advertiser must bear in mind when using all forms of direct mail.

INSTITUTE OF DIRECTORS
(116 Pall Mall, London SW1Y 5ED)

The Institute has published *The Director's Guide to Direct Marketing*. The booklet covers not only direct mail but also other forms of direct marketing, including direct selling and telemarketing.

THE POST OFFICE
(Direct Marketing Section)
(Headquarters Building, 33 Grosvenor Place, London SW1X 1PX)

The Post Office has published the following helpful booklets of practical value to all who use direct mail:

- *Planning a Direct Mail Campaign* – an at-a-glance guide;
- *Household Delivery Service*
- *The Guide to Effective Direct Mail* – this gives details of an extensive range of Post Office services. The current discount services are due to be replaced by a new programme under the collective name of *Mailsort*. Both the current and planned new services are outlined in the brochure.

CHAPTER TWELVE

Outdoor Advertising

Outdoor advertising is not restricted to consumer products and services: business campaigns have appeared on the London Underground, on backs of buses and inside taxis, at airports, and by selective use of sites adjacent to, for example, exhibition centres or distributors' showrooms. The point made earlier, that no medium should ever be ruled out, applies equally to roadside and transport advertising.

Poster sites are available in most urban areas: historically the industry divided into 'roadside' and 'transport' sections, with Advertising Association statistics showing an expenditure ratio of just under 2:1.

POSTER SIZES

Poster size terminology is historical, and 'sheets' referred to the number of sheets of paper that were pasted (or *posted*) on the hoardings. The standard poster sizes are:

    4 sheet (60" × 40")
  12 sheet (60" × 120")
  16 sheet (10' × 6' 8")
  32 sheet (10' × 14' 4")
  48 sheet (10' × 20')

There are also larger *supersite* panels: these are normally on main roads and are often illuminated. Although historically there is a wide range of sizes, the industry overhaul resulted in increased provision of the sizes most in demand – 4-sheet panels (in the majority of new towns and redevelopment areas), large 48-sheet sites, and even larger supersite panels and special displays.

The transport section of the industry offers a wide variety of sites and sizes (too many to list – think how many different types you pass on your daily travels!) on buses, trains and stations.

The term *outdoor advertising* is sometimes extended to embrace a number of fringe media. British Rate & Data, the standard reference source described on page 85, has sections dealing with car park advertising and advertising on golf courses, litter bins, livestock markets, parking meters and telephone boxes. Under the heading of transport, BRAD has sub-sections covering van posters, ships and air transport.

THE ADVANTAGES OF POSTER ADVERTISING

Posters, whether on roadside hoardings or transport sites, offer the full benefit of colour. If required, a colour quality often unobtainable in press media can be achieved, by printing in more than the standard four colours. Some sites also feature electronic displays, while supersite advertisers often achieve spectacular effects with three-dimensional constructions. The majority of poster advertisers, however, communicate effectively through standard four-colour printing.

The poster medium offers many additional advantages. The advertiser controls the area of market stimulus and can in fact book sites in exactly those locations where advertising support is most needed.

A further advantage is almost complete coverage of the active population within these selected areas, together with a high repetition factor. The greater the number of sites booked, the faster will maximum coverage be achieved, and the greater the repetition factor.

Many regard posters as the ideal reminder medium, a view reinforced by the fact that posters are usually read at a glance, and thus suited to a brief message. When the criteria of high coverage and repetition, colour and reminder close to point of sale in selected areas are considered together, it is clear why numerous consumer companies place great faith in poster advertising.

Poster advertising need not always be restricted to a brief message: on those sites where the audience is captive, as in railways and buses, there is opportunity to deliver a more detailed message.

THE DRAWBACKS OF POSTER ADVERTISING

For the medium's almost self-evident advantages there are, of course, drawbacks. One is defacement – by weather or vandals – and the work of PAB, the Poster Audit Bureau (see below), is relevant in this respect. Some traditional disadvantages – shortage of good sites due to T/C (till cancelled) bookings, and lack of research data – have largely been overcome. All these developments are described below.

BUYING POSTER ADVERTISING

Advertising rates vary according to size and site, but are subject to discounts for six-month or twelve-month orders. Sites can be bought individually (a method known as *site-by-site* or *line-by-line*), by pre-selected campaigns, or by selected packages. At one time, poster availability was a problem as many good sites were permanently booked on 'till cancelled' contracts, but the proportion on T/C bookings is now less than 15 per cent.

Restructuring the poster medium made campaign planning and buying much easier, and saw the establishment of national contractors for the poster sizes most in demand – 4-sheet 'Adshell' in bus shelters, 4-sheets in shopping precincts, and 48-sheet panels. Additionally, specialist poster agencies can put together complete poster campaigns. The activities of Poster Marketing, described on page 143, are also relevant.

POSTER RESEARCH

THE POSTER AUDIT BUREAU
(Tower House, Southampton Street, London WC2E 7HN)

As with all media, those who use posters want to check if their campaign actually appeared. With the Press it is an easy task to check voucher copies sent by media-owners. Physically checking posters is less easy, and becomes more difficult the more sites are booked and the more distant and widespread their locations. The Poster Audit Bureau can be most helpful in this respect.

PAB was established 'to bring the poster medium in line with other media by making itself accountable to advertisers in terms of demonstrating that the poster is in the *right place* at the *right time* and in *good condition*. PAB differs from other research bodies in that its information is of retrospective value, ensuring that advertisers received value for money, rather than providing audience data on which to base future planning.

There are normally two inspections each month, when approximately half of all panels are inspected, and those panels found incorrect on the last check re-examined. PAB results show the date and number of units checked, whether these were the correct design and had 'acceptable' (posted with the correct design in good condition) or 'routine damage' (which can be repaired by normal business procedures) or 'urgent damage' (which requires immediate action). PAB's definition of damaged is 'any damage which spoils the pack, the brand name, or any part of the wording means that the poster is unacceptable'.

THE JOINT INDUSTRY COMMITTEE FOR POSTER AUDIENCE RESEARCH
(c/o The Ourdoor Advertising Association, Parkgate, 21 Tothill Street, London WC1H 9LL)

JICPAR supervises the poster medium's audience measurement system: OSCAR (Outdoor Site Classification and Audience Research), is based on a constantly up-dated census of all poster sites. As implied by its title, OSCAR research covers two main criteria – *Site Classification* and *Audience Research*. Individual sites are classified and rated according to location, visibility, proximity to sales outlets etc. These figures are then adjusted according to traffic count figures, based on pedestrian and vehicular passages past each site. These combined figures provide a total weekly audience (or those with opportunities to see) for each individual panel.

Data is grouped by local government districts and areas, with contractor identification, and is available on-line from Outdoor Research Surveys (ORS) or in printed form in the six-monthly OSCAR digest published each Spring and Autumn.

OSCAR also serves as a practical planning facility: poster contractors in clients' selected areas will – given the poster sizes required, target market and number of opportunities-to-see sought – send an availability list of panels, together with audience estimates. It is intended that the dimensions of coverage and frequency be added to the existing OSCAR weekly audience data.

POSTER MARKETING
(Parkgate, 21 Tothill Street, London SW1H 9LL)

Poster Marketing is the marketing arm of the Outdoor Advertising Association, by which it is funded. Poster Marketing's activities include:

- *OSCAR*. The Outdoor Site Classification and Audience Research described above.

- *Competitive Data Reports.* ORS publishes, on behalf of Poster Marketing, quarterly reports listing the sectors/advertisers/brands that have used roadside advertising, and the numbers/sizes of panels used.
- *'Posterscene'.* This quarterly magazine highlights developments in outdoor advertising.
- *Effectiveness Awards.* Poster Marketing sponsors an annual effectiveness awards scheme.
- *Case Histories.* A growing portfolio of case histories is available, demonstrating the contribution of poster advertising to the achievement of commercial objectives.
- *Training Workshops.* Poster Marketing mounts briefing presentations, summarising the latest outdoor developments.

TUBE RESEARCH AUDIENCE CLASSIFICATION
(London Transport Advertising, 10 Jamestown Road, London NW1 7BY)

TRAC is an independent survey into the travel patterns of Underground users, commissioned by London Transport Advertising to establish a database for measuring the audience coverage and frequency of advertising campaigns on the medium.

A synopsis of the research methodology and results was published as *TRAC: The Campaign Planner* and gives audience profiles and coverage of all adults, businessmen, 15–24 year olds, AB adults, and working women.

London Transport Advertising also offers a campaign planning facility, advising on how to buy an Underground campaign which delivers the optimum coverage and frequency.

CHAPTER THIRTEEN

Television

This review of advertising now turns to the audio-visual media, commencing with television. At one time considered solely a medium for advertising consumer products and services, the medium has increasing business-to-business applications. It enables advertisers to reach 'horizontal' business markets spread across a wide range of industries, and also provides opportunities for specific targeting.

The TV medium is reviewed here under the main headings of terrestrial broadcasting, satellite transmissions, cable television, and non-broadcast sources.

As well as offering advertising facilities, these channels also present public relations opportunities through their programme provision, discussed later.

Before discussing these various categories of television, it is important to recognize that the medium is in the throes of change. A recent Government paper which will be the catalyst for a major debate on the future of broadcasting, which will eventually result in a new Broadcasting Act to be brought before Parliament. This, together with the new programme sources discussed below, plus the possibility of local television services transmitted over short distances by microwave, means that the earlier comment about a state of change is a slight understatement! Likely future consequences are nevertheless discussed below. This review also covers the relevant databases which provide audience information.

TERRESTRIAL BROADCASTING

INDEPENDENT TELEVISION

The Independent Broadcasting Authority has responsibility for administering the ITV system, and exercises control over three main operational areas:

a) The ITV network and appointment of TV contractors;
b) The programme content; and
c) The amount of advertising, and its content.

THE ITV NETWORK

Independent television is a regional system of broadcasting in which 15 IBA-appointed companies provide programme services in 14 separate areas of the country. These areas, listed in size order (in terms of percentage share of net ITV homes) are: London (which is served by two contractors on a split-week basis), East and West Midlands, North-West England, Yorkshire, South and South-East England (including the Channel Islands, sold by the same contractor), Wales and West of England, East of England, Central Scotland, North-East England, South-West England, Northern Ireland, North Scotland, and The Borders.

ITV offers regional advertising facilities, but transmitters do not recognize lines on a map and some households are in overlap areas while a *very* few are within areas which cannot receive signals.

The contractors holding franchises for the various areas also sell air-time on Channel 4, described on page 147. New contracts, lasting for eight years (but recently extended for a further three), began in 1982. When this period ends in 1993, the television map may well be redrawn with fewer and different regions. The method of awarding franchises may also be reviewed.

PROGRAMME CONTENT

The IBA ensures that each contractor provides a suitable balance of programmes, of proper quality. Whilst advertisers are not *directly* interested in programmes as such, the size and composition of the audiences they attract are of immediate concern. By the same argument, BBC1 and BBC2 programmes are of equal importance. The BBC does not carry advertising but, if audiences watch their channels, they cannot watch ITV. Both BBC and ITV, and other channels described here, must ensure their programmes satisfy the newly-appointed government watchdog: the Broadcasting Standards Council.

ADVERTISING AND ITS CONTENT

Television advertising, which appears at the beginning or end of programmes and 'in the natural breaks therein', is limited to a maximum of seven minutes an hour. This restriction on the supply of commercial airtime has important implications, discussed later. The content of the commercials must comply with the IBA *Code of Advertising Standards and Practice*.

THE TELEVISION MEDIUM

Television's great impact comes from its capacity for product demonstration, to an audience at home in a relaxed atmosphere. Additional benefits are sound and colour, while other special effects such as animation and computer graphics are also possible.

Though regional in structure, TV has an audience impact equivalent to a national medium: viewers consider television a medium of national importance, and many advertisers value it for this reason.

Television is flexible by time and day as well as area. It is possible, by making appropriate bookings, to stimulate the market on a date and at a time of the advertiser's choice. Control of timing is, however, increasingly affected by the pre-empt system and by video-recorders, both discussed later.

Advertising time is sold in standard metric units of 10, 20, 30, 40, 50 and 60 seconds duration, booked into different time segments with advertising rates appropriate to the size and composition of the likely audience. Subject to availability, longer spots may also be booked.

Television differs from other media in that rate cards are structured to obtain the maximum advertising revenue the market will bear. As the supply of airtime is limited, price is determined by demand – contrast this with the Press where a media-owner selling many pages of advertising can print thicker issues. Supply and demand of television airtime are balanced by omitting less profitable advertising: spots booked at a low cost 'broad spot advertisement rate' may be pre-empted (or displaced) by spots sold to other advertisers at a higher 'pre-emptible fixed spot' rate. These bookings may, however, be pre-empted by spots sold at rates higher up the pre-empt ladder of charges. These spots may in their turn be pre-empted by spots sold at the highest possible rate – that for non-pre-emptible fixed spots, which are the only ones certain to appear.

The pre-empt system means that television advertising – under such circumstances – demands constant attention and review. Adjustment of television schedules is virtually more important than the original plan, and most spots are repeatedly shifted as information about BBC1 and BBC2, Channel 4 and ITV programmes is released, and new audience data becomes available.

Television rate cards are more complex than those for most other media. In addition to different categories of spot rates, they include a wide variety of different discount rates as well as advertising packages.

One important package concerns GHIs, or Guaranteed Home Impressions, whereby the contractor guarantees to transmit a given number of impressions. The contractor transmits the commercial and, if – as revealed by research – it does not achieve the required number of impressions (defined as the gross number of homes receiving exposure), he keeps retransmitting it until the target number is achieved.

As well as transmitting advertising messages, many television contractors also offer numerous additional services, including production of commercials, research and a wide range of merchandising facilities. The contractors also sell commercial airtime for the fourth television channel, Channel 4.

CHANNEL 4

The Channel Four Television Company Ltd is a wholly-owned subsidiary of the IBA: it provides a national programme service except for Wales, which is covered by S4C (Sianel 4 Cymru), a separate broadcasting authority with its own network.

The programme schedule is complementary to ITV, with reasonable choice between the two channels, co-ordinated in viewers' best interests. Channel 4 seeks to provide a distinctive service to fill gaps it identified in the programming of the other three channels: for example, programmes appealing to 'light viewers' – including the AB socio-economic groups. Channel 4 is not a minority service but aims to be a channel 'for all of the people – some of the time'. It recently extended its *Business Programme* and *Business Daily* coverage to provide a complementary business service at breakfast time.

ADVERTISING ON CHANNEL 4

Although Channel 4 is a mass medium, it does not deliver conventional mass audiences. Cumulative cover builds up by a mix of audience sizes, ranging from the specialist to large, allowing advertisers to buy whatever audiences they want. Channel 4 provides the following advertising opportunities:

- *Strong up-market coverage*, particularly of the AB socio-economic groups, who traditionally are 'light viewers'.
- *Special-interest groups* – selected by considering programme content rather than standard demographic research data.
- *Coverage build-up*: the new channel, over time, delivers conventional audiences in large cumulative numbers, regardless of whether or not more specialist groups are also reached.
- *Better balanced schedules against any target audience*, providing additional opportunities-to-see for any target group inadequately covered by the ITV schedule.

Business-to-Business advertisers use the new medium in different ways and for different reasons.

Existing ITV advertisers use Channel 4 in parallel with ITV to increase their total coverage and to give better balance to their schedules. New advertisers use the channel to reach specialist target audiences, either nationally or regionally. Channel 4 is also used by new advertisers whose current budgets are insufficient to provide an acceptable weight or continuity of presence on ITV.

ADVERTISING SALES STRUCTURE

The new channel marked a new format in British broadcasting structure. Its basic source of funding is a subscription agreed annually in advance by the IBA. This subscription is provided by a levy on the existing ITV contractors (who sell Channel 4 airtime in parallel with their own) in proportion to their share of total airtime revenue for both ITV-1 and Channel 4. Although programmes are national (apart from Wales), advertising is sold on a regional basis. During commercial breaks, Channel 4 simply hands the network back to the existing ITV contractors to sell the commercial airtime. In return for their subscription, they retain all the Channel 4 advertisement revenue obtained.

Different contractors adopt different rate-card structures as regards time segments, fixed spots *versus* broad slots, pre-empt *versus* non-pre-empt pricing, and the degree to which guaranteed packages are featured.

In recent years there have been pressure groups lobbying for Channel 4 to become financially independent, and undertake the sale of its own advertising time.

BREAKFAST TELEVISION

An additional programme source was launched in 1983 when TV-AM received an eight-year franchise from the IBA, to provide a breakfast-time television service, to consist primarily of news, information and current affairs. The BBC introduced its own breakfast-time transmissions shortly before TV-AM went on air, and Channel 4 recently extended its transmission times to early mornings.

TV-AM differs from other ITV contractors in having a national franchise to broadcast seven mornings a week throughout the year. Transmission is available on the ITV-1 network, and offers the same coverage potential. (Contrast this with Channel 4, which faced two major tasks: building new transmitters and persuading viewers to adjust their TV sets and aerials.)

ADVERTISING ON TV-AM

Unlike Channel 4, TV-AM sells its own airtime and makes this available as both packages and spots. Advertisers can book national advertising from a single source rather than having to negotiate separately with numerous ITV companies. TV-AM has a policy of non-pre-emption, so advertisers do not risk having their commercials replaced by others booked at a higher rate.

TV-AM's programming reaches a high proportion of housewives, and a large proportion of advertisement revenue is accordingly contributed by manufacturers of consumer products, rather than business-to-business sources.

VIDEOTEXT

This term covers data and graphics presented on a television screen. It subdivides into two categories:

- *Viewdata* – transmitted over phone lines, eg, British Telecom's *Prestel*.
- *Teletext* – transmitted over broadcasting networks, eg, the BBC's *Ceefax* service and ITV's *Oracle*.

These alternative uses of the television screen, although not primarily advertising media, could affect conventional viewing, and also offer opportunities for business-to-business promotion.

Viewdata. An interactive system such as Prestel uses a combination of telephone, television and computer. Through a small keyboard, rather like a pocket calculator, Prestel customers have access to 'frames' (pages) of information (including many of marketing information), all continuously updated. The system represents a two-way link to the computer and Prestel customers can send messages, orders or requests for information. The system is on-line 24 hours a day, unlike Ceefax and Oracle which are available only when BBC and ITV are broadcasting.

Prestel sets have not been acquired by domestic consumers as was originally anticipated, but by business users. This alternative use of television sets is therefore likely to have only a small effect on public viewing habits, but offers promotional opportunities for business organizations to convey detailed messages, to audiences which – by the act of calling up information – indicate their interest in the product or service. This same point of a self-selecting audience applies equally to the alternative videotext system.

Teletext. This videotext system, currently much more widely used by the general public, covers the BBC's *Ceefax* and ITV's *Oracle*. Both provide news and information services whenever the two services are on air.

Like Prestel, ITV's *Oracle* has pages of marketing information, including *Mediascope* – a media facts news and comment service. *Oracle* also sells advertising space and so must be considered from two standpoints – as an advertising medium in its own right, as well as an alternative to conventional viewing.

The main brake on teletext sales is the slow rate at which people replace their sets – they do not get a new TV set before the old one breaks down. Penetration of teletext sets is now about 20 per cent, and could be accelerated by the rental market.

EXISTING MEDIA – THE ADVERTISING ROUTE

Reviewing videotext services overall it is clear that, while they offer business-to-business opportunities (see also *British Satellite Broadcasting*, page 151), their impact on conventional viewing will not compare with that of major expansion in programme provision through new television channels.

THE FUTURE OF INDEPENDENT TELEVISION – AN OVERVIEW

The ITV network has, for many years, delivered mass regional audiences at predictable times. Some contractors' areas are admittedly larger than others, but advertisers could nevertheless stimulate mass audiences in these regions at required times simply by booking appropriate transmissions with the contractor holding the franchise for that area.

Numerous developments are changing this pattern. An increasing number of channels will compete for these mass audiences, and transmission areas themselves are changing – television will cease being solely (apart from TV-AM) a regional medium, since there will also be community size, national and pan-European coverage. In short, the mass regional audiences of past years may be whittled away by viewers switching to other channels, which in turn may cover smaller or larger areas. Furthermore, TV audiences will no longer be delivered on predictable dates, since many viewers now use video-recorders as a 'time-shift' device.

These developments directly affect those already using the TV medium for business-to-business purposes and, at the same time, present new opportunities to those for whom television was previously not viable.

TV RESEARCH

The regular flow of television research information enables advertisers to gauge the size and composition of the audience they are likely to reach.

BROADCASTERS' AUDIENCE RESEARCH BOARD
(Knighton House, 56 Mortimer Street, London W1N 8AN)

To measure television audiences, BARB utilises a system of electronic meters attached to television sets in a representative sample of homes throughout the UK. The meters record minute-by-minute whether the set is on and, if so, to which channel it is tuned. The BARB contract is held by AGB, Audits of Great Britain, which publishes weekly Reports with the following basic breakdowns:

- Population estimate and panel composition;
- Chronological list of commercials;
- Minute-by-minute TVRs (television ratings);
- Analysis of audience during commercial slots and segments;
- Holiday statistics;
- Weekly schedule of commercials, by brand;
- Network reports.

Additional information can be provided by special post-survey analyses commissioned and paid for by subscribers.

BARB also conducts research into audience reaction to programmes. This is carried out by the BBC Broadcasting Department through TOP: the Television Opinion Panel. The system used is a self-completion diary questionnaire covering the week's viewing, which invites respondents to provide both overall and specific comments on their reactions to both BBC and ITV programmes.

TV audience data is also contained in the National Readership Surveys and Target Group Index, already discussed, and in JICCAR (page 155) and PETAR (page 153). Also, some of the specialist surveys listed in Chapter 9.

SATELLITE TRANSMISSIONS

Terrestrial broadcasting is being supplemented in two ways. One is geostationary communication satellites which 'bounce' TV (and radio) signals back to earth, either to individual homes – *direct* broadcasting by satellite (DBS) – or to centralised stations, from where the final link to the home is via the other supplement to traditional broadcasting: Cable TV.

Satellite transmissions differ from terrestrial broadcasting in that coverage is national (or rather international). The reception areas covered are known as 'footprints' or 'groundprints' and, to give an idea of their size, UK transmissions will overlap Northern France, while France's groundprint reaches into the UK not far short of Scotland. The larger the aerials used to receive these signals, the greater the reception area. Alternatively, some viewers beyond the true groundprint might be satisfied with a weaker signal. The net effect is a web of overlapping transmission areas, which become even larger if the signal is then spread further by cable.

Although discussed separately for ease of analysis, the two supplements to traditional broadcasting are clearly inter-related.

DIRECT BROADCASTING BY SATELLITE

UK DBS was officially launched in 1987 when British Satellite Broadcasting (BSB) signed its 15-year franchise with the Independent Broadcasting Authority. BSB plans to start broadcasting towards the end of 1989, when the service will offer higher quality pictures, stereo sound, and teletext, available by means of a 12-inch diameter disc and decoder. This relatively inexpensive (around £200) package is a key part of BSB's marketing strategy to reach an audience of four million homes in the fourth year of broadcasting.

A budget of £60 million has been allocated to the BSB launch, which is thus likely to be one of the 'noisier' events of the advertising and PR world during 1989! BSB was pre-empted by Sky Channel, which started DBS transmissions in February 1989. The new service provides additional consumer programmes and so may affect conventional audiences, but does not provide specific business services.

VIEWER SERVICES

BSB will compete with ITV for UK audiences and advertising expenditure by providing four services over three channels, appealing to a wide variety of tastes. One service will provide 24-hour news, sport and current affairs, and a second light entertainment programmes. A third channel will be divided between a daytime service aimed at children and younger viewers, and a film channel showing recent releases and current films. The first three services will be financed by advertisement revenue, while the movie channel will be on subscription.

The programming will be structurally different from ITV (in the same way that Channel 4 is structurally different). BSB's structural difference will take the form of 'thematic stranded programming'. This means there will be separate strands of programme schedules designed to appeal to specific audiences, such as up-market males for example. BSB aims to maximise these stranded target audiences by broadcasting themed programmes over longer viewing periods, rather than at particular times of day or evening.

BSB intends to provide BARB quality audience research information. Efforts are being made to include BSB in the BARB audience sample and, if this is not achieved, an equivalent alternative will be provided.

BUSINESS SERVICES

In addition to its viewing audience transmissions (with their possible business advertising uses), BSB's *DataVision* service will provide facilities for business users to send whatever material they want to broadcast (sound, video, text or data) to BSB's earth station, which will beam signals to a satellite which will then broadcast that material across the UK. These business services could be broadcast for general viewing or, through encryption, with access restricted to those closed user groups able to unscramble the signal. BSB DataVision will also provide high speed digital telecommunications circuits in competition with British Telecom and Mercury.

Reception of BSB's transmissions will link to appropriate equipment at each location – audio signals involve an amplifier and loudspeakers, video signals will link with VCRs and television monitors, text messages will be processed through personal computers and associated printers, while information and data services may communicate with large computer installations.

Business communications possibilities include corporate communications to overcome the usual complaints that staff are never kept informed (about, for examples, the latest trading figures, major re-organizations, key personnel changes, or new policy). Also possible are centrally transmitted training sessions, video newsletters to customers and staff, in-company and customer product information, sales force communications, and new product demonstrations.

These transmissions could be live or pre-recorded. They could be watched as transmitted, or alternatively recorded for later viewing: the latter practice could obviate the need to duplicate videocassettes and then distribute them across the country.

There will be opportunities for business communicators to 'bundle' the services they receive from BSB, when they use its multiple facilities of advertising slots, programme sponsorship, and DataVision communications.

This *direct* broadcasting by satellite, which BSB will provide, should be distinguished from the satellite services offered to cable operators.

SATELLITE/CABLE TRANSMISSIONS

Sky Channel and *Super Channel* transmit programmes specially for the cable networks described later, and also to SMATV (Satellite Master Antenna Television) systems in apartment buildings and hotels. The services are provided free, with income derived from advertisement revenue.

The two 'pan-European' channels are received by cable networks in 22 and 15 countries respectively (including, of course, the UK). Both offer viewers wider choice, with different programmes for different audiences at different times of day, designed to complement rather than compete with existing national channels. Advertising is kept to the UK model of not more than seven minutes per hour. Rate cards allow advertisers to buy specific days and times with programmes targeted at specific audiences. There are also opportunities for sponsorship, and the usual range of 'packages' and discounts.

All commercials must conform to the rules and regulations and guidelines laid down by the Cable Authority discussed below. Both channels retain ultimate editorial control over the form and content of sponsored programmes. Commercials and sponsored programmes are subject to normal copy clearance procedures.

Several other channels also offer advertising slots, including MTV (Music Television) which broadcasts pop videos to pan European cable audiences, CNN (Cable News Network) broadcasting round-the-clock news, Screen Sport with a sports channel and so on, and additional satellite/cable channels are likely to be launched in the future.

Audience research information about both the size and composition of satellite channel audiences is available from PETAR (described below), and also JICCAR (page 155).

SATELLITE/CABLE AUDIENCE RESEARCH

PAN EUROPEAN TELEVISION AUDIENCE RESEARCH
(Chairman's Office: 19/21 Rathbone Place, London W1P 1DF)

PETAR represents the first comprehensive study of satellite television in Europe: the most recent report covered twelve countries and researched the viewing of individuals living in households capable of receiving at least one commercial satellite station. The survey utilised individual weekly diaries, personally placed and collected over a four-week period.

The plan is to have two surveys a year, and PETAR has issued a tender specification for a 3-year research contract to measure the audience for satellite television in Europe. The tender proposes use of push-button meters (as does BARB) which will replace the diary system. The PETAR committee hopes that by the end of the three-year period it will be able to incorporate data from national measurement systems into its own results.

CABLE TELEVISION

Communication satellites are one way to supplement terrestrial broadcasting: the other is cable television. DBS will be available nationwide to all who want it, but cable is likely to cover only major population centres.

EXISTING MEDIA – THE ADVERTISING ROUTE

THE BACKGROUND

There are already a number of old cable systems, with limited 4–6 channel capacity, installed many years ago when sizeable areas of the country suffered from poor reception. Cable operators were originally restricted to acting as relayers of existing television programmes, but official attitudes have now changed.

The Government decided to let the private sector invest in cabling Britain, with opportunity to recover costs and eventually make a profit through the sale of 'wideband' cable services. To control and supervise this development, the government established a new Cable Authority.

The Cable Authority's task is not to divide the country into TV areas nor to ensure all areas (even uneconomic ones) are covered, but rather to facilitate rapid and orderly cable expansion. The Authority's initial franchises are for 15 year periods (longer than the IBA's eight years, in view of the uncertainties involved) but subsequently renewable on an eight-year basis. The Authority does not specify franchise area sizes, but each must cover a recognizable community.

The Authority draws up guidelines for programming, advertising and sponsorship, and exercises oversight to ensure that these rules are obeyed. There are to date upwards of twenty franchises, and the Authority is considering other possibilities.

THE CABLE OPERATORS

Cable operators are obliged to carry all existing (and future DBS) public television channels, but can offer viewers additional pay-channels, or even pay-per-view programmes. Most franchise holders offer their subscribers a range of different packages of channels at varying prices. Additional revenue may come from other business and domestic non-entertainment services. Services to advertisers could include many new opportunities discussed later.

ADVERTISING SUPPORT

As with local press (and radio), much advertising revenue is from local traders. Cable can additionally provide a variety of important new opportunities for national advertisers. These include small-scale test-marketing by franchise area, direct response advertising, advertising within specialist channels, and longer 'informercials' with emphasis on communicating information about products or services. There is also the possibility of sponsored programmes (subject to the Authority's code).

SALE OF ADVERTISING TIME

Many advertising executives (particularly those in agencies) want cable to be highly flexible (with time purchasable by individual franchises, by groups of systems, or across the entire cable network) and as simple as possible to plan and buy. The future may thus see the setting up of sales houses to sell the network on radio advertising lines, as described in the next chapter, or perhaps the formation of an 'Association of Cable Operators' offering a single order service as does the Association of Free Newspapers.

INTERACTIVE SERVICES ON CABLE

As official papers made clear: 'The Government is not prepared to see the introduction of wideband cable systems solely in terms of the provision of more entertainment channels. The range of non-broadcasting services . . . which the new systems can support is seen as a crucial aspect of these new systems.' These non-entertainment services could be provided at marginal price levels, basic systems costs having been absorbed by the entertainment services. This review therefore concludes by looking briefly at the other services which could operate over the same cable networks.

New cable technology can give each household a control box, through which subscribers send information back to the cable station. This wideband interactive system allows for the development of additional services, which could include business services (including video-conferencing, data and facsimile transmission), home banking, home shopping, video and voice telephone, and videotext services. Furthermore, subscribers could use their cable system to call up audio or video libraries, play interactive games, or make use of microcomputer software libraries. Services could extend to consumer market research and/or voting, to reading meters, or to link in with burglar or fire alarm or health-care systems for the old or inform (with the appropriate authorities receiving instant print-outs of all essential information whenever urgent action is needed).

The possibilities are almost endless: cable should therefore be considered in its overall context – not simply as a means of providing additional entertainment channels, but as a communications technology which could have significant effects on marketing operations.

CABLE AUDIENCE RESEARCH

JOINT INDUSTRY COMMITTEE FOR CABLE AUDIENCE RESEARCH
(44 Hertford Street, London W1Y 8AE)

Research into audiences for cable television was undertaken for JICCAR by Survey Research Associates using individual seven-day diaries and one-day guest diaries.

Although the main JICCAR Committee was dissolved after the last round of research, the Technical Sub-Committee still exists to ensure that pan-European television audience research, currently being developed as described above, meets the needs of the UK cable and satellite industry.

NON-BROADCAST SOURCES

Britain now has one of the highest penetrations of VCRs in the world and price reductions, as technological changes take place, will increase this percentage. The more recorders there are in homes and the greater use made of them, so the greater the possible reduction in use of television sets for conventional viewing. The 'owners' (many VCRs are rented) use them to declare their independence of BBC, IBA, cable and satellite channel schedules.

The advantages a VCR presents include the facility to make recordings while the viewer is away (without switching on the TV set), to 'time-shift' programmes or make permanent copies of them, to view pre-recorded videograms, or even to 'film' the viewer's own programmes by means of portable video cameras. Additional VCR facilities have further implications: viewers may edit out commercials by use of the 'pause' button if present while the recording is made. Alternatively, if the recording is made during the viewer's absence, commercials may be 'zipped' (or avoided by use of the fast-forward button) during subsequent screenings. All these facilities directly affect conventional viewing habits.

NEW GOVERNMENT PROPOSALS

The Government's Plans for broadcasting legislation, published in November 1988, listed the following main specific proposals:

- Most viewers will have a major increase in choice with the authorisation of a new *fifth channel*, to be operated as a national channel, with different companies providing the services at different times of day. *A sixth channel* will also be authorised should technical studies show this to be feasible.
- The present ITV system will be replaced by a regionally based *Channel 3* with positive programing obligations but also greater freedom to match its programming to market conditions.
- Provision will be made for at least one body which is effectively equipped to provide high quality *news* programmes on Channel 3.
- Options are canvassed to the future constitution of *Channel 4* on the basis that its distinctive remit is preserved and its advertising is sold separately from that on Channel 3. The *Welsh Fourth Channel Authority* will continue to provide the Fourth Channel in Wales.
- There will be a new flexible regime for the development of multi-channel *local services* through both *cable* and *microwave transmission* (*MVDS*). This will provide a further major extension of viewer choice.
- The UK's two remaining *Direct Broadcasting by Satellite* (*DBS*) frequencies will be advertised by the Independent Broadcasting authority (IBA) early next year. This will provide scope for two further UK DBS channels in addition to the three being provided by British Satellite Broadcasting (BSB).
- Viewers will continue to be able to receive *other satellite services* directly, including those from the proposed medium-powered Astra and Eutelstat II satellites. Steps will be taken to ensure that the programme content of all such services is supervised.
- All television services (including those of the British Broadcasting Corporation (BBC) will be given freedom to raise finance through *subscription* and *sponsorship* (subject to proper safeguards)). All services (except the BBC) will also be free to carry *advertising*.
- A new agency, the *Independent Television Commission* (ITC), will be established in place of the Independent Broadcasting Authority (IBA) and the Cable Authority to licence and supervise all parts of a liberalized commercial television sector. It will operate with a lighter touch then the IBA but will have tough sanctions.

- The BBC will continue as the cornerstone of public service broadcasting. The Government looks forward to the eventual replacement of the *licence fee* which will, however, continue for some time to come.
- The *night hours* from one of the BBC's channels will be assigned to the ITC. The BBC will be allowed to retain the other set on the basis that it uses it as fully as possible for developing subscription services.
- The part played by *independent producers* in programme making in the UK will continue to grow.
- The Government will proceed with its proposals for the deregulation and expansion of *independent* radio, under the light touch regulation of a new *Radio Authority*.
- All UK television and radio services will be subject to *consumer protection* obligations on such matters as taste, decency and balance.
- The *Broadcasting Standards Council* (*BSC*), established to reinforce standards on taste and decency and the portrayal of sex and violence, will be placed on a statutory footing.
- The exemption of broadcasting from the *obscenity* legislation will be removed.
- There will be a major reform of the *transmission* arrangements, giving scope for greater private sector involvement.

THE CONSEQUENCES OF INCREASED PROGRAMME PROVISION

Predictions always sound a risky proposition, but if events follow the predicted course then the writer is covered in glory, whereas if they do not then the same things can always be predicted again for the future. Under such circumstances, the writer's only fault is looking too far ahead!

- *Time-shift audiences*. The new media will necessitate a rethink of the marketing concept. TV will no longer deliver mass regional audiences delivered at predictable times. Increasing VCR usage will spread message delivery over time, and there will be alternative inroads into mass regional audiences.
- *Segmented audiences*. One alternative to mass regional audiences is minority viewing groups, as new programme sources will segment the total audience into smaller and more selective viewing groups. Wider choice will lead to diversity rather than uniformity, allowing advertisers to pinpoint markets with greater accuracy. This could be by cable TV's community-size areas or alternatively by programme types, some of which will permit specific business targeting. There will be great opportunity for advertisers who think in terms of 'narrow casting' rather than broadcasting.
- *Transcast audiences*. The other alternative to mass regional viewing is 'transcasting' to even larger audiences: satellite/cable channels overlap international boundaries and give pan-European coverage, while direct broadcasting by satellite will mean a single channel covering all 14 ITV regions.
- *Restructured audiences*. New satellite channels may be launched in addition to those discussed and, furthermore, the component parts of the existing TV structure may be moved about. Furthermore, as mentioned above, the Government is likely to introduce a new Broadcasting Act.

- *Volatile audiences.* The more programme choice is increased, the greater the likelihood of viewers switching from one programme to another. This possibility is increased by remote control facilities, which make it easier to change channels. The greater the possibility of losing audiences, the harder programme companies – and advertisers – will have to work to *keep* their audiences, quite apart from attracting them in the first place. Unless a commercial is interesting, viewers may well 'zap' to other channels.
- *Interactive audiences.* New opportunities arise through teletext and viewdata services, and will be far broader than telesales commercials giving phone numbers for viewers to place orders by means of credit cards. Interactive services such as cable television and viewdata make direct purchases easier, and business-to-business direct marketing could thus extend to the television medium.
- *Sponsorship opportunities.* There are likely to be increased opportunities for programme sponsorship on all channels – but not for advertisers to control programme content. UK channels want sponsors for programmes that viewers want to watch, rather than to transmit programmes imposed on them by advertisers. There will also be opportunity for new types of advertising and promotional methods – for 'informercials' such as sponsored videograms, for the integration of products and services into 'how to' programmes, and through 'ad mags' which will be the audio-visual equivalent of printed magazines.
- *Business-to-business uses.* These opportunities are not restricted to consumer marketing: television services can offer facilities for closely targeted communication to private 'closed user-groups', through new subscription programme services for selected target groups (with viewers using a special decoder to video overnight scrambled signals). The new programmes will carry advertising, and could be transmitted on a pan-European as well as a UK basis.

CHAPTER FOURTEEN

Radio

Radio is another medium often considered primarily suitable for consumer products and services, but which also serves business-to-business purposes. The medium is used at 'drive time' to reach business people on their way to work, and also for more specific targeting: to geographically concentrated markets such as farmers, for example (through selection of relevant programme breaks in suitable areas), or small builders/decorators (most of whom listen on transistors while working). The campaign to builders, for paint, was an interesting use of radio in that it had a *pull* as well as a *push* effect, as the builders were aware that the radio commercials were also heard by members of the public.

This advertising medium is available on a local and national basis through the independent local radio (ILR) network, and also through Radio Luxembourg and other stations covering Ireland and the Isle of Man.

Like other media, radio also presents public relations opportunities, through its numerous programmes.

THE STRUCTURE OF INDEPENDENT LOCAL RADIO

ILR is under the official control of the Independent Broadcasting Authority (IBA), which is responsible for administering the independent local radio system. At time of writing, there are 44 local radio stations, and the IBA has awarded franchises to provide independent local radio services for three additional areas.

The frequency, amount and nature of the advertisements must comply with the Broadcasting Act and the Authority's rules and regulations. These require that advertising must be clearly separate from programmes and obvious for what it is. Advertising is limited to a maximum of nine minutes in each hour. Programmes may be co-funded (sponsored) provided they are factual portrayals of doings, happenings, places and things that do not contain an undue element of advertising.

RADIO ADVERTISING

One of radio's great advantages is its ability to communicate advertising messages at very short notice (provided airtime is available). A commercial can be scripted, cleared in relation to the IBA Code of Advertising Standards, recorded and transmitted in a matter of hours. Frequency of market stimulus is also possible, simply through repeat transmissions.

People listen to radio at home, in parks or on beaches, in the car or at work in offices and factories or on building sites. It thus reaches different people at different times and in different moods from other media. Careful selection of transmission times as well as areas is essential if commercials are to reach business targets.

Radio is frequently a 'companion' to its listeners, so the promotional message is received in a personal atmosphere. Successful advertising requires an appreciation of radio's one-to-one relationship. The medium is a transient one: messages on the whole should usually be brief, and clearly it is necessary to make maximum effective choice of words. Their actual delivery and supporting sound effects or music are equally important.

ILR advertising time is sold in standard metric units of 10, 20, 30, 40, 50, 60-second or even two-minute commercials. On Radio Luxembourg and Manx Radio, as well as 'spot' advertisements, a limited number of sponsored programmes is available, subject to individual negotiations.

Radio is flexible by area, as well as by time and day. It can serve the needs of local firms, and equally give area boosts where necessary for national advertisers. Airtime can be booked with individual local stations, and also through regional rate cards covering stations within a coherent region. National packages can also be negotiated. A recent development is 'Newslink', which offers spots on every station within the morning news breaks – a facility clearly of interest to those wishing to reach business markets.

Airtime can be booked direct with individual local contractors or, where appointed, through national sales offices. These are:

CAPITAL RADIO SALES
(356 Euston Road, London NW1 3BW)

INDEPENDENT RADIO SALES LTD (IRS)
(86/88 Edgware Road, London W2 2EA)

BROADCAST MARKETING SERVICES (BMS)
(7 Duke of York Street, St James's Square, London SW1Y 6LA)

SCOTTISH RADIO SALES AND IRISH RADIO SALES (SIRS)
(86/88 Edgware Road, London W2 2EA)

SOUND ADVERTISING SALES (SAS)
(50 Long Acre, London WC2)

A further advantage is that radio can be relatively inexpensive to use, and commercials are normally cheap to make. Although many radio production companies are available, all ILR stations and Radio Luxembourg can make commercials on clients' behalf. For advertisers seeking a low-cost medium, radio advertising is thus often extremely attractive.

OTHER RADIO ADVERTISING

The pattern of ILR listening differs according to each station's programme pattern. This contrasts with Radio Luxembourg which declares that it is 'unashamedly a night-time entertainment medium with a much higher proportion of casual listeners'. A direct comparison of the weekly audiences to ILR and Radio Luxembourg is, however, not valid because independent local radio is often on the air 24 hours per day, whereas Radio Luxembourg is national and only available for eight hours per night. Radio Tele-Luxembourg (RTL) and Radio Telefis Eirean (RTE) recently joined forces to launch a new commercial radio station, *Radio Five*. The new programme schedule will be broadcast daily until 7pm, when a link will be provided to *Radio Luxembourg*'s existing 208 service.

From time to time there are invitations to advertise on 'pirate' radio stations (so-called because they usually transmit without licence, from ships moored outside British territorial waters). The audience reached is usually of the pop music variety. Tighter provisions in British and international regulations usually succeed in driving most of these illegal radio operators off the air. Radio advertising may, however, become more widely available through national and 'community' radio stations: The Broadcasting White Paper announced that 'The Government will proceed with its proposals for the deregulation and expansion of *independent radio* under the light touch regulation of a new Radio Authority.'

RADIO AUDIENCE RESEARCH

JOINT INDUSTRY COMMITTEE FOR RADIO AUDIENCE RESEARCH
(44 Belgrave Square, London SW1X 8QS)

JICRAR has commissioned and published radio audience surveys since the start of ILR. The research contractor, Research Surveys of Great Britain, is appointed by the Radio Marketing Bureau described below. The methodology provides continuous reporting, using random location sampling of individuals within each ILR station area, with personal placement and collection of seven-day diaries. The survey gives, for each station area, average and cumulative audiences, and analysis is provided in terms of age, social class, etc.

ASSOCIATION OF INDEPENDENT RADIO CONTRACTORS
(46 Westbourne Grove, London W2 5SH)

AIRC is the trade association for companies holding IBA independent radio franchises, which it represents in their dealings with government, the IBA, trade unions, copyright societies and other bodies. The Association provides a forum for industry discussions and an advice and information service to members on all aspects of radio.

Through its wholly-owned subsidiary, the Radio Marketing Bureau, it promotes Independent Radio to advertisers and agencies.

RADIO MARKETING BUREAU
(46 Westbourne Grove, London W2 5SH)

The Bureau's brief is to expand the base of radio advertisers, particularly at national level, rather than to sell airtime (which remains the responsibility of the stations and sales organizations).

RMB uses a wide range of media to present the case for radio advertising, including seminars, presentations to clients and agencies, direct mail and trade press advertising. The Bureau's activities include case histories, research studies, and sales material designed to make the medium better understood and more accessible.

RMB contracts for and publishes on behalf of the ILR companies the research conducted by JICRAR, and produces a range of items designed to be both useful and informative in the buying and planning of the medium. These include:

- *Radio – The Facts* – which provides station information and maps, mixed media schedules, and general marketing and media information on radio;
- *The Planning Guide* – which gives a comprehensive guide on reach/frequency levels achieved by either rating levels or numbers of spots, and includes a cost index. The data is presented for the ILR network and standard JICRAR regions.

RMB also acts as a clearing house for information on UK radio and from abroad, and has established itself as the central source for ILR-relevant marketing information.

CHAPTER FIFTEEN

Cinema

For this review of advertising to be complete, it must include the cinema, even if this medium is unlikely to have a high place on most business-to-business schedules. As always, however, no medium should ever be ruled out: some companies, for example, use cinema advertising to recruit workers in their local area. The medium can extend to in-flight movies to contact senior business executives. Films can also make an invaluable contribution to exhibitions, conferences and seminars: these variations are considered later, in Chapter 18 on created media.

The UK cinema industry has, over recent years, undergone a modernisation programme. Less attractive and less profitable cinemas were closed and many single-auditorium cinemas converted into multi-unit complexes, while new developments include multi-unit cinemas within new entertainment complexes. The explosive growth of 'multiplex' cinemas at a faster rate than ever, with a further 300 or more screens scheduled to open within the next two years, in addition to the current 100+ multiplex screens. One of the main features of these new multiplexes is that they are mostly being built in suburban areas with good car parking facilities, away from the traditional high street locations.

The cinema audience is a distinct one, composed largely of young adults. This provides an attractive market for many companies, but one unlikely to appeal to the majority of business advertisers. Furthermore, coverage build-up is slow, and full penetration of even the young age groups is by no means complete. After many years of decline, however, recent attendance figures have shown a steady increase.

Cinema advertising commercials are shown within one reel screened at all performances (except children's matinees), with the house lights down, prior to the main feature film. Advertisers can buy screen time in this reel on the basis of standard time lengths. The basic booking unit is one week's advertising on one screen, but more campaigns cover a number of cinemas over a period of several weeks or months.

Cinema advertising offers colour, sound and movement, giving creative scope to demonstrate products with high quality reproduction on the large screen, with music and the human voice heightening the effect. Other creative approaches such as animation and computer graphics are also possible. In addition, the message is screened to a captive audience, sitting facing the screen in a darkened auditorium – contrast this with television viewing.

In some cases, additional advantages stem from the fact that cinema advertising can be localised: the campaign can be screened in a town, an area, a region, or alternatively mounted nationwide. The benefit to the local advertiser is obvious – he can appeal to the local audience and feature his company name and address on the cinema screen. Other organizations with broader distribution follow the same principle by advertising in cinemas that match their particular locational requirements and, after demonstrating their products, conclude the commercial with the local dealer's name and address, perhaps on a shared-cost basis.

For advertisers with more general needs, cinema contractors offer special packages, which ease administration and often include bonuses or discounts. Operations vary slightly between contractors, but it is relatively simple to match comparable packages offered by different contractors, to build a total cinema schedule.

A number of packages relate to defined marketing areas, within any of which two alternative schemes qualify for discounts – area coverage plans (which use all cinemas in the area) and run of cinema plans (which do not specify the cinemas to be used, but allow contractors to spend a specified sum within a given time period).

Other facilities include new product discounts (for products new to the cinema) and packages in which commercials can be screened exclusively in programmes with different categories of film certificate. Other facilities include packages built around particular feature films. Another development is the Audience Delivery Plan (ADP), which basically guarantees a given number of admissions at a fixed minimum rate.

A final point is that cinema advertising can also reach specialist groups such as the services, holiday camps, ethnic communities or, of greater relevance to this book, in-flight audiences. Furthermore, a business organization can always create its own audiences – see *Created Media*, Chapter 18.

FURTHER INFORMATION

CINEMA ADVERTISING ASSOCIATION
(127 Wardour Street, London W1V 4AD)

The CAA, the cinema advertising contractors' trade association, is devoted to developing and maintaining high standards of cinema practice and presentation. One aspect of its work is conducting regular checks to ensure cinema advertising bookings are screened as scheduled, and under the optimum conditions.

Cinema admissions information is available from the CAA under various headings: total within UK, by cinema seating capacity, and by Registrar-General's Standard Regions. The CAA also provides information (based on the National Readership Surveys), about cinema audience composition, penetration, and coverage – the coverage and frequency obtained by typical cinema campaigns. Also available (based on Target Group Index sources) are index figures of product usage by cinema-going frequency.

To back up the data available from these sources, the CAA in recent years commissioned its own research to strengthen the case for cinema advertising: this research was the forerunner of the annual CAVIAR studies described on page 165.

CINEMA

CINEMA AND VIDEO INDUSTRY AUDIENCE RESEARCH COMMITTEE
(Cinema Advertising Association, 127 Wardour Street, London W1V 4AD)

CAVIAR is an annual survey of cinema-going and video film watching in all age groups, and of newspaper reading among 7–44 years olds. It is sponsored by leading firms in the cinema and video industries. The CAVIAR report appears in several volumes:

- *Cinema Report* – covering how often and when, specific films, visits in the last two months, and other information;
- *Video Report* – covering equipment, video film watching, and hiring and purchase of video tapes;
- *Abridged Media Demographics* – covering media demographics, coverage of general and specific film audiences, and video watching and cinema-going.

MISCELLANEOUS ADVERTISING MEDIA

This brief section is appended to coverage of cinema simply because the review of advertising media is now complete, and 'miscellaneous' does not merit a chapter of its own.

The range of advertising media is considerable, and within this book it has been possible to review only the major categories. Overseas media have deliberately been omitted, since it would call for a separate book to give them proper coverage, while created media are covered in Chapter 18. This chapter could be extended to include a whole range of miscellaneous media. Furthermore, as communications technology is fast-changing, and the media world an innovative one, there are constant offers of new advertising facilities which may not correspond to any standard media categories, and for which audience research data is not yet available. If any Promotion Manager is concerned with evaluating these media, the basic questions remain the same and apply equally to new and existing media. The fundamental questions to be asked were discussed in Chapter 6.

PART 3C: EXISTING MEDIA – THE EDITORIAL ROUTE
16. Public Relations.
17. Public Relations Reference Sources.

CHAPTER SIXTEEN

Public Relations

Public Relations practice was defined by the Institute of Public Relations as:

'The planned and sustained effort to establish and maintain goodwill and mutual understanding between an organization and its public.'

By this definition, marketing communications encompasses far more than selling messages. Public Relations includes community and consumer affairs, as well as government, international and industrial relations. With so wide a field to consider, how best to plan a public relations programme? A logical start is to consider the groups with which any business organization should communicate, and then review the public relations media by which it can reach them.

PUBLIC RELATIONS 'PUBLICS'

At fundamental level, most PR activity is directed to four overall target categories, within any one of which a company might wish specifically to target opinion-formers and perhaps pressure groups:

- *People the company sells to* – target markets, existing and potential, also distributors or agents.
- *People the company buys from* – suppliers of materials or services.
- *People who work for the company* – employees, existing and potential, as well as management and trade unions.
- *People who finance the company* – shareholders and financial institutions including stockbrokers, merchant and clearing banks.

These four groupings are not watertight compartments, however, since staff may also be shareholders, for example. Furthermore, these different individuals are all members of 'the public' and may well read about company activities in the editorial columns of general media. Any business organization would be unwise, however, to restrict Public Relations activity to general media – imagine how you would feel if, on reading a national or local paper, you found by chance a news item which affected YOU personally. You are directly concerned, but nobody had bothered to tell you. In such circumstances there would be no 'goodwill and mutual understanding': on the contrary, considerable ill-will would result.

The four categories, and sub-groups thereof, each merit separate PR activity – 'planned and sustained' – to ensure they are kept fully informed about matters which affect them. To restrict public relations to these four groupings may, however, be insufficient. Between the two extremes of specific target groups and the 'general public' are other groupings which merit separate attention.

Business organizations do not exist in isolation, but operate within a community which in turn exists within a government-directed economy. Overlap may arise again, since individuals in the four primary groups may also play significant roles in the community, or in local or national government. Public Relations activity should therefore extend to members of the community in which the organization is located, to ensure they are informed about matters of concern to them. Similarly, it may be necessary to direct PR activity towards government – local and/or national. In some cases, public relations may have as its objective not passing information, but influencing government policy. Political lobbying is, however, a tightly regulated activity.

No single checklist can cover every possible 'public' for every type of organization: the promotional task, before undertaking any public relations planning, is to ensure that none of an organization's particular publics – internal or external – has been overlooked.

The concept of marketing communications encompasses communications from as well as to the market, and the principle applies equally to public relations. 'Mutual understanding' necessarily involves researching the views of target groups, as well as communicating with them.

As earlier chapters made clear, internal marketing can be as important as external marketing, and marketing communications can no longer be treated in isolation. Promotional considerations should play an important part in influencing company policy rather than merely reflecting it. This is particularly true of public relations, where access to the views of target groups sometimes necessitates bringing unwelcome home truths to management attention.

Also cited earlier were those authorities who suggest that marketing planning is more important than the actual plan. This applies equally to public relations planning, because it disciplines loose thinking into rigorous analysis, reveals any gaps in information, and ensures consultation between key people. A joint planning process assists in resolving possible differences of opinion and getting all concerned to agree and work to a common objective. As this book repeatedly stresses, it is essential that all aspects of marketing communications inter-relate – unless advertising, merchandising, public relations and sales promotion all interlock with the company's positioning and marketing planning, no business operation can operate to maximum effect.

PUBLIC RELATIONS MEDIA

The PR media that can communicate with target markets include the very ones reviewed in the various advertising chapters. The media may be the same, but promotional activity is now directed to the *editorial* rather than advertising columns. Third party endorsement can strengthen marketing communications messages – target markets view favourable editorial references very differently to advertisements for which they know the company has paid.

Much public relations activity is therefore aimed at supplying journalists in press and other media with material of interest to their readers or viewers, in the correct format, in good time for them to use it. The chapters on advertising stressed the need for an in-depth editorial (as well as statistical) knowledge of media, and this is as true for public relations as it is for advertising. This involves the simple expedient of *studying* each publication over time. Only by regular reading can a Promotion Manager get a feel for the kind of stories that will interest the news desks. This appreciation should go beyond the type of story: it is equally important to appreciate the length of articles carried and the types of photographs featured. A detailed understanding of how each publication operates is unnecessary, but the Promotion Manager must appreciate the constraints under which journalists work, as outlined in Chapter 5.

A great deal of so-called 'public relations' activity is alas wasted – companies concentrate on what *they* want to say, rather than what the journalists need to know. Furthermore, many supposed 'news releases' go straight into the wastepaper basket – they contain no news, and are sent to the wrong individuals in the wrong media in the wrong format at the wrong time. The organizations concerned then wonder why their PR efforts are unsuccessful!

Fortunately, there are helpful sources and guidelines to assist business organizations in ensuring their news releases do not suffer the same fate.

ISSUE OF NEWS MATERIAL

The Institute of Public Relations has published a number of 'Recommended Practice Papers' which give truly professional advice:

> No. 1: *News Releases* – this practice paper (see Appendix 1) gives guidelines for the format and presentation of releases.

Format and presentation must be based on genuine news content. The title (not headline) is vital, and is the signal which at a glance causes a journalist to pause and read the release rather than put it in the bin. No journalist will use an actual headline: if he did, he might find the same thing in a competitive journal. The release's title should attract attention by putting the essential news into the fewest possible words.

News release content should be written in the same style as the journalist would write it, giving the news as it will interest the publication's readers. A good system to follow is the inverted pyramid, with really important news at the top and supporting information further down. This enables a News Editor to 'sub' paragraphs from the bottom and still leave intact the main thrust of the story.

PHOTOGRAPHS

On many occasions photographs are sent together with News Releases – here too, are mistakes to avoid. The photograph must have genuine 'news' value, and be submitted correctly. The IPR again gives professional advice through another Recommended Practice Paper:

> No. 2: *Photographs Accompanying News Releases* – this Practice Paper (see Appendix 2) advises how best to submit photographs to the media.

National newspapers rarely accept contributed photographs, and so the Promotion Manager will need to arrange photo opportunities.

PRESS KITS

Public Relations is not restricted to the issue of news releases and photographs. It may be more effective to hold a press conference and/or invite the media to visit company premises, and – to back up organized activities – issue each journalist with a press kit. The Institute of Public Relations has valuable advice to offer in this field, also:

No. 3: *Press Kits* – this Practice Paper (see Appendix 3), contains the Institute's guidelines for issue of press kits.

Issue of News Releases and photographs, holding of Press Conferences and preparation of Press Kits all imply the Promotion Manager *does* have news of interest to the media.

SOURCES OF AN INDUSTRIAL NEWS STORY

Many executives overlook the wealth of events taking place within their organizations which, if properly presented to the media, could result in valuable editorial coverage. The following list may help in locating material within any organization:

- A new product or service.
- An important development of an existing product or service.
- A new use for an existing product or service.
- Additions to an existing range of products or services.
- An ingenious method of meeting some unusual demands.
- Use of the product or service by some personality or prestige organization.
- Important price changes.
- Large and unusual orders – home or export.
- Trade mission participation.
- Business visits overseas by management.
- Appointment of agents, home or overseas.
- Dealer and stockist promotions.
- Sponsored events and competitions.
- Sponsored events in conjunction with other organizations.
- Company awards.
- New advertising campaigns, packs, television commercial films, etc.
- Participation in exhibitions, home and overseas.
- New factories or offices.
- Extensions to existing factories and offices.
- New production plant.
- Production records.
- Technical developments.
- Management and staff appointments.
- Promotions and achievements by employees.
- Long service awards and retirements.
- Anniversaries.
- Speeches and appearances by management.
- How material and world events will affect the company.
- How local events will affect the company.
- Company charity, educational sponsorship, etc.

The problem which faces other PR practitioners is not lack of newsworthy events, but ensuring that they know about them in good time to take action. It is important, therefore, to ensure that, within an organization, *everybody* keeps the Promotion Manager fully informed. The head of an organization renowned for its excellent reputation, in response to the question 'How many public relations staff do you employ?' replied 'X thousand' – this being the total number on his company's payroll! This response, however, masks two distinct PR considerations – one is staff being aware of the need to keep the PR manager informed, and the other is that staff themselves, through their behaviour, affect the company image and thus directly influence an organization's public relations. The need for internal marketing is again apparent.

WHAT TO PUBLICISE?

Which of these many events should a company publicise? Some events are so newsworthy they merit public relations action under any circumstances. Overall, however, much depends on the company's promotional objective. Depending on this objective, the Promotion Manager may wish to publicise – and indeed actively seek out – newsworthy events of one type rather than another. Should the potential of a multi-use product not be fully appreciated, for example, promotional effort may concentrate on publicising its manifold applications. This and many other possible PR objectives are discussed in Chapter 20.

DESTINATIONS FOR NEWS RELEASES

News releases (in the correct format) should be sent to the right media – those to which they are of interest. Furthermore, it is more effective to address material direct to the relevant journalist rather than to 'The Editor'. This saves valuable time, and also ensures that material finds its way to the correct desk.

Fortunately, a number of reference sources tell just whom to contact. These are listed in the next chapter: the same sources also help locate receptive media for feature articles.

FEATURE ARTICLES

Much consumer PR seeks to obtain brief – but very valuable – mentions in news columns. With business operations, however, there is often scope for fuller coverage through feature articles. These may be written by the media subsequent to public relations contact, or alternatively prepared by company staff – perhaps the technical experts who pioneered new developments, with a by-line giving their company's name and the position they hold.

TOP TEN ERRORS

According to the country's leading journalists, most Public Relations Officers:

1. Write long boring news releases that don't stand a chance of being published.

EXISTING MEDIA – THE EDITORIAL ROUTE

2. Send dull and boring photographs which don't stand a chance of being printed.
3. Send these boring news releases and dull photographs to the wrong people anyway – bad targeting.
4. Send these boring news releases and photographs not only to the wrong people but also at the wrong time – normally after the deadline.
5. Hold press conferences unnecessarily – 90 per cent are a waste of time, money and effort.
6. When they do hold potentially interesting conferences they do so in a long-winded, badly-organized and ill-timed fashion.
7. When they have got something to say they do not individually 'tailor' their PR approach, even though this always succeeds over mass rallies.
8. Rarely think up creative suggestions – or 'angles', of the type that might titillate the interest of a journalist.
9. Don't know how to handle 'bad news' – they clam up instead of saying something positive.
10. Spell the Editor's name incorrectly, or get it wrong altogether: psychological suicide.

PR'S GOLDEN RULES

To counter the ten top errors, there are fortunately ten golden rules!

1. Write short, sharp news releases. And get to the point immediately.
2. Get press photographers to take your photographs. And arrange photo opportunities for the nationals – they don't accept contributed photographs.
3. Send the release to the right journalist – not just to 'The Editor'.
4. Find out journalists' deadlines and 'dead days' – and work to them.
5. Only hold a press conference if you really need one.
6. If you must have a press conference, keep the presentation short.
7. Tailor news releases to appeal to specific media.
8. Be creative – make stories newsworthy.
9. Interviews: anticipate the negative questions and have your answers ready. Focus on making three key points, whatever the questions.
10. Remember – developing personal relationships with journalists beats everything.

OTHER PUBLIC RELATIONS ACTIVITIES

Public Relations is by no means restricted to planned activities which publicise newsworthy events within the media. This assumes three things:

- One is that there *are* suitable media;
- A second is that only planned PR activities have public relations implications;
- The third is that all PR activities can be planned.

Firstly, Public Relations activities often extend well beyond existing media – consider for example, the importance of seminars, facility visits, and house journals. These and many other forms of marketing communications are considered later in Chapter 18.

The second point concerns the PR implications of any organization's day-to-day activities: the concept of message sources stresses the many ways in which existing and potential target groups receive impressions about the company. These include advertising, correspondence, direct mail, factory maintenance, house style, printed material, office appearance, receptionists, sales literature, service and other staff, telephone contacts, vehicle livery – and the public relations aspects of business marketing's seven P's.

The third point is that not all PR activity can be planned in advance, however much a company seeks to have a public relations programme that is 'planned and sustained' – what about those unforeseeable events for which it is impossible to make detailed plans?

The concept of 'crisis management' is vital, but demands more attention than can be given within a single book encompassing the full gamut of marketing communications. All that can be achieved here is to alert readers to the possibility of a crisis occurring within their own organization. Think of the many recent events which have brought some unfortunate organizations into the national or international headlines, following – for example – radiation or chemical leaks, or industrial injuries. To believe that such crises occur only in *other* organizations is to have a false feeling of security. Crisis management calls for advance preparation at the highest possible company level, with serious attention given to many practical issues. Disasters do not restrict themselves to the working week when staff are available to deal with them and, should such an event occur within your own organization, do you have out-of-office-hours phone numbers to contact top management? Who would be responsible for giving information to the many media which might besiege you, and demand information *now*? What procedures ensure the nominated executive is supplied with essential information, and knows how this should best be communicated to the media? Hopefully, your organization will never have to face this predicament, but do remember Top Error number 9 (most PROs don't know how to handle 'bad news' – they clam up instead of saying something positive). Fortunately, there are practical books on this very topic, advising on how to prepare for such an eventuality.

PUBLIC RELATIONS ORGANIZATIONS

PUBLIC RELATIONS CONSULTANTS ASSOCIATION

See page 45.

INSTITUTE OF PUBLIC RELATIONS
(Gate House, 1 St John's Square, London EC1M 4DH)

The IPR represents and regulates professional practitioners in the United Kingdom, and is the largest organization of its kind in Europe. Its concern is to maintain and raise the standard of professional practice, so ensuring that public relations practice achieves and deserves status, recognition and understanding.

The Institute provides regular opportunities for members to meet to exchange information and ideas, and organizes both regional and vocational groups.

There are eleven regional groups spread throughout the country, and vocational groups for members working in local government, City and financial public relations, and as consultants. There are also a number of special interest groups covering, for example, the construction industry, food & farming, government affairs, health & medical, international, technology & engineering, psychology & PR, trade associations & professional bodies, and tourism & leisure.

The various elements of the IPR organize more than 100 events each year including seminars, debates and workshops, lectures, lunch and evening meetings, discussion groups and facility visits.

The Institute has published various Recommended Practice Papers, some of which are reproduced in the Appendices as well as a number of Guideline Papers on practical topics including:

- Public Relations & the Law
- Public Relations Practice – its Role & Parameters
- Resolving the Advertising/Editorial Conflict
- The Use, Misuse & Abuse of Embargoes
- Fees and Methods of Charging for PR Services
- Interpretation of the Code of Professional Conduct

CHAPTER SEVENTEEN

Public Relations Reference Sources

Numerous sources provide Public Relations data or services of business-to-business relevance – details of publications about to publish features on particular business topics, for example, and which journalists concentrate on different business areas. There are also service organizations which can assist in distributing PR messages. Readers are advised to make a quick check of this chapter, rather than read it in its entirety, and then return to those sources of interest for detailed study later. Public Relations sources and services include:

ADVANCE
(2 Prebendal Court, Oxford Road, Aylesbury, Bucks HP19 3EY)

This bi-monthly source of information about forthcoming editorial programmes covers:

- *Advance Extra*, featuring personnel changes in the media, new addresses and publication launches and closures.
- *Editorial Features*, detailing forthcoming features and special supplements. All information is verified with Editors, and lead time is provided to take advantage of these opportunities.

BENN'S MEDIA DIRECTORY
(Benn Business Information Services, PO Box 20, Sovereign Way, Tonbridge, Kent TN9 1RQ)

The UK volume of this annual Media Guide covers publishing houses, national newspapers, provincial newspapers, periodicals and free consumer magazines, broadcasting, media agencies services, and media organizations.

A second international volume is a guide to international media contacts in the UK, as well as to the overseas media themselves.

Purchasers of the Directory can take advantage of BEMIS (Benn's Media Information Service) for free advice by telephone, telex or letter.

BLUE BOOK OF BRITISH BROADCASTING
(Tellex Monitors Ltd, 47 Gray's Inn Road, London WC1X 8PR)

This annual publication provides details of TV and radio contacts in the UK, for both national and regional broadcasting, as well as cable and satellite channels. In addition to indexing programmes of different types, it lists station output, producers, presenters, executives, job titles, addresses and phone numbers.

EXISTING MEDIA – THE EDITORIAL ROUTE

EDITORS MEDIA DIRECTORIES
(9–19 Great Sutton Street, London EC1V 0BX)

Editors Media Directories publish a UK Media Directory in six volumes:

1. *National Daily Newspapers, National Sunday Newspapers, Radio & Television* – published monthly;
2. *Business & Professional Publications* – published quarterly;
3. *Provincial Newspapers, and News Agencies* – published quarterly;
4. *Consumer & Leisure Magazines* – published quarterly;
5. *Town & Country Local Media* – published twice yearly;
6. *Writers' Guilds and London Correspondents of Foreign Press* – published annually.

In addition to the Named Editors listings, the directories also feature:

- Forthcoming special features (titles and dates);
- Special features diary (for volumes 2, 3 and 4);
- A publication and readership profile (for volumes 2 and 3);
- Percentage of editorial content of free weekly newspapers;
- Indication of colour, spot or mono editorial pages.

EXPORT

See *International Operations*, below.

HOLLIS PRESS AND PUBLIC RELATIONS ANNUAL
(Contact House, Sunbury-on-Thames, Middlesex TW16 5HG)

In addition to a subject index/classification guide, this directory divides into six main sections:

1. *News Contacts* – commercial, industrial, consumer, professional, financial & corporate;
2. *Official & Public Information Sources*;
3. *Public Relations Consultancies, UK and Worldwide*;
4. *Reference & Research Addresses for Communicators*;
5. *Services for the Communications Industry & The Media*;
6. *Sponsorship* – sponsorship consultants, who sponsors what, sponsorship venues, sponsorship services.

INTERNATIONAL OPERATIONS

International Public Relations calls for a book in itself, if the topic is to be covered properly: all that can be achieved here is to mention sources which can provide valuable assistance, including:

BRITISH COUNCIL
(10 Spring Gardens, London SW1A 2BN)

PUBLIC RELATIONS REFERENCE SOURCES

BRITISH OVERSEAS TRADE BOARD
(1 Victoria Street, London SW1H 0ET)

CENTRAL OFFICE OF INFORMATION
(Hercules Road, London SE1 7DU)

INSTITUTE OF EXPORT
(64 Clifton Street, London EC2A 4HB)

OVERSEAS MEDIA

Numerous overseas publications and other media have London contacts: various directories listed in this chapter contain details.

MONITORING

Numerous firms provide cuttings services, and monitor the various media: the various directories listed in this section contain details.

Any Promotion Manager should of course monitor the media closely himself – how else can he get the 'feel' of the public relations (and advertising) opportunities within individual media, or keep fully up-to-date with target markets' (and competitors') activities, and with changes within the media themselves?

The administrative chore of clipping cuttings can, nevertheless, most certainly be delegated, and various services will undertake this on a company's behalf. It is important, however, for the Promotion Manager to provide a tight brief on *precisely* what he wants clipped, if he is to avoid being inundated with unwanted information (for which he has paid unnecessarily).

PIMS LONDON PLC
(PIMS House, 4 St John's Place, London EC1M 4AH)

This organization provides a number of Public Relations services, including:

- *PIMS Media Directory*. This monthly publication provides information on UK media, covering daily national and regional press, trade and technical magazines, consumer magazines, television and radio, and weekly local newspapers. Each entry contains the name of the medium, circulation details, address, editor's or correspondent's name, phone number and frequency of publication. It also includes UK correspondents of overseas media, news and photo agencies, journalists' guild membership lists, and specialist freelance writers.
- *PIMS Media Townlist*. This quarterly publication covers, as its name implies, local media. It lists for any town the local daily and weekly papers, freesheets, regional BBC television offices and ITV stations, BBC and independent local radio stations, local news and photo agencies, and local business publications. As with the Media Directory, contact details are provided.
- *PIMS Financial Directory*. Published quarterly, this directory divides into four main sections covering:

EXISTING MEDIA – THE EDITORIAL ROUTE

- Financial & business media
- City financial institutions
- Associations, local authorities and government lists
- British and European members of Parliament.

Other PIMS services include issue of news releases on clients' behalf, on-line direct customer access to the databases listed above, news photography, and press clippings.

PNA
(13–19 Curtain Road, London EC2A 3LT)

This organization provides a complete press release distribution service, including:

- *PNA Media Guide*. This bi-monthly guide covers all UK editorial media, listing editors' names, editorial addresses and telephone numbers, plus circulation and frequency details. Full details of specialist editors and correspondents are included. *Media Guide* divides into the following sections: National Newspapers, Regional daily & weekly newspapers, Trade & technical journals, Consumer magazines, News agencies, Radio & TV stations and specialist programmes, Freelance writers, and London correspondents of foreign media.
- *Media Guide* is produced from PNA's continuously updated computer database. Special features include:
  - A special City and financial section including named Investment Analysts. In addition, the *City News* division of PNA distributes financial press releases, reports and documents to the media, and also to stockbrokers and other important City contacts;
  - Access to PNA's *Media by Town* system. PNA's computer is programmed to select regional and local media relevant to any town, county or TV region in the UK – it identifies media read, seen or heard in each town, not just media published there. In addition, PNA's *Newspac* provides a weekly mailing service to all the local press.

Other PNA activities include photography, word processing, printing and a computerised media database and electronic communications package tailor-made for the PR industry, called *PNA Targeter*.

PR PLANNER-UK
(Media Information Ltd, Hale House, 290–296 Green Lanes, London N13 5TP)

PR Planner-UK is a comprehensive guide to the British press, and lists names, addresses, telephone numbers and other relevant information concerning:

- National dailies, Sunday newspapers, local weeklies (by county), consumer magazines, trade and technical journals;
- Radio and television networks, programmes, newsreels and news agencies;
- Editors, correspondents, features and specialist writers by publication.

PR Planner-UK is published on a subscription basis and comes in a loose-leaf binder, the contents of which are constantly updated. *Mediadisc* is a new service containing PR Planner on an updated disc service. 'Peel-off' addressed labels are also available, with a choice of editorial contact by name and covering newspapers, magazines, and radio/TV stations.

PR-TEL
(52 Poland Street, London W1V 3DF)

Pr-Tel is an on-line videotext news and information service designed to meet PR practitioners' needs via a viewdata terminal. Information can be instantly accessed on advance features, sponsorship, exhibitions, finance and broadcast media. It is updated throughout each working day, and available 23 hours every day of the week.

Pr-Tel's database features the following 'content headings': What's New, Newsline, Newsfile, Forward Features, National Press, Business Press, Regional Media, Sponsorship, Exhibitions, Broadcast (television and radio), Financial Supplement, Sporting Events, and pages provided by the Institute of Public Relations.

The Features sections include numerous categories of immediate business-to-business relevance.

The Business Press databank covers more than 600 titles across six major press areas: Agriculture, Business/Finance, Doctors, Industrial, Retail and Computers. The information covers basic facts, editorial assessments, circulation trends, and readership research.

Pr-Tel is a division of MediaTel, described on page 92, which provides an on-line service for advertising media planning.

UNIVERSAL NEWS SERVICES
(Communications House, Gough Square, Fleet Street, London EC4P 4DP)

This organization is a wholly-owned subsidiary of the Press Association, the UK's national news agency, and its services are all carried over the PA network. It provides a number of services to facilitate distribution of newsworthy information, including:

- *UNS National Newswire.* This can transmit news to newsrooms of the national press, broadcasting stations and news agencies in London, regional morning and evening newspapers in England and Wales, associated weekly newspapers, and newsrooms in Scotland (via *UNS Scotwire,* Scotland's own Newswire).
- *UNS City Wire.* This serves the City desks of national and regional newspapers and broadcasting services.

Other UNS services include *Features* (for feature material on a wide range of topics including Business), *Appointments* (for distributing information about key staff changes), *News Alert* (to publicise news conferences or photo opportunities), *Radio Services* (for recorded interviews and features, or live link-ups), and *UNS International* (which serves some 138 countries worldwide, in all the principal languages).

WHO'S WHO IN TECHNICAL JOURNALISM
(Broad Street Associates Public Relations, 30 Furnival Street, London EC4A 1JE)

This media directory details the major technology and computing publications, and pin-points the journalists most relevant to various industry sectors. There is an extensive list of 200 magazine profiles, looking at circulation figures, target audiences and key staff. Entries outline individuals' careers, personalities and the sort of stories they write.

WILLINGS PRESS GUIDE
(British Media Publications, Windsor Court, East Grinstead House, East Grinstead, West Sussex RH19 1XA)

This annual directory divides into various sections:

- *UK publications* – covering newspapers, periodicals and annuals, giving description of contents, year first issued, frequency of publication, selling price, subscription rates, average circulation, address and telephone numbers, and names of key contacts;
- *Overseas publications* – giving details of major newspapers and magazines from more than 100 countries;
- *Classified index* – listing publications alphabetically under subject headings;
- *Newspaper Index England* – covering both free and paid-for, grouped under geographical areas of distribution;
- *Publishers and their titles* – comprising an alphabetical list of UK publishing houses and the titles they own;
- *Services and supplies* – giving details of suppliers of products and services relating to the publishing industry.

PART 3D: CREATED MEDIA
18. The Range of Created Media.

CHAPTER EIGHTEEN

The Range of Created Media

Although numerous media exist through which to communicate with target markets, through both advertising and editorial columns, a Promotion Manager may find that even this wide range does not fully meet his company's needs and he must therefore create new media.

There is literally no limit to the range of created media, and this book can review only selected major categories. Before so doing, it is important to consider them in context, in the light of communication objectives.

Earlier chapters distinguished between advertising, public relations, merchandising and sales promotion. Reviewed at simplistic level:

Advertising = Specific Communication
Public Relations = Mutual Understanding
Merchandising = Pushes products towards people
Sales Promotion = Pulls people towards products

These are not tight definitions, and different created media might serve any or all of these different communication objectives at different times.

PLANNING CREATED MEDIA

Created media present a paradox as many executives forget that, as well as creating a medium, they must also create an audience for it. This, however, raises matters in illogical order, since nobody should create a medium without first having a specific target audience in mind. Equally, the Promotion Manager should decide in advance how to deliver the created medium to this created target market. Booklets, films, leaflets, or videos – however well created – cannot deliver their message from inside a cupboard!

A final point is that those who create media become media-owners in their own right. Some house journals are subsidised by sale of advertising space. Other companies' created media may present the Promotion Manager with advertising and public relations opportunities, and his own media may present such opportunities to others. When considering other organizations' created media as promotional vehicles, they should be evaluated in the same way as normal media.

THE RANGE OF CREATED MEDIA

ADVISORY BUREAUX

Some organizations, either individually or on an industry-wide basis, communicate with their target markets through advice centres which, as well as meeting the needs of existing buyers, also serve to 'grow the market' by providing guidance to new users. Leaflets and manuals, as well as personal advice, often form an important part of the advisory service. Some extend this service to the provision of teaching aids for technical courses. The information should of course be prepared with target market needs in mind – any material which too obviously 'blows its own trumpet' could be counter-productive.

THE ANNUAL REPORT

The main purpose of any Annual Report is to communicate financial results, and it is the key source of information for investors and shareholders. Clearly it must take note of regulatory practices and changing standards of disclosure. It is increasingly recognized however that, if treated in a purely accounting fashion, its contents may be incomprehensible to many and boring in the extreme to others. Many organizations therefore treat the Annual Report, or a simplified version of it, as an opportunity to present the company in its best light, and for communicating about other matters: new product development, staff activities, and changes in company policy, charting successes (or explaining failures).

AUDIO-VISUAL DEVICES

Audio-visual media range from the simple to the complex. This heading covers audio tapes, charts and diagrams, chalk boards, computer graphics and other electronic displays, films, flip charts, overhead projectors with pre-prepared transparencies, slides (perhaps with live voice-over commentary), co-ordinated tape-slide presentations (perhaps multi-picture), and video.

Words, sound and pictures can have a powerful impact on any audience, particularly when supplemented by colour and demonstration (this combination is of course present with cinema and television, but these media may not deliver suitable business audiences). The combination in created media can be as effective for the sales representative with a one-man audience of the buyer in his office as with large conference audiences.

Those creating audio-visual material must also consider the *created* audience. Think of presentations you attended, only to find the slides illegible from where you were sitting! Audio-visual material must be prepared in as practical a fashion as possible, in relation to cost and the contribution it can make in specific circumstances. Conferences, demonstrations, exhibitions, open days, sales presentations, and seminars are each likely to call for different types of audio-visual material.

It is equally important to consider the practicalities of presentation – films can be 8, 16 or 35 mm, while videos can be VHS, BETA, or UMATIC (and, in overseas markets, other systems may operate). Many embarrassing moments can be avoided by checking compatibility of audio-visual material and equipment, along with voltages and electrical cycles – this is important within the UK, and absolutely vital in overseas markets. A rehearsal before the event can also prevent embarrassing mistakes such as back-to-front or upside-down slides!

AWARDS & PRIZES

Many companies achieve effective marketing communications through the awarding of prizes. These could be for created competitions, discussed below, or to recognize outstanding achievement in other areas, perhaps in conjunction with an academic, professional or scientific institution. The benefits of many students, executives or members striving to win a company's medal, and the consequent publicity received at the awards ceremony, can be invaluable. Some firms, rather than give medals, award presentation sets of their own products as much sought-after prizes.

COMPETITIONS

See also *Awards & Prizes*, above, and also *Sponsorship*, page 194.

Some companies, rather than sponsor other people's awards, mount their own competitions with awards for, as example, research and development work in their area or new uses for their product. Many companies benefit from such association with the pioneering concept.

CONFERENCES

The term 'conference' is an all-embracing one covering, as it does, people who come together to confer! Sales conferences can be a most effective means of communicating with representatives. If properly organized, the occasion can deliver a technical briefing about a new product or service, tell representatives about sales targets (and incentives), and build enthusiasm and confidence by explaining the promotional activities (including media created for their use) which will assist their selling efforts.

Dealer conferences can be equally effective in briefing and enthusing sales agents or distributors.

In other circumstances, a company may organize conferences for ultimate customers, or perhaps take advantage of an existing trade or professional event, using the occasion for technical staff to present a paper on new developments, which is subsequently published. This then provides an ideal platform for Public Relations activity to gain wider editorial coverage.

In every case, any comment on the benefits of different types of conference must include the vital words 'if properly organized'! Some conference venues provide practical and down-to-earth check-lists, to assist in organizing effective events.

Press Conferences: see the earlier chapter on Public Relations.

DEMONSTRATIONS

See *Exhibitions*, below.

DESIGN & CORPORATE IDENTITY

This term in fact embraces *all* items discussed within these covers. The design of products, their packaging, the livery of delivery vehicles and drivers, company premises, advertisements, letterheads, news releases and other printed material, all contribute to corporate identity. Creating a total and consistent image for any organization, covering all the marketing mix P's, is a matter which demands expert advice.

DIRECT MAIL

This created medium was examined in Chapter 11.

DISPLAY MATERIAL

See *Point-of-Sale Material*, page 190.

EXHIBITIONS – IN-HOUSE AND MOBILE

The exhibition medium is not restricted to participation in commercial events: many firms find it effective to mount exhibitions in-house, or to have portable units which they erect in premises hired for the occasion. Some even have mobile displays in specially-prepared trailers or buses: if customers do not (or cannot) visit conventional exhibitions, it is always possible to take exhibitions to them. Some business firms mount 'road shows', visiting all important centres or even individual customers direct. These extensions of the exhibition medium were discussed in Chapter 10.

FACILITY VISITS

Many organizations find it advantageous to open their doors from time to time, to let people see for themselves what goes on. As always, different arrangements are necessary for different groups, according to their different interests. The local community have a general interest, whereas shareholders have financial matters in mind. Journalists seek news of new developments. Visits from school parties, or from careers teachers and advisers, may bring long-term recruitment benefits. Such events often necessitate creation of other media discussed within this chapter: audio-visual presentations, in-house exhibitions, and printed material to take away as a permanent reminder of the visit.

FILMS

See *Audio-Visual Devices*, above.

INCENTIVES

See *Gifts* following, also *Merchandising* (page 189) and *Sales Promotion* (page 193).

GIFTS

Business gifts represent a controversial area. Small gifts may be thrown away as worthless, while more expensive items may be viewed as a step on the road to unfair inducement or even bribery! The answer to this problem is, as always, to take a logical approach – why consider business gifts, to whom will they be presented, and what are they intended to achieve? Some firms find a *functional* approach effective – one leading printing supplier distributed printers' aprons: these were welcomed by recipients, and competitors' sales representatives found it daunting to see everyone wearing their rival's emblem!

It is important to establish what competitors are doing. When selecting business gifts it often pays to be the odd one out: if a target group receive calendars or diaries from all competitors, something different might be more welcome. An alternative approach, to ensure a gift is not wasted, is to personalise it: recipients often appreciate diaries embossed with their personal initials, for example – and it is difficult to give away such a gift!

HOUSE JOURNALS

A company may create its own newspaper or magazine to inform certain key groups about on-going activities and to ensure that, in the terms of the Institute of Public Relations, there is 'mutual understanding'. Apart from 'mechanical' considerations such as format (covering page size, number of pages, method of printing, black and white or two or full colour), the Promotion Manager must also consider frequency of publication, method of distribution, and editorial content. The latter of course depends on the target audience, and here house journals can serve two purposes – internal and external. Publications prepared for internal consumption serve to keep staff fully informed, while external journals may be targeted at existing or potential users, shareholders, distributors or agents, or the community within which the organization operates. A mistake to avoid is trying to satisfy too diverse a range of readers: this can lead to much of the content being of little interest to many recipients. Under such circumstances a house journal, however attractive in superficial appearance, will attract a low readership. BAIE, the British Association of Industrial Editors, includes relevant training courses among its many activities, to develop members' skills and to improve standards of communication. Some organizations have successfully pioneered house journals in video rather than in printed format.

HOUSE STYLE

See *Design & Corporate Identity*, page 187.

MERCHANDISING

As with Sales Promotion, it is best to avoid a 'something for nothing' approach. 'Something instead of nothing' is more productive – rather than spend money on advertising from which the target group does not directly benefit, some tangible incentive is offered as a reward for performing a specified action. The important thing is to establish precisely what action distributors/agents/sales staff should take.

Merchandising incentives can take many forms – some perhaps financial (free stock, 13 for the price of 12, free sample of another product, sale or return, money-off discount, or extended credit), all of which would be considered when deciding one of marketing's original four P's: Price.

The Promotion Manager must beware of inexact planning. Contrary to popular opinion it is *easy* to stimulate response, simply by offering a large incentive – but it may bring the wrong response from the wrong people for the wrong reason! Respondents do indeed want 'something for nothing': they want the free gift, and have no real interest in performing the specified action. Hence the vital need – as with advertising and public relations planning – to analyse the problem, set a specific objective, and consider how best to achieve it.

NEWSLETTERS

See *House Journals*, page 189.

OPEN DAYS

See *Facility Visits*, page 188.

POINT-OF-SALE MATERIAL

Even though it delivers an advertising message, display material appears under created rather than advertising media, since there is no rate card on which to look up costs, and it is – quite literally – a created medium.

Adequately display at the place of purchase can make or mar the success of any campaign – particularly for those firms selling to the reseller market. Display material can serve a vital reminder function, delivering its promotional message at the time and place most likely to result in sales. The range of display material is vast, and extends from showcards of various shapes and sizes, through window stickers and crowners, shop and showroom television units, and dispenser units which both sell and display the product.

It is important to recognize, however, that point-of-sale material differs markedly from other advertising media, where payment to a media-owner ensures delivery of the promotional message. With display material, on the other hand, message delivery depends entirely on the recipient who selects, from the vast amount of material available, the few display units he will use.

It has been said, with justification, that 90 per cent of all display material is wasted. Unless a company controls its own showrooms, this high wastage rate usually arises from one or both of two basic faults – production of poor material, and failure to merchandise this material.

In this context poor material means not only inferior quality, but also high-quality material that does not meet the agent's or distributor's needs. Much display material is based on what the company would like, and ignores the hard fact that only the material the recipient thinks functional is put on display. Furthermore, even when a company has produced exactly the right display material, the Promotion Manager must still devise a merchandising programme to ensure its effective use at point of sale. Sending out a showcard with the products, to be unpacked in the warehouse and thrown away, its existence unknown to the showroom manager, illustrates failure to appreciate this point. There are many ways of ensuring dealers' co-operation, considered under the heading of merchandising: all have the common aim of making dealers confident that products will sell, and eager to use relevant display material to promote them to best advantage.

PRINTED MATERIAL

Company literature or manuals can play various vital roles in marketing communications: perhaps paving the way for the representative's call, functioning as a sales aid, delivering detailed or technical information, acting as a 'textbook' guide for new users, or performing a post sales reminder function. Some printed material may serve as a sales promotion incentive: the offer of an informative booklet (featured in both advertising and public relations) can lead to enquiries from prospective customers. These enquiries can in turn serve a merchandising function as leads for sales representatives.

Printed material – like all promotional items – must be carefully planned and the usual questions asked: which executives comprise the target market, what is the purpose of the material, what information must be conveyed to achieve this objective, and how best to convey it?

Many business products and services are necessarily complex, and the technical content of any printed matter must be totally accurate. Unfortunately the technical staff who provide and must check the content are rarely skilled communicators, and the wording they provide often reads like a badly-written text-book. If their dull text is then poorly presented, printed material will fail to achieve its objective. Visual appeal should be added to factual data, and the text presented in a way which makes it easy to digest, while at the same time matching the 'house style' adopted for all company communications.

Multi-lingual publicity material demands careful consideration to keep print and production costs within reason. It is very wasteful to print split runs in different languages, especially when taking into account the expense of colour origination, let alone printing costs. If language text is printed in black only (with no coloured or reversed out headings) this can result in massive cost savings, because only one set of colour scanning and origination work is required. Colour material is left standing for the whole print run, with only an additional (fifth) black plate for each language version required.

Page layout should also allow for language differences: preparing material for overseas markets is a matter of length just as much as language – English text when translated into Spanish, for example, may require 25 per cent more space. This reinforces the point, made in the later chapter on creativity, about the importance of adequate white space in any layout.

Content and presentation depends also on method of delivery – a booklet prepared as a sales aid should differ from one intended to be self-explanatory, or to accompany a direct mail shot.

Printed matter need not necessarily be produced externally by professional printers – although they can of course make a valuable contribution. The advent of 'desktop' publishing, and the graphic facility of many computers and word-processors, means that much effective material is now produced in-house.

PROVISION OF EQUIPMENT OR SAMPLES

Many firms look to the future and achieve effective marketing communications by donating or making permanent loans of equipment to educational institutions. To have future generations receive their training on a company's equipment can prove a valuable long-term investment.

SALES FORCE

Some readers may be surprised at finding the sales force under the heading of created media. Like telemarketing below, its inclusion is justified on the grounds that neither means of communication have editorial columns nor do they sell advertising space or time. Both nevertheless play a vital role in marketing communications. Furthermore, organizations do of course 'create' their sales force through their recruitment and training policies.

Personal selling permits a dialogue to take place. Two-way communication, where customers can ask questions and salesmen react to particular situations, is more effective than one-way contact such as advertising or editorial comment.

Sales representatives can, however, deal only with a limited number of people, and each contact costs a great deal. The high cost of industrial sales calls led many companies to re-examine their total selling and communications strategies. Furthermore, it takes a long time for the sales force to complete their journey cycle of existing customers, and longer still when prospective purchasers are considered.

The sales force role varies according to the type of selling undertaken, which could include any of the following:

- *Product delivery* – milk is the classic consumer example, but certain industrial companies sell supplies on the same basis;
- *Inside order taking* – showroom or depot staff (or those employed by agents or distributors) may undertake this function;
- *Outside order taking* – where sales representatives visit existing and prospective customers;
- *Goodwill building* – where sales staff perform a merchandising function, 'pushing' products or making follow-up calls to reassure those who have just made the purchase;
- *Consultancy* – where representatives sell advice;
- *Selling intangibles* – such as insurance;
- *Seminar selling* – where sales staff undertake an educational function;
- *Conference selling* – where sales force teams meet with groups of client company staff;
- *Telephone selling* – discussed under *Telemarketing*.

Clearly the representatives' role varies with the type of selling and (as already established) sales of industrial products and services are often inseparably linked, the product being so complex that purchasers cannot buy it without a representative's expert advice.

Within these different types of selling, representatives may have different objectives, including:

- *Prospecting* – finding customers. This can often be undertaken more efficiently by use of mass media, to obtain sales leads;
- *Communicating* – conveying product/company information. This task could be facilitated by created media such as printed and/or audio-visual material;

THE RANGE OF CREATED MEDIA

- *Selling* – the art of salesmanship. Many representatives might object to earlier references to *order-taking* and would, quite correctly, prefer the term 'order creation'. Other forms of promotion – back-up advertising, audio-visual or printed sales aids – can, however, assist representatives in this vital task;
- *Servicing* – technical assistance or back-up problem solving. Other forms of promotion may have only a minimal contribution here;
- *Information gathering* – marketing intelligence. Marketing communications is a two-way process, and representatives' reports should feed back into the marketing database, and provide valuable information on which to base future promotional planning;
- *Allocating resources* – representatives must manage their time effectively. Whilst marketing communications is not directly involved, one basic planning stage – determining specific objectives – is directly relevant. Without a specific objective, on what basis are representatives to allocate their time?

This book is primarily concerned with the sales force as a created communications medium, although this cannot be divorced from the vital selling function.

The Promotion Manager, working with the Sales Manager, must ensure that sales representatives are kept fully up-to-date with whatever information they must communicate, and provided with sales aids which assist them in this task. Hence the vital importance of internal marketing and of other entries under the general heading of created media: audio-visual devices, conferences, and printed material.

Other sales force activities may provide opportunities for marketing communications activities. Some business firms utilise driving/travelling time to communicate with representatives by means of audio-tapes. Conversely, other promotional activities can provide opportunities for sales staff – sponsorship, described on page 194, often facilitates client entertainment and consequent building of goodwill.

SALES PRESENTATIONS
See *Conferences*, page 187.

SALES PROMOTION
See *Gifts* (page 188) and *Merchandising*, (page 189) – the same comments apply, but here the 'something instead of nothing' tangible stimulus is aimed at pulling target markets towards products (rather than using incentives to push products towards them). As with merchandising, it is important to avoid imprecise planning. ISBA, the Incorporated Society of British Advertisers, has recently published a *Guide to Sales Promotion*.

SAMPLES
See *Provision of Equipment or Samples*, page 191.

SEMINARS

See *Conferences*, above.

SPEAKERS PANELS

A number of organizations achieve effective marketing communications by providing expert speakers for events organized by, for example, local Chambers of Commerce, Rotary Clubs and other organizations. Speakers can similarly be provided for conferences, seminars and training courses. For effective communication, this may involve other created (audio-visual and printed) media.

SPONSORSHIP

Sponsorship has been defined as:

> 'The provision of financial or material support by a company for some independent activity, not directly linked to the company's normal business, but from which the sponsoring company hopes to benefit.'

The two parties concerned should view sponsorship as a business deal which works to their mutual advantage.

Association with the particular qualities evoked by the sponsored activity can win recognition for a company, enhance its corporate image, and improve the reputation of its goods and services.

Sponsorship can be an effective and memorable means of communicating with current and potential customers, the general public, the local community, employees, opinion-formers, and decision-makers. It can also provide imaginative and unusual opportunities for client entertainment outside the normal business environment, and can be equally effective with other VIPs.

In the early days most sponsorship opportunities were of a sporting nature, but the range has since extended to encompass arts festivals, ballet, beauty contests, charities, community services, cultural exhibitions, expeditions, film festivals, jazz and rock concerts, literary awards, and orchestral performances. These events, properly planned, often achieve extensive media coverage. For organizations whose target markets are 'horizontal' rather than vertical, with large numbers of prospective customers across a wide range of industries, sponsorship can prove most effective. Where organizations provide parallel services for consumer as well as industrial markets, sponsorship can prove even more cost-effective.

Other organizations approach sponsorship in a different way, by sponsoring books or leaflets giving guidance on their product area: see *Advisory Bureaux*, page 185.

The growth of sponsorship into a complex and sophisticated business created a need for specialist and professional services. Sponsorship consultancies, information services and brokers now offer expertise and experience in every aspect of sponsorship. Any company considering sponsorship for the first time would be well advised to seek specialist advice. Having said this, the need for a practical approach and down-to-earth questions still applies – why consider sponsorship, what is the image of the event sponsored, who will receive the sponsorship message, how many will receive it, and what will it cost?

Further information on Sponsorship is given at the end of the chapter.

TELEMARKETING AND TELESALES

As with the sales force, some readers may be surprised at telemarketing appearing as a created medium. The medium does not sell advertising space or time, however, nor does it have editorial columns: it is accordingly reviewed under this heading.

Telemarketing can be a highly cost-effective medium, particularly bearing in mind the increasingly high cost of industrial sales calls, which led many firms to make more extensive use of the telephone as a means of marketing communication.

Three quantitative marketing variables – existing and potential purchasers, the number of sales representatives, and calls made per day – all inter-relate. Without a corresponding increase in sales force size, an increase in customer numbers necessarily means the longer must be the interval between calls, or the shorter the visit itself. To avoid too long an interval or too short a visit, the telephone can provide a most positive alternative or addition to conventional sales calls.

Telemarketing can serve numerous business-to-business functions, including database building, screening prospective purchasers, arranging sales appointments, converting enquiries, handling routine re-orders, servicing marginal accounts, or market research. If the many roles of direct mail are considered in telephone terms, the benefits of telemarketing become apparent.

There are, however, additional benefits. It is direct, as telesales staff actually talk to the target market. It is flexible, since they can find out what respondents want, and adapt the message accordingly. The company knows what happens on every call, and so the medium can be directly evaluated. Furthermore, distance is no object: phone calls cost money, but save travelling time and expenses. It is one of the few media where competitors don't know what a company is doing, and finally it is fast, as there is no waiting for print or production.

Drawbacks are that it is non-visual, as it is not possible to 'show' a new product over the telephone. Furthermore, while it is easy for someone to say 'yes' on the telephone, marketing requirements may call for a signature on a contract.

Telemarketing is not, however, simply a matter of sales representatives making phone calls. The medium is becoming increasingly sophisticated and, as such, often treated as a distinct operation with separate staff.

A recent development in market research – CATI, or Computer Assisted Telephone Interviewing – has been adapted, for marketing needs, into CATS – Computer Assisted Telephone Selling. Various companies specialising in telemarketing services now provide information technology systems which both speed up the operation and increase its efficiency. Automated telemarketing systems can maintain an interactive database of customer and market information (as discussed earlier under database marketing), but with autodial and automatic recall facilities. Calls can be scripted, and follow-up sales information automatically generated or product literature despatched, as soon as each call is completed. Campaign results can be analysed and evaluated, while the campaign is running.

TELEPHONE

While the telephone can play a most positive role in outward contacts through telemarketing, its importance as an incoming medium is often overlooked. For many prospective customers, their first personal contact with a company is the switchboard operator. It is important that all such telephone contacts leave a good impression, otherwise much of what promotion does to build a positive image is *undone* with each incoming call.

Staff training should ensure that switchboard operators (and their coffee and lunch break substitutes) realise the importance of treating every caller as an important person.

Internal marketing must play its part here, ensuring that switchboard staff are aware of promotional activities, and not suddenly deluged with a flood of unexpected phone calls for a new booklet about which they know nothing!

TRAINING

Many firms selling complex products or services (information technology, for example) provide training services for existing and potential users. The created medium is often a purpose-built training centre, with its own extensive facilities and even residential accommodation.

VIDEO

See *Audio-Visual*, page 186. Some specialist broadcasting and production companies, working with hotel chain groups, now offer extensive video-conferencing facilities.

SUMMARY

Created media must be planned as carefully as other promotions, and it is vital to adopt the planning approach stressed throughout this book.

No Promotion Manager would ever say 'It's time we did some advertising, so let's buy some space somewhere at some cost and say something to somebody about something at some time!'

But alas some organizations do (believe it or not) approach created media such as merchandising and sales promotion in this haphazard fashion. 'Things are tough, so let's have a Promotion' – they then wonder why things went wrong!

A company may create promotional media for various reasons – to improve mutual understanding, to push its products towards people, or to pull people towards these products. As with other marketing communications media, the company must determine a specific objective, and then plan how best to achieve it.

FURTHER INFORMATION ON SPONSORSHIP

DATABASES

Several of the advertising and Public Relations references sources listed earlier contain information about sponsorship.

ASSOCIATION FOR BUSINESS SPONSORSHIP OF THE ARTS
(2 Chester Street, London SW1X 7BB)

The Association is the national independent organization established to promote the concept and practice of business sponsorship of the arts and to represent sponsors' interests. It also administers the Business Sponsorship Incentive Scheme on behalf of the Minister for Arts.

ABSA has more than 200 business members and four offices in London, Edinburgh, Belfast and Cardiff. It maintains a Register of Sponsorship Opportunities, and advises on sponsorship programmes.

The Association also sells various publications, including *The Sponsor's Guide'* (for business), and the ABSA/W. H. Smith Sponsoring Manual (for arts groups), and will advise any business interested in this field.

SPORTS SPONSORSHIP ADVISORY SERVICE
(16 Upper Woburn Place, London WC1H 0QP)

This Advisory Service was formed by the Sports Council and Central Council for Physical Recreation to provide, at no cost, professional and objective advice and expertise on the use of sport as a communication medium.

INCORPORATED SOCIETY OF BRITISH ADVERTISERS
(44 Hertford Street, London W1Y 8AE)

ISBA has published a *Guide to Sponsorship*, which gives practical guidance and lists statutory and non-profit organizations which have sponsorship advisory services.

PART 4: EFFECTIVE MARKETING COMMUNICATIONS

19 Research & Investigation.

20 Setting Specific Campaign Objectives.

21 Purchasing Patterns.

22 Budgeting.

23 Preparation of Campaign Proposals – The Message.

24 Preparation of Campaign Proposals – The Media.

25 Approval of Promotional Proposals.

26 Execution of Promotional Proposals.

27 Follow Through.

28 Evaluation of Results.

CHAPTER NINETEEN

Research & Investigation

Before planning any marketing communications, the Promotion Manager must brief himself fully on many functional business aspects, for unless his company's campaign reflects these practicalities it cannot work to full advantage. This essential planning stage is henceforth referred to as 'R & I' (or, for variety, as research or alternatively investigations).

THE ORGANIZATION

A full knowledge of the firm is essential. A long-established company could place promotional emphasis on years of experience, while another might promote itself as a newly-formed pioneer. Outstanding research facilities and staff could be featured, as might achievements recognized by awards, royal warrants, or appointment as official suppliers to prestigious users. The organization may perhaps comprise a range of companies, rather than function as a single business operation. These in turn might operate nationally, internationally or multi-nationally. Organization size, financial strength, profitability and growth rate (overall and division by division) are all important, as is management structure. Some companies have a distinctive management philosophy which is featured in promotional messages. Clearly such considerations affect promotional planning, so an in-depth knowledge is essential.

THE PRODUCT OR SERVICE

Complete knowledge of the products or services to be promoted (both individually and over the range) is equally important.

Business marketing can be categorized under various broad headings, including production machinery, raw materials, components, consumable supplies, capital equipment, and services. Whatever the heading, it is important to have answers to many questions. What does the product actually do? Does it have a single application, or is it a multi-use product? Sales of multi-use products might be increased, for example, by promotion which points out additional product applications. Raw materials used, method of manufacture, quality control systems – all are important, as are product range, prices and delivery. Perhaps the organizations offer some special guarantee or pre- or after-sales service. The service might be more important than the product itself, as far as users are concerned. The company may market a service as such, and is a service organization rather than a manufacturer.

The relationship between new and existing products or services can be a significant one. In promoting financial services or business travel, for example, this relationship could be vital since organizations competing for business markets often provide parallel services for private consumers. In such circumstances, two distinct promotional campaigns can be mutually beneficial – one aimed primarily at the business market (but with the added benefit that it influences private consumers), whilst the consumer campaign re-inforces the frequency with which the business community is reminded of the company name. Where an organization mounts separate campaigns for different products as well as different markets, their inter-relationship is again important. Planning such a complex campaign structure is no easy matter: the promotions must be so planned that they re-inforce each other.

Whether the necessary facts are supplied by production staff or, as is more likely, the Promotion Manager checks products or services himself, he must obtain all this vital information. He must further ensure he is notified, well in advance, of any impending changes.

The Promotion Manager should also, together with the Marketing Director, analyse the company's portfolio of products. Which are the stars of the future? Which should be milked now? Which need to be replaced, or developed? And by what dates?

Having thoroughly studied the products, the Promotion Manager can then study potential purchasers, known in marketing terminology as 'the market'.

THE TARGET MARKET

When a housewife says she is going to the market (or perhaps supermarket) she is referring to the place where she will make her purchases. In marketing terminology, however, 'market' is the people (or organizations) who purchase products, rather than the place where they buy.

Consumer companies define their markets in terms of age, sex or socio-economic groupings, or perhaps their interest, sports or hobbies. Business-to-business firms, however, sell to organizations (and executives within them) rather than to private individuals, and so define their markets differently.

Whichever way markets are classified, the Promotion Manager must have a clear picture of the customers likely to be interested in his company's products. Borrowing from consumer marketing terminology, he must have a clear picture both *demographically* and *psychographically*. If he does not know which organizations and individuals comprise his target market, how can he select media to reach them? Equally important is a psychological picture for, unless he understands how the target group reach purchasing decisions and what motivates them, he is in no position to create marketing communications messages.

DEMOGRAPHIC MARKET CLASSIFICATIONS

'Demographics' should indicate a clear target for marketing communications messages, and various approaches are possible: one is Standard Industrial Classifications. Government employment statistics, for example, show the numbers engaged in the following industrial divisions (some further sub-divided into classes):

- Agriculture, forestry and fishing
- Coal, oil and natural gas extraction and processing

- Electricity, gas, other energy and water supply
- Metal manufacturing, ore and other mineral extraction
- Chemicals and man-made fibres
- Mechanical engineering
- Office machinery, electrical engineering and instruments
- Motor vehicles and parts
- Other transport equipment
- Metal goods
- Food, drink and tobacco
- Textiles, leather, footwear and clothing
- Timber, wooden furniture, rubber, plastics etc
- Paper products, printing and publishing
- Construction
- Wholesale distribution and repairs
- Retail distribution
- Hotels and catering
- Transport
- Postal services and telecommunications
- Banking, finance, insurance
- Public administration etc.
- Education
- Medical and other health services, veterinary services
- Other services

This approach to classifying markets is a 'vertical' one, implying the wish to reach executives at various management levels within a particular industrial sector. This could well be the case with machinery specific to, for example, the brewing industry. Other organizations classify their markets 'horizontally': they wish to reach executives who perform similar functions (accountants, for example) across the full range of industry and commerce.

When classifying market horizontally it is possible to utilise, as numbers increase, demographic descriptions usually applied to consumer purchases. The standard socio-economic groupings of A, B, C1, C2, D and E, adopted in many media surveys, can serve in defining business markets. A, B and C1, for example, all refer to 'Managerial, administrative or professional' occupations – the difference between the three being that they are respectively *Higher*, *Intermediate* and *Supervisory or clerical and junior*.

Whether the market is classified vertically or horizontally, or a combination of the two (accountants within a selected range of industries, for example), further demographic measures can affect promotional policy. Customer location – local, in another part of the country, concentrated in certain areas, national, or spread throughout the world – clearly affects where to aim promotional messages.

PSYCHOGRAPHIC ANALYSIS

To aim marketing communications messages, demographic details are needed: to decide message content, it is necessary to understand the target market's motivation and decision process.

When do customers buy, and how often? This influences campaign timing and message frequency. Is the product bought on impulse (unlikely, perhaps, but applicable to a minority of business purchases) or only after careful consideration? If the latter, how long is this consideration period? This too clearly affects timing, and the type of campaign to be mounted.

Why do purchasers buy a product or service, and why do they select one supplier in preference to others? How strong is their brand loyalty? Are some groups more likely than others to adopt new products? Within each group, how are purchasing decisions actually reached?

Without answers to these questions, the Promotion Manager is in no position to create communications messages, and the purchasing decision-process is therefore examined in detail in Chapter 21.

MARKET SEGMENTATION

It is often effective to *segment* the total market into different groupings. This helps give better understanding of the market, and of how and why customers buy. It also helps in selecting for attention those most likely to respond, and in planning promotions to stimulate the selected segments. Market segmentation is a crucial tool in promotional planning and, as always, there are various ways of approaching this task. Markets might be segmented by:

- *Demographics* – industrial classification, occupation and geographic locations and concentrations;
- *Operating variables* – technology, and user applications;
- *Size* – current and potential consumption;
- *Type* – first time, repeat use, or one-off;
- *Purchasing approach* – size of decision-making unit, ease (or difficulty) of obtaining decisions, purchasing criteria, price elasticity;
- *Ease (or difficulty) of communication*

Another segmentation approach is to classify organizations under one of two headings, one of which further sub-divides. Organizations are either Users or Non-Users of products. If Users, they can then be classified as Light, Medium or Heavy.

A later stage in promotional planning is to determine campaign objectives, and segmentation is clearly important here – a company might seek to persuade non-users to commence using its product, or alternatively aim to convert light users into medium, or medium into heavy. This will depend also on 'psychographics' – if non-users will never have need for the product, the Promotion Manager should have better uses for money than waste it in trying to convert them! At the other end of the scale it might seem attractive to aim for heavy users – but if they are loyal to competitors, promotional effort might be better directed at a more responsive market segment.

A different approach to segmenting existing and potential buyers is to consider their 'message sources' and *media* habits and attitudes. Marketing communications is a two-way process, and so markets can be classified in terms of how they use the media being used to reach them – target groups may be heavy, medium, light or non-users of specialist press, newspapers, or other media.

MARKET AND SEGMENT SIZE

A great deal depends on the total size of the market, and of individual segments which comprise it, by whichever criteria these are categorized. Equally important are the *trends* behind the figures. Such considerations are a starting point for determining whether to use mass or selective targeted media.

With a market or segment size of only single or double figures, promotion would clearly concentrate on personal contacts backed up by selective media such as direct mail. If market size increases to a few hundreds the situation remains much the same, but when target market numbers reach the thousands, then personal contact must become selective (with whom should sales representatives make contact, and how often?) and promotional planning would consider additional means of communication. When target markets reach tens of thousands, personal contact can no longer cope, as mass markets call for mass communications.

OTHER TARGET GROUPS

For PR purposes, promotional briefing is both broader and narrower.

Overall Public Relations planning must cover a wider market than actual or potential purchasers, and should include others who are *affected* either directly or indirectly. This could include many groups important enough to call for further campaigns which deliberately inform them (rather than leaving them to find out by chance) of developments. This extensive list could include, for example:

- Educational bodies
- Employees
- Government departments
- Local authorities
- Local communities
- Opinion formers
- Potential investors
- Pressure groups
- Shareholders
- Suppliers
- Trade unions

There is, however, no sharp distinction between primary and secondary target groups: some individuals might be both employees and shareholders, for example, while others could serve on local councils. All will of course see the campaigns aimed at existing and potential purchasers. The important thing is to consider ALL target groups marketing communications should reach. The promotional plan should in turn encompass all their message sources.

Conversely, PR briefing is sometimes narrower, in that the Promotion Manager wishes to issue a news release. This should cover, and he should therefore brief himself on, the five traditional questions asked by journalists – *Who, What, When, Where and Why?*

MARKETING POLICY

Investigations have so far covered the organization and its product or service, and equally the markets which might buy it – but as yet there is no link between the two. Promotional policy is directly affected by, and should reflect, distribution and selling and other aspects of marketing policy. Equally, when deciding marketing policy, the Board should remember Promotion is one of the original four P's, and consider its vital role in successful marketing.

Various 'marketing mix' components, outlined earlier, directly affect marketing communications planning. Distribution may be national, regionally biased, or even restricted to certain areas: this clearly affects where promotional messages should be delivered.

Many companies divide their selling territory into areas, and the total marketing operation thus comprises a number of individual sales drives.

A 'rolling' launch may be phased over a period of time, successively covering one area after another until national (or sometimes international) distribution is achieved. This clearly affects campaign planning, since it calls for heavy promotion in appropriate areas during the launch period, followed by reminder campaigns during the months that follow. Message content too will change, with informative launch announcements followed by reminder messages in local media, until such time as distribution is wide enough for national media to be used. Even where distribution is nationwide, the objective may be to increase sales by pin-pointing a particular target market segment (as distinct from geographical area) for special attention. Clearly, such marketing decisions directly affect promotional planning.

Sales force structure, the number of salesmen employed, and the time taken for them to complete their round of calls, can all affect promotional planning. It is equally important to know if they call on all customers, or whether the company relies on distributors or agents to reach smaller buyers. The number of sales outlets will influence promotional policy – the need to list distributors' names and addresses has a marked influence on both media selection and the message to be delivered.

Promotion can be affected by the discount/margin/mark-up position, and whether the organization has a competitive advantage (or disadvantage) over rival suppliers. The earlier review of marketing pointed out that companies may adopt 'push' or 'pull' promotional policies – the latter give minimal discounts and use heavy promotion to pull merchandise through the distribution chain. The agent gets only a small profit per unit, but the prospect of heavy sales stimulated by heavy promotion makes him stock the merchandise, ready to meet the demand stimulated. With a 'push' campaign, on the other hand, little is spent on promotion, but attractive discounts persuade the agent to promote the goods, in view of the large sum he gets for every unit sold. In practice it is rarely a question of operating at either extreme of this push-pull scale but at some intermediate point. Most business campaigns tend to push rather than pull, although some 'horizontal' business services (such as industrial cleaning or staff health care) have been advertised on mass media such as television – such advertisements not only reach employers but, as management know their staff (and unions) also see the commercials, the campaigns also have a strong 'pull' effect.

Promotional planning will vary according to whether the marketing objective is to launch a new product, sustain an existing one, or halt a decline in the market. If the marketing objective is to increase sales of an existing product, is this to be achieved by converting non-users into users, light users into medium, medium into heavy, or by some other means? Hence the importance of market segmentation, discussed earlier.

When planning promotional effort, it is clear that different marketing policies call for different campaigns, in terms of both messages and media.

PREVIOUS PROMOTION

R & I should involve a careful check on what promotional activities were undertaken in the past and with what results, to see what lessons can be learned.

Future effectiveness can be increased by evaluating which media proved productive, and what the campaign called for in terms of advertisement size, position, use of colour, timing and duration. Evaluation should equally cover which publications carried the company's news releases. Also what promotional messages were transmitted, whether through editorial comment or advertising, merchandising or sales promotion.

Money is alas often wasted through failure to keep adequate records. Careful evaluation can lead to better results for the same money, or achieving the same results for less outlay. Either way, the benefit is obvious. Future plans must be prepared in the light of what was learned from the past, and the results of this year's campaign should provide the basis for next year's planning. This preliminary R & I stage thus links with the final *Evaluation of Results* stage, to which Chapter 28 is devoted.

CONSTRAINTS

Two categories of constraint can directly influence promotional planning: internal and external.

INTERNAL

The constraints encountered here would arise when checking through the five previous headings: firm, product, market, marketing policy, and previous promotion.

One constraint could be that the firm has insufficient funds to mount an extensive promotional campaign. Alternatively, if financial restraints are not the problem, will management in fact authorise the expenditure – many industrial companies are notoriously production-orientated.

Regarding product, there may be limits to the amount the factory can supply. If so, there is no point in over-promoting and thus boosting competitors' sales.

The market itself may be a constraint: if one market segment is loyal to the competition, promotional effort would be better aimed at another group, more likely to respond.

Marketing constraints may mean promotional planning must take account of restricted distribution areas, fewer outlets or a longer sales journey cycle than that of competitors.

Equally important a constraint may be competitors' promotional activities – an organization which is being out-spent, or whose rivals dominate a particular medium, must under such circumstances spend its limited funds where they will make maximum impact.

EXTERNAL

A number of legal constraints and voluntary codes limit promotional activities.

For some manufacturers the constraint is fundamental and dictates media policy; eg, cigarette advertising is not allowed on television. It is unlikely that any business supplier will encounter a barrier of this kind, but various trade restraints may be imposed. In the past, for example, firms offering certain professional services were forbidden to advertise. An increasing number of governing bodies now take a more enlightened view and permit members to promote themselves, subject to strict guidelines.

In other areas, the offer of financial advice services, for example, strict legal requirements must be observed. There are also numerous laws relating to all marketing communications activities, whether business-to-business or consumer campaigns. Legal advice should always be sought when necessary, particularly as regards merchandising and sales promotion schemes.

Almost all promotional activities are covered by self-regulatory controls, such as the Advertising Standards Authority's Code of Advertising Practice, the IBA's Code of Advertising Standards and Practice, and the British Code of Sales Promotion Practice. Some media have their own additional specialist standards.

Finally there are the marketing communications professional bodies' own Codes of Conduct – most of the trade and membership organizations listed in various chapters have strict codes of professional practice.

Research must ascertain just what the company is (and is not) allowed to do – how else can the Promotion Manager prepare a campaign that satisfies these requirements?

COMPETITION

Investigating competition necessitates not just one study but at least six, since each rival organization must be considered under the same headings – firm, products or service, market, marketing policy, previous promotion and constraints.

The Promotion Manager must check the strengths and organizational weaknesses of rival firms and also their products, and how they compare with those of his own company. The strong and weak points of each can provide the basis for comparison campaigns.

He should also ascertain who his competitors' customers are, and how they differ from purchasers of his own company's products. And, most important, why they purchase rival brands in preference. This may be due to product differences or perhaps because of marketing policy, the next aspect of competitor's activity demanding analysis.

Competitive firms' marketing policies must be carefully studied, by the same criteria utilised when checking his own company's policy.

Equal attention must be paid to the promotional campaigns mounted by rival firms, and whether they concentrate on advertising or public relations, and in which media. It is also important to check which sales points they stress in these campaigns, and in their merchandising and sales promotion activities.

If competitors face any restraints on, for example, delivery or product range, this could give a competitive advantage on which promotion might be based.

Before planning his company's campaign, it is vital that the Promotion Manager has a thorough knowledge of the competition his organization faces from others. A clear understanding of the indirect competition which his firm and its rivals face from other product groups can be equally important.

MARKETING COMMUNICATIONS MEDIA

Investigations should include gaining a first-hand knowledge of promotional media: this must be both quantitative and qualitative. A sound understanding of circulation and readership statistics will indicate whether a medium is likely to reach the target market, while an in-depth appreciation of each medium is equally important. The editorial features carried and their regularity will indicate whether the publication merits a news release, or might perhaps carry a feature article. The advertisement positions available on different pages also influence promotional planning. Readership statistics (as emphasised earlier) relate to *average* copies – where an advertisement is positioned within the publication influences its effectiveness: an advertisement on the management page, for example, picks out from total readership those with management interests, and reaches them when they are mentally 'tuned in' to management matters, and thus more likely to be receptive to promotional messages about management products or services.

BACKGROUND

The Promotion Manager must recognize that his firm does not compete with rivals in isolation, but against the background of a national economy increasingly influenced by international factors. There are two useful acronyms to assist in reviewing this background – P-E-S-T and S-W-O-T.

P-E-S-T

These initials signify four background aspects with direct implications for marketing success (or failure): Political, Economic, Sociological and Technological.

Political. This analysis does not concern party politics, but simply recognizes that political decisions directly affect any business's day-to-day operations and long-term objectives. Changes in tax structure, capital allowances, development grants and in overall monetary policy all illustrate how political decisions have immediate business implications. Changes in the law, brought about by Parliament, can be equally important.

Economic. This area overlaps the first, as different political parties have different policies for economic ills such as unemployment, inflation, or recession. The

UK economy is, however, influenced by others: American budget decisions about internal and trade deficits, OPEC action on oil prices, and consequent changes in exchange rates, all have far-reaching effects on UK business activities.

Sociological. This heading covers considerations such as the changing roles of women or young people, the increase in single-parent households, the development of Britain's multi-racial society, or the trend to health-consciousness, all of which have direct implications for any promotional campaign. Although business-to-business firms sell to other organizations rather than private individuals, many such purchasers buy business products in order to market consumer products or services. The concept of *derived demand* means any business organization must keep abreast of changes in the overall market from which much business-to-business demand stems. As example, an organization which manufactured specialist encapsulation machinery achieved success by planning its promotion so as to benefit from the growth in sales of health products.

Technological. Many business products are subject to constant scientific development. Whether or not this is the case for a particular firm, *all* business organizations are affected by technological change: by, for example, information technology – computers and word processors. Promotional media are themselves undergoing a technological revolution: different printing methods, regional editions and shorter copy-handling periods all affect the possibility of using their editorial and advertising columns for marketing communications messages. Other media are similarly affected.

The various *P-E-S-T* factors often overlap, and this is an opportune moment to mention 1992, when 12 countries in Europe become one vast trading zone, with a market of some 320 million consumers.

Many goods and services which British companies produce for the UK market must satisfy official national standards, but at present other countries can impose their own regulations on UK exports (and the UK sometimes does the same for imports). The barriers to international trade imposed by national standards will be removed by 1992, thereby affecting most products and services. The physical barrier will also be removed in 1993, when the Channel Tunnel joins the UK physically to the rest of Europe.

Business firms should be preparing themselves for market expansion: this involves a complete review of many factors just discussed – organizational structure, product/service (including product name and packaging), marketing policy, and promotion – and analysis to determine the degree to which they are suitable (or must be adapted) for these new markets. UK firms should also recognize the likelihood of strong competition for the home market from continental rivals.

This vital matter demands more attention than can be given within this book: all that can be achieved here is to remind readers of these forthcoming changes, and draw attention to information available from various sources, including:

THE DEPARTMENT FOR ENTERPRISE
DEPARTMENT OF TRADE AND INDUSTRY
(1–19 Victoria Street, London SW1H 0ET)

The Department has published 'The Single Market' information packs, as well as 'An action checklist for business'.

THE INSTITUTE OF PRACTITIONERS IN ADVERTISING
(44 Belgrave Square, London SW1X 8QS)

The IPA has published, within its *How to Succeed in Industrial Advertising* series, a booklet on 'Industrial Advertising and Marketing in Europe'.

THE INCORPORATED SOCIETY OF BRITISH ADVERTISERS
(44 Hertford Street, London SW1Y 8AE)

ISBA includes among its publications a 'Guide to Advertising Overseas'.

LONDON ENTERPRISE AGENCY
(4 Snow Hill, London EC1A 2BS)

S-W-O-T

These initials come from a well-known marketing analysis which applies equally to deciding promotional policy. Bearing in mind the many factors just reviewed and likely future trends, R & I should conclude with a SWOT analysis of *S*trengths and *W*eaknesses, and of the *O*pportunities and *T*hreats facing the organization.

THE IMPORTANCE OF RESEARCH

The first planning task is to carefully check the many points just discussed. Without such investigations, it is impossible to plan future promotion effectively.

Research is vital for accurate media selection. Promotional planning can be likened to aiming a gun: a marksman cannot hit a target unless he knows what and where the target is, and research can provide this information. Research also helps in timing the campaign, by indicating when any product is purchased and how frequently.

R & I can also help in creating suitable promotional messages. Most products offer many benefits, any of which could be stressed in promotion: it is vital to select the key attribute that will attract readers' attention and lead them to study the material more closely. Stressing the correct selling proposition attracts attention and, equally, featuring the wrong 'copy platform' loses attention – and sales.

Research can contribute significantly to media planning and creative work by ensuring it is soundly based. Its function, however, is only preparatory: it will not produce a media schedule or press circulation list, nor the content of promotional messages. Research does not dispense with the need for good planners or writers, but provides an efficient tool to make their work more effective.

Market research has been defined as 'the systematic study of products (and services) – existing or potential – in relation to their markets'. Information could be obtained by interviewing potential customers personally, but field research is both costly and time-consuming, and valuable information may already be available from other sources.

Research does not necessarily imply heavy expenditure on field research, by calling in a professional market research company – although naturally the information resulting from such action can be invaluable. R & I also includes desk research, and the number of information sources is extremely large: numerous government surveys and reports, and the many data sources listed in various chapters of this book. If to this list is added the research undertaken by trade, professional and technical associations and institutions, and the reports, publications and on-line databases available from other sources, then the wealth of desk research information will be apparent. A good librarian can provide invaluable help in locating relevant information sources, either direct or through various directories in which such sources are listed.

Desk research can also reveal unexpected public relations opportunities. If any reference sources do not include or give sufficient coverage to a Promotion Manager's own organization, there is scope for PR activity, supplying Editors with the information their readers need, ready for the next edition. Other firms may well consult these same information sources, in search of the very products or services his own organization provides.

Desk research could perhaps make field research unnecessary by locating information, perhaps bit by bit, in many different published sources. This would save the several thousand pounds required for a field survey, and save vital time as well. If, however, desk research cannot answer all the questions, if different sources give conflicting data, or if some available information is out-of-date, then field research may be essential. To prevent this book becoming a research methodology text, comment is restricted to the fact that there are two possibilities open – one is to commission a field survey, and the other is to 'buy in' to services already undertaking on-going research and providing information on a regular basis. The Specialist Readership Surveys chapter (Chapter 9) cited several research organizations offering such an 'omnibus' facility.

THE NEXT STEP

With investigations complete, the Promotion Manager now has a firm base on which to undertake the next task – determining his organization's promotional strategy.

RESEARCH AND INVESTIGATION

RELEVANT ORGANIZATIONS

ASSOCIATION OF BRITISH MARKET RESEARCH COMPANIES
(c/o Peter Hodgson, Travel & Tourism Research Ltd, 39c Highbury Place, London N5 1QP)

ABMRC members include leading operators in computer technology, specialist and business-to-business research companies, fieldwork and coding agencies and research consultancies, in addition to many major full service research houses.

As well as representing the professional and commercial interests of its 106 member companies, ABMRC is concerned with enhancing professionalism in market research and in promoting confidence in market research among both clients and the public. ABMRC is the largest trade organization of its type in the world.

The Association produces a number of publications, and a copy of the ABMRC Handbook is available on request for research buyers.

DATABASES

The many databases listed in various chapters can provide valuable market as well as media coverage data.

INDUSTRIAL MARKETING RESEARCH ASSOCIATION
(11 Bird Street, Lichfield, Staffordshire WS13 6PW)

IMRA is the professional body for people engaged in searching for and analysing information relevant to marketing goods and services to corporate and institutional users. The growth of research into such markets and its distinctive nature (compared with consumer goods) led to the Association's formation in 1963, since when it has developed into the recognized national body representing the industrial market research profession in the UK.

Regional sections and specific industry groups (eg, building & construction industry, electrical & electronics, and packaging) meet regularly, giving opportunities for discussion and the development of personal contacts.

MARKET RESEARCH SOCIETY
(175 Oxford Street, London W1R 1TA)

An extremely useful guide to market research organizations and the many services they provide is the MRS's booklet: *Organizations and individuals providing market research services*. The Society has a business-to-business special interest group.

CHAPTER TWENTY

Setting Specific Campaign Objectives

Having completed his research and investigations, the Promotion Manager should have a full knowledge of his firm and its products or service, its target markets and marketing policy, previous promotional activities, any constraints imposed, the competition faced, and business background. He is now in a position to take positive action, and determine his organization's specific campaign objective.

Marketing communication is a means of achieving business objectives, and there is an extensive range of practical reasons for mounting promotional campaigns. *How British Business Advertises*, the study undertaken by British Business Press (see page 104) investigates the role of the business press in relation to 12 key advertising tasks. Another well-known analysis, *Defining Advertising Goals for Measured Advertising Results* by R. Colley (see Chapter 28), lists 52 advertising goals! Bear in mind that this range from twelve to fifty-two possible objectives relate to *advertising* alone, whereas the Promotion Manager is concerned with the full range of marketing communications media – not just advertising, but also created media, merchandising, public relations, sales promotion, the sales force itself, and indeed all the marketing 'P's'. The range of possible promotional objectives is thus even wider, making a detailed examination of possible campaign objectives all the more important.

The fundamental reasons for mounting promotional campaigns are a surprising blind spot for many business executives. Any enquiry about campaign objectives often results in the reply 'To increase sales' – and a look of surprise, as if the question is a foolish one. But increased sales is only an optimistic hope for the future, and not a business objective! How are these increased sales to be achieved? The same loose thinking applies to a campaign to 'improve our image'. If increased sales or improved image are, in fact, to be achieved, then it is essential to define a specific objective, since this affects the type of promotional campaign mounted, the media used, and the message content.

A useful exercise is to select at random a number of advertisements (press, television, direct mail or whatever) or indeed news releases or merchandising or sales promotion incentives, and then try to deduce (from the message and the media, and manner in which these media are used) just what is the campaign's *specific* objective. Few would-be analysts will achieve a high success rate, which surely proves one or both of two points:

1. Many executives have a blind spot when analysing campaign effectiveness.
2. Many promotional campaigns are ineffective, for lack of a clear objective.

This argument may be a 'heads I win, tails you lose' one, but why else should such analysis not be successful? Hence the importance of this and Chapter 25 on *Approval of Campaign Proposals*, which gives guidance in this respect.

Creativity must never be underestimated, but it is functional only when applied to campaign objectives. A clear objective assists creative staff by setting the parameters within which they should work: it indicates the creative approach necessary, and is essential for good media selection and planning.

ANALYSIS OF SPECIFIC OBJECTIVES

Analysis of a wide range of promotional campaigns in many media revealed numerous distinct objectives. These are discussed here, but not in any universal order of importance. The list is not exhaustive and different objectives may sometimes overlap. A company may wish to achieve two or more purposes simultaneously, and thus needs to run two or more concurrent communications campaigns, or perhaps has an objective not included in the list. Furthermore, these objectives may change over time, as circumstances change. The main point is the essential need to set out clearly, before starting to plan, *precisely* what objective the campaign should achieve. Planning and creativity then follow on logically.

One leading advertising agency for which I worked insisted on a firm discipline to this process. The first stage was to obtain the client's agreement that agency staff clearly understood the research elements outlined earlier. The next stage was client's agreement on the specific objective to be achieved – and this was *before* communications media or messages were considered. Some critics argue that such disciplined analysis must inhibit the creative process. To the contrary, it should assist creative staff, by concentrating their efforts on providing the ideal creative solution to the *real* problem facing the company. The point that the planning process is as important as the plan applies to creativity just as much as other aspects of marketing.

POSSIBLE CAMPAIGN OBJECTIVES

As has been made clear, there is a very wide range of possible objectives. A starting point for analysis is the list of 12 key tasks in the British Business Press study. To achieve any of these requires answers to many questions, thus emphasising the importance of earlier discussions of *Criteria for Media Comparison* (Chapter 6), and *Research & Investigations* (Chapter 19).

Many of these BBP objectives are re-examined later, and their interrelationship discussed, through my own marketing communications matrix, prepared to assist promotional planning analysis.

CREATE DIRECT SALES LEADS

The purpose of promotion may be to provide representatives with sales leads on which to call. Salesmen's time is both limited and costly, and following up contacts who have indicated interest by, for example, returning a coupon is far more productive than cold canvassing.

To achieve this objective the Promotion Manager must return to the R & I stage for the answer to a basic question – from which market segments are replies sought? This objective has other implications for promotional planning, since it may dictate use of media which facilitate direct response, and some media are more inter-active than others. Furthermore, it might demand flexible media, which permit turning the promotional tap on when necessary, or off when representatives have more business than they can handle.

PROVIDE EFFECTIVE SUPPORT FOR YOUR SALES FORCE

Promotion can give a valuable psychological boost to salesmen who, in the field all day, may feel cut off and become dispirited. Where representatives sell to industrial buyers (rather than to retailers, who may be influenced by consumer campaigns) this back-up role can be vital. A McGraw-Hill advertisement, designed to promote advertising in its specialist magazines, showed a steely-eyed industrial buyer staring at the reader and saying:

> *'I don't know who you are.*
> *I don't know your company.*
> *I don't know your company's product.*
> *I don't know what your company stands for.*
> *I don't know your company's customers.*
> *I don't know your company's record.*
> *I don't know your company's reputation.*
> *Now – what was it you wanted to sell me?'*
>
> **MORAL** – Sales start **before** your salesman calls –
> with business publication advertising.
>
> **McGRAW-HILL MAGAZINES**
> BUSINESS · PROFESSIONAL · TECHNICAL

INCREASE POTENTIAL CUSTOMER BASE

Like sales leads, this objective calls for an answer to the target market question – in which segments of the overall market is the increase sought? This specific objective is re-examined later. It is in fact left until last: not because it is unimportant – on the contrary – because it demands more detailed analysis than other possible objectives.

REACH SPECIFIC TARGET AUDIENCE

To achieve this campaign objective, the Promotion Manager must revert to earlier chapters for answers to two specific questions – precisely which executives comprise this specific target audience, and which media reach them? The importance of earlier analyses immediately becomes apparent.

COMMUNICATE DETAILED INFORMATION ABOUT YOUR PRODUCT OR SERVICE

This objective calls for the same comment as the last, and similarly two questions – one, as with the previous objective, asks for a target market definition. The second asks what capacity have the various media for delivering this detailed information. A third question, *what* detailed information should be communicated, is considered in Chapter 23.

ADVERTISE NEW PRODUCT LAUNCHES

For new products or services, the promotional task is one of basic education – informing potential customers of the benefits they will reap by purchasing a new product, about which at present they know nothing. A side effect of this may be, in due course, a counter campaign by competitors whose sales decline in consequence.

This BBP key objective could extend to cover new product developments, as well as launches. Present customers may already know the products, but not about improvements made, or new lines added to the range. Furthermore, such changes often open up new market segments, for whom the original products were unsuitable. Potential customers do not become purchasers if they do not know of such changes, and marketing communications help keep them informed.

There are again clear media and creative implications, and need for full target market and product information, as examined at R & I stage.

CREATE PRODUCT AWARENESS

This objective calls for the answer to one question already posed – precisely *who* should be made aware, and to a second: aware of *which* particular product benefits? This latter question is tackled in Chapter 23.

IMPROVE THE BUSINESS-TO-BUSINESS STATUS OF YOUR COMPANY

The McGraw-Hill advertisement can be cited again here: not for the psychological boost it can give sales representatives, but for its direct effect on the target market – the advertisement cites many important operational areas which can improve a company's business-to-business status.

This objective can sometimes start from a negative base: the organization may need to restore confidence, counter criticisms or attacks, or correct misconceptions.

See also *Build company reputation*, below.

PROVIDE THE RIGHT BUSINESS ENVIRONMENT FOR YOUR PRODUCT OR SERVICE

Environment was one of the criteria for media selection discussed in Chapter 6. Certain media, through their editorial, deliver a target audience already mentally 'tuned in' to a product or service. Furthermore, when delivering the promotional message to this already receptive audience, they add an atmosphere of authority and expertise which enhances the product benefits featured in either advertising and/or editorial columns.

BUILD COMPANY REPUTATION

This campaign objective to some extent overlaps the earlier Status objective. This kind of promotion has various titles – people often refer to image-building, and to prestige, corporate or institutional campaigns. Some organizations may need to concentrate on their image rather than their products – but what sort of reputation should the organization seek? This approach is, alas, often misused, or even taken as the easy way out. One cynical Creative Director remarked that, when all else fails, he could always rely on the old stand-by of an aerial view of the factory and a picture of the Chairman to keep the client happy! But for this type of promotion to be effective, the Promotion Manager must ask very fundamental questions:

- Whose opinions should he be concerned about?
- What opinion do these individuals hold now?
- What view does his company wish them to have in future?

Without answers to these questions, it is not possible to select media nor to decide creative content.

Some companies, bearing in mind 'P-E-S-T' considerations, have concentrated on creating the image of organizations fully aware of social and environmental responsibilities.

On the other hand, if a company's image *is* bad, is this in fact deserved? If it is, then no amount of so-called prestige promotion can rectify matters. If a firm is notorious for late delivery or for poor after-sales service, there is little point in publicising 'strength' in these areas: this will make matters worse rather than better. The true solution is to put things right, and then mount a promotional campaign which convinces the target market that matters have indeed been rectified.

GET COST EFFECTIVE ADVERTISING

This campaign objective reaffirms the importance of earlier *Criteria for Media Comparison* discussions – which marketing communications media are in fact most cost effective? It also reveals the importance of *Evaluation of Results*, examined later.

DEMONSTRATE YOUR PRODUCT OR SERVICE

This objective, like the last, affirms the importance of a clear understanding of media comparison criteria. Two obvious questions must be asked: to whom must the product or service be demonstrated, and how effectively can different media demonstrate it?

OTHER CAMPAIGN OBJECTIVES

British Business Press's 12 objectives clearly call for different promotional messages, different media to deliver them, and different ways of using these media.

The BBP list by no means exhausts the possible objectives which might underly promotional campaigns – there are others which call for equally specific proposals. These are also co-ordinated in my marketing communications matrix, which concludes the chapter.

REMIND EXISTING USERS

Those business executives who use products or services need reminding: human memory is short, and innumerable distracting factors soon make it fade. In some cases, it may be the advertising of rival firms. Suppliers of totally different products also compete for target market attention. Taking a still wider view, thousands of non-selling influences work to make memory fade – domestic problems, office pressures and politics, the latest home and foreign news, interest or exchange rates changes, and alterations to many different practical aspects of government policy such as tax structure and business allowances. Reminder campaigns can help maintain sales momentum and this objective, like all others, has clear implications for media choice and creative content. Furthermore, constant reminders can enhance a firm's reputation and play their part in cementing customer loyalty.

REASSURE PREVIOUS PURCHASERS

Re-assuring those who have already purchased differs markedly from simply reminding existing customers. In many purchasing decisions, particularly those involving major expenditure, current users often play a key role in influencing potential purchasers. Much promotional planning therefore recognizes the theory of 'cognitive dissonance'. This title stems from the roots of cognition – to know, and dissonance – not in harmony. Or, more simply, a clash of knowledge. The theory is based on the concept that if a business executive knows various things about a product or service that are psychologically incompatible, his mind will, in a variety of ways, try to make them consistent to reduce the dissonance.

Those who read advertisement or editorial features always include a high proportion of people who have just purchased the product in question. Few products are *so* outstanding that they are in every way better than rivals – if they were, competitors would soon be out of business! All products have advantages and drawbacks: those who purchase are concerned that they make the correct decision and, having made it, seek reassurance in this respect. If you reflect on any recent major personal purchase, you will realise you most probably sought the advice of somebody who had already bought the product: their view was far more influential than any salesman. Much the same applies when an organization makes a purchase. As negative reactions would soon discourage prospective purchasers, much promotional activity aims at reassuring previous purchasers just as much as attracting new ones. For products in this category, the need to 'keep customers sold' has clear implications for both media choice and creative content.

COUNTER THE NATURAL DECLINE IN THE MARKET

Reminder campaigns can help maintain sales, but many organizations overlook the fact that existing customers, through no fault on the company's part, steadily decrease in number. Product quality may remain as high as ever, but sales will fall through natural diminution of the market. Lord Keynes once summarised this for consumer companies by pointing out that in the long term we're all dead! The same principle applies to business markets – firms leave the area, change their requirements, or simply go out of business. For every business mailing, some will always be returned marked 'Gone away' or 'Not known at this address'. New customers must be attracted to counter this decline, and promotion is an effective means to achieve this end.

INFORM THE CONSTANT FLOW OF NEW POTENTIAL CUSTOMERS

Any business market changes ceaselessly. Just as people change from schoolchild to teenager to young married to parent, so organizations change in size and scope of operations, and need to purchase new equipment or facilities. They become prospects for products previously not of interest, and marketing communications can convert them into customers. Many firms mistakenly assume that, just because they have been promoting themselves over the years, prospects know about the products they offer. This ignores the fact that many potential purchasers entered the market *today*, and earlier promotion therefore had limited effect. Business executives read advertisements and editorial concerning products which interest them, and ignore others: yesterday these potential purchasers were not in the market, so were unlikely to respond to promotion of the products in question.

THE CONSTANTLY CHANGING MARKET

Many organizations overlook the ceaselessly changing market. Markets steadily decline through natural causes, a constant flow of new prospects need information and, in the meantime, existing users need reminding and perhaps reassurance.

The reader's own organization is a market for other business products or services. At every stage of development it represents a lost customer for one producer, a possible repeat purchaser for another, and a prospective buyer for yet a third. Promotion, if it is to be effective, must take account of these never-ending market changes.

STABILISE PRODUCTION

A number of organizations seek not to increase sales but to stabilise demand. If product demand is unsteady, the factory may have to work at full capacity (perhaps even overtime) while sales are high, but when demand falls off machinery lies idle. A sales graph with great peaks and troughs makes for uneconomic production, and the same applies to a fluctuating staff workload. Promotion can help even out the graph in two different ways.

One solution is to plan promotion to fill the troughs. There is a net increase in sales, but the campaign aims to stimulate the market only at specified times of year (or even days of week).

The alternative route to a more even sales graph is by shifting sales from peaks to troughs: there is no net sales increase but, by using promotion to persuade customers to make their purchases in slack rather than peak periods, expenses are reduced with obvious increase in profits.

Promotion can facilitate efficient use of plant or staff, and such considerations directly affect campaign timing and creative content.

OVERCOME RESISTANCE

Some companies mistakenly assume their target groups merely await a suitable promotional message to stimulate them into buying. Firms are, however, wary of buying unfamiliar products, and retailers (who represent a major business-to-business market) are equally shy of stocking merchandise unknown to their customers.

If a product encounters resistance so strong that it cannot be overcome by promotion alone, it may be necessary to solve the problem on the broader front of all the marketing P's. Some manufacturers of revolutionary products had to 'grasp the nettle' and, to quote a famous Hollywood film producer, 'Make 'em an offer they can't refuse'. Equipment was installed free on a trial basis, backed by guarantees, on condition that the outcome could be quoted. This then provided the basis for PR-generated editorial features and testimonial advertising.

'UMBRELLA' CAMPAIGNS

Many corporate campaigns aim to link separate business operations, particularly for those multi-structure organizations active in various fields, when separate divisions sell separate products to separate market segments via separate promotional and sales campaigns.

Many such organizations now link the self-contained business operations, to the joint benefit of all component companies. As a hypothetical example, divisions A, B, C and D of a multi-structure organization might each mount campaigns to their separate industrial markets, with appropriate promotion in the relevant specialist press. National media would normally be ruled out as too few readers come within the specified buyer categories. But as many industrial purchasers buy not only product A but perhaps also B, C and D as well, the separate specialised campaigns can be made more effective by an 'umbrella' promotion in more general media, on the message theme of 'If you need advice on A, B, C or D, we are the experts.' Sales representatives from individual divisions then cross-refer enquiries as necessary. Such a promotional objective clearly has a more functional aim than a so-called 'prestige' campaign, and there are clear implications for both media choice and creative content. The same effect can apply, however, even within a single company, as explained below.

BENEFIT TO OTHER LINES

An effect similar to an umbrella campaign may apply, on a smaller scale, within a single organization. One obvious effect of promotion is to increase sales of the product featured, but a secondary result may be increased sales of *other* lines. Multi-product manufacturers benefit when the publicity afforded by promoting one item helps other products in the range.

If promotion is likely to have beneficial spin off for other products, this added advantage must be borne in mind. Planning should strive for a 'synergistic' effect whereby each product's promotion benefits all others. There are many opportunities to arrange promotional matters so that 2+2 equals not 4 but 5 or even 6! Some organizations overlook this to their cost — there is no 'house style' to individual campaigns, nor any mention that 'We are a member of the Such-and-Such Group'.

EXTEND DISTRIBUTION

In some cases, promotion can be directed at distributors or agents, rather than the target market. An organization with insufficient outlets would seek wider distribution, and could use promotion as a tool to achieve this objective. Specialist press advertising or direct mail are obvious in this respect, but promotion aimed at target markets is equally effective, when representatives take round proofs of advertisements which they employ as a sales aid in getting distributors to stock and display. If extended distribution is the campaign objective, it is often advantageous to book advertisements of a larger size than that required to convey the creative message, simply because of the impact this larger size has on potential distributors.

Indirect influence was one of the criteria for media comparison considered earlier. This can be as important for existing as for potential new distributors.

STIMULATE EXISTING DISTRIBUTION

As in the previous case, promotion is used for its effect on distributors rather than the target market. The difference is that the product has wide distribution, but stockists are insufficiently active in promoting sales. In such circumstances, heavy promotion can be used to persuade hitherto passive agents to give products more of a 'push'. As before, larger sizes than are strictly necessary can be helpful when using advertising as a sales tool for representatives.

In both this and the previous case, it is often efficacious to feature stockists' names and addresses, perhaps on a co-operative shared-cost basis. In both cases, merchandising activities could play a major part in the promotional programme. Such considerations clearly influence media choice, the way in which selected media are used, and campaign finance.

BUILD A MAILING LIST

Many organizations use promotion to obtain sales leads for representatives. Others use response media for 'selling off the page'. Some find it profitable to vary this pattern for direct marketing purposes. Promotion serves to build an initial mailing list, and direct mail and direct selling are then used to obtain orders from those who expressed interest. Direct sales are the primary campaign objective, and general promotion used to 'top up' the mailing list from time to time, since this must necessarily suffer the natural decline inherent in every market. This approach can profitably be developed into database marketing, discussed earlier.

MARKET RESEARCH

On occasion, a Promotion Manager must accept that the necessary R & I information is alas not all available. In such circumstances, two possibilities present themselves. One is to commission the necessary field surveys into relevant market segments. The other is to proceed despite this lack of data, using promotion as a research tool. Some new products, with application to a wide range of business markets, were launched in this way. The manufacturers spent money on promotion in horizontal media (rather than on investigating possible markets). They then carefully evaluated customer response, to identify suitable market segments for individual development through subsequent specialist campaigns in targeted media. As the database marketing section pointed out, this approach could in fact replace conventional market research, by planning promotional campaigns in such a way as to obtain the necessary information. Even for those unable to develop their database so directly, this objective clearly links with the later planning stage of *Evaluation of Results*. As Chapter 28 makes clear, evaluation is a vital stage, whatever the campaign objective.

CLEAR SURPLUS SUPPLIES

Promotion sometimes serves an occasional rather than a continuing purpose. The 'sales' which feature so prominently on the retail scene reflect this, but the same objective can apply from time to time in business-to-business operations. Sales advertising often serves two quite distinct purposes – one is to boost sales at an otherwise slack time (as described above), while the other purpose is to clear old stocks to make way for new. The old stock is made more attractive by cutting prices, and this reduction is announced through promotion. Additional benefits come from release of valuable storage space, and improved cash flow.

DISPOSE OF BY-PRODUCTS

In other cases, the campaign objective may be to market by-products rather than to clear old stocks. In manufacturing their main product, many organizations produce by-products which they wish to sell at a profit.

This exercise differs from the main selling operation in that sales volume is dictated by the main product, demand for which determines production levels. This in turn controls the amount of by-products produced. Rather than 'derived demand' discussed earlier, the Promotion Manager faces 'derived supply'. The campaign aim is thus to sell fixed amounts and no more, since there is little point in stimulating massive demand for these secondary by-products when supplies could not be increased without creating an unsaleable surplus of the main product. Any campaigns thus have 'cut-off' points dictated by the main sales programme, which emphasise the importance of earlier R & I clarification of possible restraints.

UTILISE OTHER MARKETING STRENGTHS

There are other circumstances in which promotional planning is determined by the overall marketing programme, rather than by demand for the product in question. When manufacturers review both product range and sales force effectiveness they may find, for example, that representatives are not working to full capacity: this is no reflection on their efforts, but simply recognizes that the present product range does not keep them fully occupied. There is thus spare sales force capacity and the marketing question then arises of 'What additional product, of interest to current buyers, could sales staff carry and sell effectively?' When a further item is added to round out the product line, promotional planning is again determined by R & I factors outside the usual considerations.

AS AN AID TO BUYING

Promotion usually performs a selling function, but sometimes the aim is the very opposite – not to sell, but to buy. Many government and business projects are put out to tender, the contract being advertised and featured in news releases, with the order going to the firm submitting the best bid.

Similarly, 'Situations Vacant' advertisements are placed to locate suitable applicants for staff vacancies. This chapter's preamble mentioned that two or more promotional objectives might apply at any one time: 'Situations Vacant' is an example. Viewed functionally, such advertisements comprise three components – job specification (a description of the task to be performed), person profile (outlining the qualifications and experience expected) and company offer (rewards and conditions). Such a three-part advertisement could be brief but many would-be employers realize that, whilst a small classified might adequately convey the bare facts, they face competition for the best applicants. 'High flyers' are more likely to respond to a prestige advertisement which conveys that they would be working for the leading company in the field.

Employers also realise that many others see these advertisements, including existing and potential purchasers, suppliers, distributors, shareholders, and the public at large – all could be favourably impressed by a recruitment advertisement outlining a company's outstanding achievements and track record. Such advertisements can also have a disheartening effect on competitors! 'Situations Vacant' are therefore correctly treated more as a public relations and prestige exercise rather than simply filling posts, although this task in itself calls for specialist skills.

ARBITRARY REASONS FOR PROMOTION

This section should not be here but, whilst there are many sound marketing communications objectives, there are other reasons which are less rational.

It is not unknown for a senior executive to advertise out of personal pride: he likes to see his company name (or even his own picture and an aerial view of his factory!) in print or other media, and to feel business acquaintances think him an important man.

Media selection is sometimes influenced by arbitrary factors – the motivating force may be tradition, as the organization has always used the medium in question. Alternatively, an executive may feel 'forced in' because he does not wish his organization to be the odd one out. In other cases, by booking space in special programmes, firms use advertising as an indirect means of making charitable donations.

FIGHTING DECLINING SALES

This final section analyses a promotional blind spot which comes in two versions – the pessimistic (sales are falling, so lets have a campaign), and the optimistic (let's have a campaign to increase sales). In neither case is there any firm base for promotional planning – *why* are sales falling, and *how* are increased sales to be achieved? These so-called objectives have deliberately been left till last not because they are unimportant – far from it – but because they demand more detailed analysis than other objectives so far discussed. This analysis tackles the pessimistic version first.

The overall campaign aim may be to counter falling sales, but this masks various types of decline, for which different promotional approaches are necessary. Sales may in fact fall for one of four reasons:

- *A natural decline.* The ever-changing market was discussed earlier: if this accounts for a drop in sales, then reason and solution are both self-evident – the organization has failed to inform the constant flow of new entrants to the market, and must mount a promotional campaign to achieve this objective. The creative message in this case will be educational – 'These are the benefits you get from using this product'.
- *Losing out to competition.* The campaign objective may be to sustain a particular supplier against rivals. This calls for a different promotional message (part building brand or source loyalty, and part comparison approach, pointing out benefits over rivals) as well as different promotional media.
- *A temporary set-back.* Promotion can help counter a temporary drop in sales. The Chancellor's budget, for example, may bring tax changes adverse to specific groups of products, reduce financial allowances or increase interest rates. The target market must eventually accustom itself to these new conditions, but promotion can hasten the adjustment process.
- *A permanent decline.* When a product has exhausted its life cycle, it is unwise to expect promotion to reverse a permanent trend. It may, however, make some contribution by giving time to seek new opportunities. Earlier 'Research and Investigation' stressed the importance of P-E-S-T background factors – if technological changes make products obsolete, it is pointless hoping that promotion will overcome reality.

Technological and other changes also raise possibilities for new products and new markets, for which the optimistic version of the same blind spot is more relevant.

INCREASED SALES

The so-called aim of 'increased sales' is a blind spot for many firms, large and small, which mistakenly regard this as a sufficient basis for promotional planning. But 'increased sales' is only an optimistic hope for the future, rather than a specific objective. What percentage increase is the target figure, and by which date? Just as important, how are these increased sales to be achieved? Answers to these questions directly influence promotional expenditure, media choice, the way in which the selected media are used and, equally fundamental, the communications message.

Many executives overlook the fact that different routes to increased sales call for different types of promotional campaign. One well-known marketing matrix suggests four basic ways of increasing sales:

- Existing products to existing markets
- Existing products to new markets
- New products to existing markets
- New products to new markets

These possibilities can then be evaluated against a 'risk' scale, with the fourth clearly being the most risky.

SETTING SPECIFIC CAMPAIGN OBJECTIVES

While we accept this matrix from a purely marketing standpoint, it is unsatisfactory for promotional planning since it fails to take account of competition, nor does it consider campaigns which persuade customers to switch supply sources. An alternative approach is therefore necessary, and the following matrix (which re-examines some objectives discussed earlier) should facilitate promotional planning.

A first essential is to stop thinking of increased sales, and to think instead in terms of increased *purchases* – or, more specifically, possibly purchasers and their purchasing patterns.

Viewed in purchasing terms, there are many ways to increase sales:

INCREASED PURCHASES BY EXISTING USERS

Such a campaign converts light into medium users or medium into heavy, and the promotional aim is to extend the range of uses they make of the product, or increase their frequency of use. This increases the value of the market, but not its size in terms of numbers of purchasers.

PURCHASES BY NEW USERS

With such a campaign, the promotional aim is to educate non-users (who have not used the organization's product nor that of any rivals) about the product's basic benefits, thus converting them to its use. Such campaigns increase market size in terms of numbers of purchasers, as well as market value.

PURCHASES BY COMPETITORS' CUSTOMERS

The campaign aim here is to persuade buyers of rival products to switch supply sources, and the company must fight to overcome established purchasing patterns and existing goodwill. This will not increase the size of the cake: only the way it is divided.

These three routes to increased sales of existing products facilitate promotional planning more effectively than the earlier matrix, which suggested only two, existing and new markets, and ignored source-switch possibilities.

This new matrix does not yet allow for *new* products. This term could encompass replacements for existing products, or extensions to an existing range, as well as entirely new product lines, so clearly promotional analysis must be extended beyond the three possibilities so far considered. A full planning matrix should also allow for:

PURCHASES OF NEW PRODUCTS BY EXISTING CUSTOMERS

There are many advantages when planning such a campaign – the company knows who its present customers are and could reach them through, for example, direct mail. Furthermore, promotional messages can build on existing knowledge: there is (hopefully) a wealth of goodwill to assist in launching the new product.

PURCHASES OF NEW PRODUCTS BY NEW USERS

This is similar to the second possibility (purchases of existing products by new users) in that the target group has not used the new product, and needs education about its benefits. One significant difference is that as the product is *new*, there is no track record on which to build, so the testimonial approach of 'thousands of satisfied customers' is not applicable.

PURCHASES OF NEW PRODUCTS BY OTHER COMPANIES' CUSTOMERS

Although similar to route number three (purchases of existing products by competitors' customers) the differences is again significant – there is again no track record on which to build, and furthermore the organization must fight established goodwill to rival companies.

This new matrix gives six (rather than the original four) routes to increased sales, and the difference is more than a numerical one – it has vital implications for promotional planning.

If the increased sales/increased purchases analysis is reduced to fundamental level, media policy and message content can be entered on the matrix shown on page 229.

If the new product is a multi-use one, this six-route matrix can be extended by subsequent campaigns which suggest new product uses (or, for a single-use product, reasons for more frequent use). This completes the circle by returning to the first route to increased sales – existing users to use more.

A campaign designed to meet one objective is unlikely to achieve others as effectively, since all call for different promotion in terms of both media and message content.

From the message standpoint, a campaign aimed at existing users, suggesting further uses for a product, may not be understood by new users, who are unaware of the product's basic function. A campaign designed to explain basic product benefits to potential purchasers may have minimal effect on existing users, who are already well aware of its function. Neither will effectively influence those who buy from rival sources. Equally, a campaign aimed at persuading buyers of rival products to switch supply sources, by stressing the advantages of one product over others, is likely to be less successful in educating new users to the product group's basic benefit.

Campaigns planned for new products call for similar basic differences in creative content.

Similar comments can be made about media policy: to increase sales to existing customers, any organization would clearly continue (but strive to improve) its present media pattern, whilst to reach new prospective buyers may call for new media. Playing 'follow my leader' rarely results in effective promotion, but a company seeking source-switch sales will clearly wish to influence competitors' customers and would *deliberately* aim at the same market – and is thus likely to use the same media (but strive to use them more effectively). This is a very different matter to blindly following a rival's lead, for lack of anything better to do.

SETTING SPECIFIC CAMPAIGN OBJECTIVES

Type of sales increase	*Media policy*	*Message content*
A. Existing Products		
1. Existing product to existing users	Maintain activity in current media	Suggest new uses for the product, or reasons for more frequent use, building on existing contacts and goodwill.
2. Existing product to new users	Consider new media	Explain the basic benefits of the product and company record to people unaware of them.
3. Existing product to users of rival products	Consider competitors' media patterns	Comparison campaigns pointing out the advantages of the product over rivals, and overcoming established purchasing patterns.
B. New Products		
4. New products to existing customers	Maintain activity in current media	Explain basic benefits, building on existing contacts and goodwill.
5. New products to new users	Consider new media	Explain basic benefits, and company record in other fields.
6. New products to other companies' customers	Consider competitors' media patterns	Explain basic benefits, and overcome established goodwill.

This new matrix of course over-simplifies for ease of analysis, and the six types of increase are not self-exclusive. Furthermore, certain promotional campaigns successfully increase sales in two or more ways simultaneously. Much successful promotion recognizes the distinct routes to increased sales and accordingly the campaign is not a single entity but several inter-related components, each aimed at one distinct target group. The campaign components are not only successful in their own right but, because they are clearly linked, each reinforces the effectiveness of the others. Synergistic promotion such as this can be achieved only by careful planning, never by accident.

Promotion should clearly be planned in context, as a vital part of the total marketing operation. It is not an isolated activity but must be based on clear and detailed marketing objectives. Advertising, merchandising, public relations, sales promotion, and selling itself should be complementary, and all aimed at achieving the identical objectives.

SUMMARY

The essential message of this chapter is the need to define clearly, before starting to plan any promotion, the precise campaign objectives. Different types of sales increase call for different media choice as well as different creative content. Like most fundamental truths this is very obvious – once it has been pointed out! A great deal of current promotion is, alas, ineffective simply because this basic principle has been ignored. Analyse marketing objectives properly, and promotional effectiveness must increase.

THE NEXT STEP

Having decided what his organization hopes to achieve, the Promotion Manager must next extend the Research & Investigation stage, by analysing in greater detail prospective purchasers and their purchasing patterns. This will facilitate the later planning stage of converting campaign objectives into communication objectives – what information must his campaign convey, and to whom, to achieve its desired objectives?

CHAPTER TWENTY-ONE

Purchasing Patterns

The earlier overview of industrial marketing pointed out that the original four P's (Product, Price, Place and Promotion) were insufficient – business planning calls for three additional P's: *Positioning* and *People*, (already discussed), and *Purchasing Patterns*, examined in this chapter.

The two preceding chapters discussed campaign objectives and the information necessary for promotional planning. Both chapters necessarily overlap with this, in that research should give an understanding of the target market's purchasing patterns which, in turn, influence campaign objectives. Industrial buying behaviour is, however, so complex that it merits a separate chapter. Purchasing patterns also directly influence other planning stages covered later: creation of promotional messages, and selection of media to deliver them.

An understandable error by those new to marketing communications is self-orientation: concentration on what THEY want to say. This starts at the wrong end of the communication process, since effective promotion calls for what the target market wants to hear, rather than what anybody wants to say. This chapter therefore examines the different types and classes of purchase, who is involved in the buying decision, their motivation, the various phases of the buying process, and how these factors vary over the product life cycle.

HOW PURCHASING DECISIONS ARE MADE

There are various models of buyer behaviour, but no question of one being right and others wrong – all are applicable in certain circumstances. The promotional task is to decide which best applies to particular target markets.

Far from being theoretical, this examination should be treated as practically as possible – the Promotion Manager must try to look into the prospect's 'organizational mind' and establish what actually goes on. How else can he decide what promotional messages to deliver, how and when to best deliver them, and to whom?

Planning analysis must cover the following aspects of buyer behaviour: Buy-Types, Buy-Classes, Buy-Roles, Buy-Motives, Buy-Phases and Buy-Stages. Many organizations undertake regular tracking research to identify trends in buying and decision-making criteria within each market segment (as well as into industry-wide and corporate-level perception of their companies).

A useful practical exercise, to assist in understanding how prospective purchasers operate, is to look inside your own organization and analyse a recent business purchase: to what extent can you identify the various 'Buy' aspects discussed here?

BUY-TYPES

Most purchases of business products or services can be categorized under one of three headings:

- *The Industrial market* – organizations which acquire goods and services for the production of other goods and services;
- *The Reseller Market* – organizations which acquire goods (or services) to sell or hire to others at a profit;
- *The Public Sector Market* – Government units, national or local, which purchase or hire in order to perform their due function.

It is important to recognize differences within each market type. Supermarkets and department stores are both types of reseller, but they are by no means the same. Differences within industrial and public sector markets are equally significant.

This approach to classification reinforces the need to consider psychographic as well as demographic factors: these three market types (and sub-sections thereof) have very different buying motives, and clearly call for different selling messages as well as different media to reach them. Within each of these three buy-types, any organization might proceed to one of three buy-classes.

BUY-CLASSES

Whatever the buy-type, most business purchases can again be categorized under one of three headings:

- *Straight Rebuy* – whereby re-ordering occurs with no change in specification. In some cases, the promotional objective is to arrange automatic re-order systems of stock control. Providing the product/service performance remains satisfactory, it is very difficult for a rival supplier to disrupt the sequence. Promotion can play a significant role in maintaining source loyalty for the supplier holding the contract. For competitors, on the other hand, promotion would have a very different function, suggesting reasons why switching supply sources would give greater satisfaction;
- *Modified Rebuy* – when there is a change in selection criteria. The purchaser's needs may have altered, or revised supplier specifications have led to a re-examination. Promotion can deliver vital information about changes in price or product performance, leading to the decision to re-examine;
- *New Purchase* – where organizations consider products or services not previously purchased. Promotion may have different roles to play here – one might be to channel a prospect's need into an enquiry and then into an order. Alternatively promotion's role might be educational, in awakening the company to its unrecognized need for a product or service. Marketing communication's dual function here is to stimulate latent demand AND channel it towards the Promotion Manager's own company – he will not win any medals for increasing competitors' sales! Whatever the buy-class, a number of different individuals will be involved in the purchasing decision.

BUY-ROLES

In 1984 the *Financial Times* commissioned the Cranfield School of Management to research 'How British Industry Buys'. The Survey's introduction stated:

'The ways in which companies arrive at final purchasing decisions are extremely complex. From the point at which the need to replace existing equipment, or the need to buy new types of equipment, arises, there is a range of people within organizations who will have some influence on the final decision. This chain of people involved in the purchasing process has come to be called the Decision Making Unit.

Every salesman and marketing man needs to know who, within potential companies, are the key figures when it comes to what products will be bought, and who the suppliers will be. It is with these people that the seller, through advertising and personal selling, needs to communicate.'

I fully endorse this concise summary, apart from adding that marketing communications embrace more than advertising and personal selling alone: merchandising, public relations, sales promotion and created media all have a vital role in influencing purchasing decisions.

The Decision Making Unit may be formal or informal, and various models attempt to clarify the decision process. One DMU model suggests the following roles. The use of the plural in listing these is deliberate, as there are likely to be several people occupying each role.

- *Initiators* – those who perceive (or can be made to recognize) their need for a product or service;
- *Users* – those staff who will actually use the product or service, and may play an important part in defining purchase specifications;
- *Influencers* – those who influence decisions, either directly or indirectly;
- *Buyers* – those with formal authority for negotiating and placing orders, and possibly selecting suppliers. They may also advise on specifications. In many organizations, purchasing is recognized as a professional function;
- *Deciders* – those who have formal or informal power to select the final supplier. For relatively minor purchases buyers may also be deciders, but crucial purchase decisions are usually taken at Board level;
- *Gate-keepers* – individuals who control the flow of information to members of the DMU and may perhaps block delivery of promotional messages. The existence of gate-keepers will directly influence choice of promotional media, to overcome this barrier.

Another model suggests a simpler structure, with only four categories of DMU member:

- *Specifiers* – those identifying a need, and specifying the type of product required to satisfy the need;
- *Authorisers* – who may be senior managers or directors, or sometimes the whole Board may be involved;
- *Buyers* – purchasing executives, and perhaps the purchasing manager.
- *Users* – who may be the Plant Manager, perhaps supervisors, and sometimes even the operatives.

Whether a prospect's decision process fits the six or four role model, the Promotion Manager should recognize that the executives occupying each role in a given organization are likely to change from one purchasing decision to the next.

Selling advertising space is of course a business-to-business operation, and one media-owner commented:

> 'Some years ago we looked in detail at the media-decision process and came to the conclusion that, whilst many people had the ability to say NO, almost nobody had the ability (or was allowed) to say YES. This means that the plan which is accepted is the one nobody says NO to. According to some recent information this is how the Japanese Government was run pre-war and, as the only proposition that nobody said NO to was War, they bombed Pearl Harbor. Idiosyncratic decisions often prove more effective than democratic ones.'

This anecdote may be a cynical one, but it does illustrate the need to understand how purchasing decisions are made! Equally important are the motives behind the purchases.

BUY-MOTIVES

Here, there are two important questions to ask:

- *What are the target market(s) buying?* This is not necessarily what an organization thinks it is selling!
- *What is their buying perspective?* By what criteria do they choose between one supplier and another?

The answers to these questions have clear implications for the promotional approach, and the creative implications are examined in Chapter 23. What an organization needs is not necessarily what it wants. Whatever the motives, purchasers may be at different phases of the buying process.

BUY-PHASES

Analysis of buyer behaviour now extends to a fifth stage: examination of various 'buy-phases', each of which demands different roles for marketing communications.

As always, alternative analyses reflect different behaviour patterns, but any organization's buying phases might include the following distinct stages:

- *Problem Recognition* – identification, anticipation or recognition of need, and general need description;
- *Product specification* – establishing the characteristics of the needed items;
- *Supplier search* – locating potential suitable suppliers.
- *Proposal solicitation* – contact with candidate suppliers, to request proposals;
- *Supplier selection* – evaluation of alternative offers;
- *Decide/buy* – make final choice and agree order routine;
- *Use;*
- *Post-purchase review and evaluation*

Depending on the complexity of any particular purchase, there may be additional buy-phases – while the decision process is under way it may become necessary, for example, to re-examine purchasing criteria in negotiation with potential suppliers, in response to their comments or suggestions.

Different buy-types often have different procedures and appropriate buy-phases – government departments, for example, may utilise marketing communications within their supplier search phase, by putting contracts out to tender and inviting bids through public advertising. Such contracts would also be made known through public relations activity.

Clearly, the Promotion Manager must decide at which phase (or phases) promotion should contribute. Is its role awakening a prospect organization to a need of which it is unaware? Alternatively, if already at the 'supplier search' phase, the role of marketing communications is to ensure inclusion on the short list contacted. Another role for promotion is to reassure prospects – perhaps at the supplier selection stage, or at the later performance review, when marketing communications can play an important 'reinforcement' role.

The *Financial Times* survey of 'How British Industry Buys' makes interesting reading in that it examined a number of different product categories: plant & equipment, commercial vehicles and trailers, company cars, materials, component parts, private cars, office equipment including microcomputers, and mainframe and/or mini-computers. Within each product category, the study examined the executives involved at the various buy-phases, and illustrated the importance of these analyses.

BUY-STAGES

Another important consideration for promotional planning is the product life cycle. 'Innovation/Diffusion' analysis examines how buyers (and their purchasing patterns) vary at introduction, growth, maturity and decline stages of the cycle. Buyers at different stages are classed as early adopters, late adopters, early majority, late majority, and laggards.

Position on the product life cycle clearly affects promotional planning, as early adopters may differ from others in industrial classification as well as motivation. Different stages of the cycle again call for different messages and different media to deliver them.

An extension of the innovation/diffusion approach is to consider early adopters as marketing communications media in themselves: they often serve as 'multipliers' in spreading word of new products to other potential purchasers.

THE TIME-LAG

Organizational buying decisions take longer than consumer buying decisions. Because of the technical complexities involved, decisions require more information, undergo longer evaluation, and often involve more uncertainty about product performance. The longer consideration period required for organizational buying decisions often means significant time-lags between the application of marketing effort and obtaining a buying response.

PROMOTIONAL PLANNING

Analysis of industrial purchasing patterns must consider all six buy-aspects concurrently, since different phases may call for different messages, which in turn must be delivered to different members of the decision-making unit. This analysis of inter-related buy-aspects is made more complex by the fact that each individual buying organization is likely to be significantly different from every other. Accordingly, promotional planning might require viewing each existing or potential purchaser as a separate market segment. Few (if any) consumer goods companies must be so concerned about tailoring their promotional strategies to each individual customer.

THE NEXT STEP

Once these analyses of purchasing patterns are completed, together with R & I and specification of campaign objectives, the Promotion Manager can now consider how much his company should spend on achieving these objectives.

CHAPTER TWENTY-TWO

Budgeting

The first stage of effective promotional planning was gathering information on which to base campaign proposals. Next came setting specific objectives coupled with analysis of the target market's decision process. With these tasks completed, the Promotion Manager can now tackle the next planning stage – deciding how much his company should spend on achieving the chosen objectives.

A later task, once the promotional budget is decided, will be to divide it between different communications media – how much should be allocated to advertising, public relations, or created media?

Not all readers will be directly involved, as they work to budgets set by others. They should nevertheless understand the different ways of deciding budgets. Furthermore, if views are sought on a proposed sum, or should any Promotion Manager seek to persuade the Board to spend more, then this practical appreciation is even more important.

THE REWARDS OF PROMOTIONAL EXPENDITURE

Promotion is a cost incurred in increasing sales, from which come profits. When promotion results in increased sales, profits increase accordingly, and the additional profit can more than cover the costs of promotion. Increased sales can also lower manufacturing costs, thus improving profit margins: large-scale production brings economies such as better terms for bulk purchase of materials, and spreads overheads over more units of output. Such savings lower unit costs, and thus make possible lower prices and/or increased profit.

Chapter 20 established that increased sales is only one of many possible campaign objectives – stabilised sales also make for more economic production. Promotion can contribute to profitability in many ways, depending on particular business objectives. An organization may also wish to communicate for public relations purposes, and to measure outcome in terms of customer goodwill or staff and shareholder morale rather than money.

Few firms believe that promotion increases the price of their products, thus putting them at risk of being undercut by competitors who do not promote themselves: most accept that promotion is a cost that brings savings which more than offset the expenditure involved. The true decision is not whether to spend money on promotion, but how much to spend.

PROMOTION IN CONTEXT

The promotional budget decision must be approached as part of a business's overall operation, and there are distinct stages to the financial planning involved. First comes the marketing plan – that the organization manufacture a product (or provide a service), with advertising, distribution, merchandising, pricing, product policy, public relations, sales promotion, and selling effort all geared to achieving sales in a chosen target market.

An overall allocation of funds then follows: so much for production plant; so much expenditure on raw materials and labour; so much for selling effort; so much on marketing communications; and so forth. A total budget is thus drawn up, quantifying the various financial commitments involved. Fixing the promotional budget is clearly part of a management process of balancing expenditures, when different activities compete for funds.

PROMOTION AS INVESTMENT

The promotional budget should be viewed as investment rather than expenditure. For management to approve a budget, the Promotion Manager must convince Directors that promotion is the most productive form of expenditure and will give a better ROI (Return on Investment) or ROC (Return on Capital) than any other use of funds, thus making a positive contribution to profitability. Should the Board view marketing communications as spending without result, they are unlikely to approve any budget proposals.

The amount spent on promotion is known as the 'appropriation' and appropriation policy is usually initiated by the executive responsible, and then confirmed by the Board, some three months or so before the marketing year commences.

THE PROMOTION BUDGET DEFINED

The term 'appropriation' has been defined as 'The total amount to be spent on marketing communications during a given period'. Like all definitions it sounds simple, but two points merit comment – for very practical reasons.

One point concerns 'a given period'. If the Promotion Manager has a budget of £X,000, he can have no idea whether this is too little, sufficient, or too much unless he knows the period for which this sum must provide promotional support. Most appropriations are decided on an annual basis, either the financial year commencing in April or the calendar year starting on 1 January, while some organizations operate to different business years. Some budgets are longer term (whilst a minority cover shorter periods), but the annual appropriation is customary. Accounting practice often makes this inflexible, so that towards the end of the period it is not permitted to borrow from next year's budget: equally, accounting practice forbids carrying over any unspent funds. The Promotion Manager must, therefore, be clear about the period to be covered by the money available, otherwise he cannot budget to cover it effectively. This, surprisingly, is less frequently a problem than the second point calling for clarification: the meaning of 'marketing communications'.

In its broadcast sense, marketing communications include anything featuring the company name or symbol (and indeed *all* message sources) but for budgetary purposes the term is usually restricted to conventional communications media – advertising, merchandising, public relations, sales promotion, and so on.

Firms adopt different operational definitions of what they class as promotion. Some include advertising and public relations but exclude printed material or other 'created media', which are funded out of a separate budget. Other firms include all such items together with miscellaneous costs such as direct mail postage, all of which are borne by the marketing communications budget. In some companies promotion department salaries are charged against the budget, whilst in others they are considered general personnel costs. Even 'Situations Vacant' advertisements are sometimes classed as promotional expenses rather than recruitment costs.

There is thus no generally accepted rule as to what any budget does and does not cover, and practice varies from firm to firm. The basic rule is, however, simple – any executive with budget responsibilities must be clear what comes out of the appropriation and what does not. Failure to establish this might result in the Promotion Manager carefully planning how to spend his budget to maximum effect and then, towards the end of the year, being unexpectedly charged for something he does not consider as marketing communications, but which the accountants do.

Even minor expenses pose a major problem, as many promotional activities do not fit neatly into defined categories and can soon mount up to a considerable expense. Is the new factory sign a promotional cost, or a general building expense? What about charges incurred in printing redesigned letterheads or special livery for delivery vans? There is a strong possibility that other sections may pass unwanted invoices (and no departmental head *wants* charges against his department) to the Promotion Manager. If these invoices are then paid from the so-called appropriation, there is less money available for genuine promotional expenditure. It is therefore vital for the Promotion Manager to be completely clear on this point.

The following anecdote illustrates the need for this practical understanding. A newly-appointed Promotion Manager learned to his dismay, three-quarters through the company year, that he had overspent by several thousand pounds. He considered himself well within budget, and the dispute arose because he believed costs of publishing the Annual Report (and arrangements for the Shareholders' Meeting) were charged to the Company Secretary, whereas accounting staff classed them as marketing communications. In consequence, the Promotion Manager had no choice but to cancel planned activities to make up the deficit, so upsetting his carefully considered arrangements. This deprived his company of valuable promotional support when greatly needed, which resulted in lost sales which, in turn, meant loss of profits. A clear understanding of what the appropriation covered would have prevented this.

Equally important – although outside the bounds of this chapter – is for the Promotion Manager to plan those aspects of organizational activity which, although *not* charged against the budget, have promotional implications – the sales force has an important marketing communications function, as do all the marketing P's.

THE NEED FOR A BUDGET

With appropriation period and coverage clearly defined, the Promotion Manager can commence planning, and so deciding the budget is a vital step.

Before reviewing various methods of fixing the budget, three alternatives must be dismissed:

NO BUDGET

Inexperienced executives occasionally decide 'It's time we sent out a news release . . . or had an advertisement', or may even advertise simply because a media representative asked for an order! Such an unplanned approach is likely to result in money spent haphazardly across media and over time, and such promotion is unlikely to be productive. To be effective, marketing communications must be planned. The plan should be flexible to allow for unexpected opportunities – and setbacks – but promotion must nevertheless be planned in advance, with marketing and selling integrated with all forms of marketing communications which, in their turn, are fully co-ordinated. Sales staff then concentrate on items featured in advertising, which is backed by appropriate merchandising, public relations, and sales promotion. Effective planning ensures representatives are fully briefed about the products promoted, and know the stock/delivery position. In this way the prospect's interest is aroused by editorial following a news release, press advertisements and direct mail shots stimulate requests for further details (perhaps reinforced by the sales promotion offer of an informative booklet), the replies are merchandised to sales staff, and sales completed by prompt visits from the representatives. When sales staff are ignorant of advertising or public relations activity, bad impressions are created, and sales often lost. Clearly the Promotion Manager must ensure that this does *not* apply to his company's marketing communications.

THE ARBITRARY 'GUESSTIMATE'

Picking a figure by hunch rarely leads to successful promotion. Few organizations adopt this approach, and most give careful consideration to the amount they spend. Some executives, however, disguise this approach by claiming 'My twenty years experience tells me we should spend £X,000'. Certainly true experience can make an invaluable contribution, but all too often the term is used to defend what is only a guess. Has this individual really had 20 years experience – or one year's experience twenty times? The 'method' exists, however, and so must be mentioned – if only to stress it has little in its favour.

'CHAIRMAN'S RULES'

This 'method' is found in those companies where the Promotion Manager works to a figure dictated by his Board, and has no say in deciding budget policy. In many instances the company *does* know what it is doing, but in others there is no real basis for the Board decision: the Directors concerned have alas little idea whether they are budgeting too much or too little. The 'method' nevertheless exists and so must be mentioned if only to add that – like the 'arbitrary guesstimate' – it has no sound basis.

The last two methods, however, do have *some* merit. Both set aside a fixed sum, which in itself necessitates at least basic planning and raises fundamental

BUDGETING

questions such as 'If *X* products need promotional support, how much should be allocated to each?' and 'How should spending be spread over the year?' From the planning standpoint, somebody is forced to apportion money between advertising and public relations and other promotional methods. Within each means of communication, this individual must then decide which media to use and what message to deliver, and so on. These two methods are likely to result in some minimal planning, and so are not without merit – but either could result in too much or too little spent on marketing communications.

Most readers will know the comment attributed to Lord Leverhume – 'Half the money I spend on advertising is wasted – the trouble is, I don't know which half'. Whenever I hear this story, I always recall my visit to the head of a large American corporation. In reply to my question as to how many people worked in his organization, my host's laconic reply was 'About half of them'.

The Promotion Manager must ensure *all* his company's marketing communications money works to full advantage and, as the 'no budget/arbitrary guesstimate/chairman's rules' methods have little in their favour, he must consider more practical alternatives.

There is no ideal method of deciding the budget, and much depends on circumstances. Fixing the appropriation for an established product may be an annual ritual, while a product launch often calls for promotion to be regarded as capital investment. Many methods are in current use: each has advantages and drawbacks, and all are applied with varying degrees of success.

BUDGETING METHODS

The numerous methods can be reviewed under seven main headings, each subsuming many variations – some call only for simple arithmetic but others demand a computer to undertake complex calculations: the basic method nevertheless remains the same. The fundamental choices, together with their advantages and drawbacks, are:

PERCENTAGE OF LAST YEAR'S SALES

This is perhaps the most widespread method. Many organizations take a set percentage of the previous year's turnover as the basis for their appropriation. This has the advantage of safety as money is spent in line with established sales. The method has, however, two drawbacks. First is deciding what percentage – one, two, three or more per cent? Some firms have industry statistics which show the average for their particular product group, but this is not as helpful as it seems. If there is an *average* percentage, that is because many firms, quite correctly, spend more than the average while others, equally correct, spend less. The first drawback is thus determining what percentage to spend.

The method's second basic weakness is that it looks backwards rather than forwards. A poor year means lower sales and thus even less for promotion – in a downward spiral. One answer to falling sales might be *more* spent on promotion, in the belief it stimulates sales. Even if sales do not fall, the method has a further drawback: a sales increase of five per cent, against a market growth of 15 per cent, means the company has lost out by ten per cent.

Furthermore, it is chicken and egg – did sales rise because more was spent on promotion, or is the company spending more because sales have risen? Despite its weaknesses, many organizations use this method: others, rather than look to the past, use *expected* sales as their criterion.

PERCENTAGE OF ANTICIPATED SALES

This method leads to more realistic expenditure if, for example, the marketing objective is a marked sales increase. It suffers, however, from a previous problem: deciding what percentage. A second drawback is that over-estimation leads to over-spending. 'Expected sales' decisions comprise three broad categories:

- *The single-executive decision.* Many smaller firms' management decisions are taken by one individual: since he has responsibility for all aspects of business operations, he usually adopts a realistic approach.
- *The sales versus promotion split.* Some larger firms divide these two functions, the Sales Manager being responsible for selling operations, and the Promotion Manager for marketing communications. This frequently leads to problems, as most Sales Managers are optimists and often overestimate unintentionally. When the sales target is not achieved, the Sales Manager blames the Promotion Manager and *vice versa*. The Sales Manager asks how he can be expected to sell anything without proper promotional support, while the Promotion Manager points out that marketing communications cannot achieve the impossible and he is not to blame if the sales team do not bring in the orders. When unsold stocks come to management attention, the Managing Director reprimands the Sales Manager, who promptly takes it out on the Promotion Manager, who vents his wrath on the agency (or public relations consultancy), and blame eventually passes to the hapless media representative who sold advertising space, and whose medium 'proved' it could not bring results!
- *The marketing approach.* A single individual again takes the budget decision, but this is very different to the one-person approach described above, since the Marketing Director has reporting to him executives responsible for sales, for promotion, and for market research – and who indeed participate in the decision process. Marketing teams devote time and effort to sales forecasting in order to decide the appropriation, as well as fixing production levels, with greater accuracy. As with other aspects of marketing, the planning process ensures there is consultation between all concerned in agreeing realistic objectives.

THE UNIT PERCENTAGE METHOD

This method uses cost analysis as the basis for deciding how much to spend, thus overcoming the problem common to the last two methods: determining a suitable percentage figure. Detailed costings analyse expenditure on raw materials, production costs, overheads, packaging, and so on. These figures may total, say, £950, and a selling price of £1,000 leaves a £50 margin, of which the company can then decide to keep £10 and spend £40 on promotion, keep £20 profit and spend £30 per unit, and so on. This costing analysis often extends to agents' margins and distribution charges through to final customers rather than stopping at the factory gate. In essence, the appropriation is fixed as a residual figure with profit: the difference between costs and selling price leaves a balance which can either be spent on promotion or retained as profit. Unlike the two previous methods, this approach is unlikely to lead to unintentional overspending as a £50 margin would clearly prevent the Promotion Manager from recommending £60 per unit spent on promotion.

This apparently logical method is not without flaw, as it is strictly inward-looking, and takes little account of the outside market. Furthermore, the danger exists that costings may not be revised as raw materials prices change or wage rates increase. Additionally, overheads vary with output: the more units produced, the wider costs are spread and the smaller the charges borne by each unit. Finally, all figures are costed on the basis of a sales target which may not in fact be achieved. However, providing sales estimates are accurate and costings revised regularly (so that the same percentage does not become an in-house tradition) this method gives a practical guide to what the organization can afford.

COMPETITIVE PARITY

Another approach to fixing the appropriation is to look at what competitors are spending. When entering new markets, competitors' expenditures can give a useful guide to the amount of money needed to inform the market.

One weakness is that competitors are similar — but not *identical* in their marketing mix, and their objectives are therefore different. Finding out what competitors are spending is another problem. Press advertising expenditure can be estimated by checking competitors' advertisements against publishers' rate cards. The task is even easier with larger advertisers, as expenditure estimates are included in the reference sources outlined earlier: these also contain television billings. For other media, however, such as direct mail, exhibitions, merchandising, public relations, and sales promotion, it is far more difficult to estimate competitors' expenditure. Even press advertising estimates may be inaccurate, since it is impossible to monitor the full range of business media and, in any event, figures are at rate-card costs, whereas much space is purchased at a discount. Even if information is available, who is to say if the rival companies were correct in the first place?

A further drawback is that any new market entrant must affect competitors' sales: they might then spend more on promotion, so forcing the new firm to increase its appropriation. Competing firms should therefore not extend this method by waging a wasteful promotional 'war'.

PROMOTIONAL SHARE

This method overlaps others already discussed. The 'promotional share' approach looks not only at expenditure in relation to competitors, but also relative sales. Both expenditure and sales figures are considered in terms of 'share' and the question posed is 'Does market share, in terms of sales, match promotion share?'

Such analysis often reveals interesting information about promotion/sales ratios, and whether a company is 'working harder' (in promotional expenditure terms) than competitors, and – much more important – what results this is having on sales. This study of relative shares is often extended over time by the 'dynamic difference' approach which compares:

Sales share one year less sales share the preceding year

with

Promotion share one year less promotion share the preceding year.

Firms which increase their promotion share may also increase their market share. (Or, of course, *vice versa*.)

This method's weaknesses were outlined under the 'competitive parity' method and, furthermore, it does not *prove* that increased expenditure results in increased sales.

THE MARGINAL METHOD

The preceding five methods all pose variations of the same 'How much to spend?' question. The marginal (sometimes called zero-based) method asks a very different question: 'How much *extra* to spend?' Attention shifts from fixing a set sum to deciding 'level by level', and additional expenditure must justify itself. The claim 'Promotion increases sales' is frequently made: the marginal method asks 'How much will it increase sales?'.

The marginal method extends unit percentage calculations, based on the results of each *additional* amount spent. If, for example, each unit sold contributes £10 profit, then £1,000 spent on promotion must result in sales of at least 100 additional units in order to be worthwhile. 'Increased sales' of only 50 units would be of little appeal, since this involves a *loss* of £500. The marginal method can be extremely valuable when sales can be directly related to promotion.

It is important to bear in mind what is being evaluated, however, since promotional expenditure has, in fact, bought nothing more than blank space! Many organizations, fortunate enough to have a direct response they can measure, extend the marginal method to measure medium A against medium B, creative message C against message D, headline E against headline F, illustration G versus illustration H, and so on.

Economists refer to the 'Law of Diminishing Returns' and the marginal method applies this in practice – full page advertisements are some four times as expensive as quarter-pages, and the same applies to weekly insertions rather than a monthly appearance, and the marginal method checks if it is actually worth it. Equally, special positions cost more than run-of-paper insertions and colour costs more than black and white – are they worth it in terms of increased returns? The fundamental question this method poses is 'If it costs X per cent extra, do returns increase by more than X per cent?' A later chapter discusses evaluation of results in detail, but clearly this method ideally suits those organizations which can directly measure results. The proportion of business firms in this fortunate position is certainly higher than for consumer companies. Those organizations unable to establish so direct a connection must consider other methods of fixing their appropriation.

THE TARGET SUM METHOD

Sometimes called 'Objective and Task', this approach operates on a different basis to those so far considered. Instead of asking 'How much (or how much extra) to spend?' the method asks 'What will it cost?'

The method estimates the cost of the promotional task necessary to achieve the objective – how many news releases, how many press conferences, and what is the cost of other PR activities? Advertising expenditure estimates work back from media-owners' rate cards and, if the task calls for half-pages every week in a set number of publications to achieve a given sales target, then the appropriation is calculated by multiplying the cost of these advertisements by the number of insertions. Thus a weekly schedule of advertisements totalling £10,000 for each appearance in a selected list of publications gives an annual appropriation of 52 × £10,000 or £520,000, plus production costs. In practice, of course, the calculations would be more complex, particularly when extended to include costings for merchandising, public relations and sales promotion activities, together with agency or consultancy service fees.

The method, like all others, has both strong and weak points. It is realistic in recognizing actual costs, thus overcoming a weakness common to earlier methods by which, if media rates increase by, say, ten per cent, the organization can then only afford to book ten per cent less space or time. By the same argument, an increase in postal charges means fewer news releases, and the same restriction applies to other promotional media.

The problem underlying the target sum method is deciding the variables – are half-pages the correct size, is weekly frequency necessary and which media should be included? Who is to say whether a news conference *is* necessary, how many media should be invited, and what standard of hospitality should be extended? The danger obviously lies in being over-ambitious and seeking saturation campaigns in advertising, public relations, merchandising and sales promotion, and so on! In such circumstances, *all* the company's money could be spent on promotion. However, if a realistic view is taken of the weight of campaigns really necessary in different promotional media, this is a sound method of fixing the appropriation.

THE COMPOSITE METHOD

This chapter stated earlier there were seven main approaches to budgeting, so readers may well be surprised at finding an eighth! The eighth 'method', however, simply uses several methods simultaneously. When considering budgetary approaches, some methods immediately appear relevant to a particular situation, and others less practical. The necessary calculations for the methods selected then give a range of figures indicating minimum and maximum expenditure levels. The Promotion Manager then selects a figure within the range indicated by the various calculations – a range which in any event is likely to encompass a relatively narrow span. Rather than any arbitrary guesstimate it is clear that, whatever the circumstances, the company should not spend less than a certain sum. A maximum figure has been calculated equally logically. This practical approach narrows down the range of uncertainty, at which point experience becomes truly valuable.

There is a world of difference between vague claims that 'My experience tells me we should spend £X,000' and the practical application of true experience, which tells the Promotion Manager where, within the range, he should fix his company's appropriation. A depressed economy, for example, might indicate the need to spend the maximum affordable sum. If, however, his company's products have distinct technical and price advantages, and the main competitor's sales force and distribution are currently weak, the Promotion Manager (after a *SWOT* analysis of strengths and weaknesses) might then recommend to his Board a budget at the lower end of the scale, rather than the higher level which at first seemed necessary.

British Business Press's research into 'How British Business Advertises' asked respondents to rate various influences on budget decisions in order of importance. These, in rank order, were:

1. Sales targets
2. New market or product development
3. = Profit requirements
3. = % of total turnover
5. Public image/company reputation
6. Analysis of sales
7. Previous year's budget
8. Objectives set by research
9. Competitors' spend

Experience can be an invaluable aid in evaluating these variables, and certainly the results of the previous year's promotion should also be considered. Appropriation policy is thus a circular procedure, with the results of one year's budget serving as a basis for deciding the subsequent year's expenditure which, in its turn, is revised to meet the needs of the following year.

IN SEARCH OF THE PERFECT METHOD

Various budgetary methods, all with many variations, are thus currently in use, each with advantages and drawbacks. The outlines given perhaps over-simplify some variations, which are based on econometric approaches and complex mathematical models.

I make no apologies to any reader seeking the impossible – a single perfect method. I recall, however, a consumer product colleague who took me to task after reading my earlier writings on this subject – why was I so general, when his organization calculated its budget precisely? Upon my enquiring how, he proudly produced a complex mathematical model which required estimates of some dozen variables, and a lengthy computer run to resolve these into a recommended budget figure. When I pointed out that most industrial companies did not have access to estimates of so many variables, nor a formula to inter-relate them even if they had such data, and that the market research budget to acquire this information (let alone the cost of devising the formula and then processing the data) far exceeded most business-to-business budgets, he did admit his 'perfect' method was specific to *his* firm and that having a vast promotional budget did make a difference!

In the absence of a universal perfect method then, these are the main methods from which the Promotion Manager can choose. Indeed, any method is preferable to the 'bit-here-and-a-bit-there' approach, in that it must lead to planning and thus to more effective promotion.

Even if a single ideal method were available, there is a considerable difference between fixing a sum, and then a) spending it and b) using it. All that has been achieved so far is to decide how much to spend, rather than to consider what use to make of the money. A budget spent effectively gives more value for money or, viewed another way, the same results for less money. The media buying skills with which the budget will later be spent should thus influence the initial decision on how much to spend.

Creative skills are equally important: if the Promotion Manager can create compelling campaigns (either in-house or through external services) then clearly he need spend less than competitors whose promotional messages do not convey their products' benefits to good effect.

BUDGET DIVISIONS

Various further points must be made about budgetary policy, before turning to the next stage of promotional planning. One is that an organization may have several appropriations, one for each product or division, rather than a single figure. There may also be an additional budget to finance an 'umbrella' campaign covering all component companies of the group, rather than individual products.

Furthermore, the appropriation may be divided between 'above the line' expenditure by external services and a 'below the line' budget retained for in-house use.

The budget may further sub-divide for another reason: to provide funds for manufacturer/distributor co-operation. Many firms find it productive to share with agents the cost of local promotions which announce they stock the products featured in the campaigns. Some companies also help finance industry-wide promotion: rather than fight each other for market share, they contribute finance to co-operative campaigns aimed at increasing demand for their product group as a whole.

Additionally, part of the budget – described as a 'Contingency Reserve' – may be retained to cater for unexpected opportunities or setbacks. All these sub-divisions of the overall appropriation are discussed elsewhere.

LONG-TERM PLANNING

The various methods discussed all imply *annual* decisions, but this somewhat artificial custom arises from accounting practice. Many companies now take a longer-term view, since it is unrealistic to expect a new product to realise a profit within a calendar year, especially taking into account the heavy development costs incurred in most new business-to-business ventures. As long-term prospects are important, the marketing plan accordingly covers several years, depending on the estimated time needed to capture the market. The first year of operation may involve a deficit, in the second year the company breaks even, the third year's profit offsets the first year loss, and a true profit is made in the fourth year. The initial deficit is a calculated situation, and the appropriation regarded as an investment to be recouped by subsequent sales. Conventional accountants, however, sometimes resist the concept of promotion as investment, since it provides no tangible assets they can sell off as they could machinery, stocks or equipment.

Long-term budgeting calls for two cash flow calculations – the rate at which money is spent, and the rate at which it will return. The marketing plan therefore includes a 'payout schedule', showing how much capital is required to finance operations until a profit situation is achieved: it would be poor financial management to run short of capital on the eve of the first true profit. A marketing-orientated accountant can make a most valuable contribution in preparing these financial estimates.

Equally, any Promotion Manager who understands financial practice will find this accounting knowledge a most useful asset – even if only in persuading conventional accountants not to give way to their instinctive reaction in times of recession, which is to cut the promotional budget. Most promotion personnel have this argument more than once during their careers!

This chapter opened by stressing that fixing the appropriation is a management decision, and it concludes on the very same point. The appropriation was decided at Board level, and promotion staff must learn to work to this figure. The temptation to ask for more money, to take advantage of some special opportunity, must be resisted. If the Promotion Manager does ask for more money, there may be no immediate Board meeting scheduled and, in any event, the Directors are unlikely to view this special offer (a very minor event in the company's total operation) with the same enthusiasm. Such events should be covered by the contingency reserve mentioned earlier, and are a very different matter to a *major* policy review. Should the company situation change to such a degree that the marketing plan is no longer valid, the Board would meet as a matter of urgency, to review all aspects of business activity – production levels, prices and, of course, promotion. Such a major review is very different from coping with the inevitable minor setbacks which are an unavoidable feature of business life.

THE NEXT STEP

Now that the budget is decided, the Promotion Manager's next task is preparation of campaign proposals to achieve company objectives.

CHAPTER TWENTY-THREE

Preparation of Campaign Proposals – The Message

Having established campaign objectives in the light of buyer behaviour, the next step is to consider how best to achieve these objectives, within the restraints of the budget. This stage comprises two distinct but inter-related activities:

- *Preparation of message proposals* – discussed within this chapter;
- *Preparation of media proposals* – to be covered in the next chapter.

No book can make the reader an expert advertising or news release writer, graphic designer or media planner, but it can establish fundamental principles so that promotional planning – whether of created media, or existing media through advertising or editorial columns – is soundly based.

It is misleading, however, to talk of creative or media planning, since this implies a single campaign, whereas effective promotion is more complex: it is more correct to talk of *campaigns* in the plural.

Before purchasers can buy a product it must be available: before distributors can stock it representatives must sell it to them, and before they can do so they must be fully briefed. Any promotional plan thus has multiple components – a campaign to potential purchasers, a second to agents and a third directed at sales staff. Firms which sell direct have two rather than three campaigns, but each should encompass the full range of marketing communications. Within each promotional category are two distinct but linked aspects: the messages to be delivered, and media to deliver them. Each campaign component must interlock with others. This chapter concentrates on creative content of the various messages, and the next chapter examines the media aspects.

Although messages and media are separated for ease of analysis, it is important to treat them as inter-related. There is little point in striving to create a pursuasive message and then just dropping it into a media plan in the hope that target groups will see it. Business executives are bombarded by many thousands of promotional messages each week: they react to very few per year, and act on fewer still. It is important therefore to cut through all the noise and clutter to ensure target groups actually *receive* the message. Positive steps are considered both within this and the media planning chapter following, since both message and/or media means can serve to attract attention.

THE ATTENTION FACTOR

It is insufficient to create a strong message and then simply place it in a suitable medium. Before the message can communicate, it must attract the target market's attention. Various devices can serve this purpose: all have one thing in common, however – they call for knowledge of media which goes far beyond circulation or readership statistics.

This book has repeatedly stressed that, whether planning advertising or public relations activities, the Promotion Manager must know the format of each individual medium, and this is as important for the message as for other aspects of promotion. What regular (or occasional) features are carried? Which relate to his product area, and indicate fertile ground for receipt of news releases? What advertisement positions are available, and on which feature pages? Equally important, do competitors appear in either editorial or advertising columns? Without such an in-depth understanding, it is impossible to decide how best to attract target market attention.

ATTENTION DEVICES

There are numerous devices which can attract attention. Although considered under the heading of message, they also have media planning implications. Some 'mechanical' devices are inserts, gate-folds, stick-ons, slide-outs and tear-offs. Other devices include:

SIZE

A large exhibition stand in itself attracts attention (and is more impressive to those who see it), as well as giving greater scope for creativity and demonstration. The same principle applies equally to press and other media. The decision to use size as an attention device has clear planning implications. Sheer size is no substitute for creativity, however, and can be extremely wasteful – double-page spreads in press media may be ignored as being 'only advertising', while full-pages in broadsheet publications may be too big to be read comfortably, except at arms length.

POSITION

A press advertisement on the front page, or in a solus position without competition from other advertisers, is likely to be seen by more people than an advertisement appearing alongside others in the body of the publication. Those adjacent to or facing editorial will also receive more attention. Similarly, more exhibition visitors are likely to see a stand in a prime location facing the entrance, than one poorly sited. Again, the decision to use position as an attention device directly affects the media plan.

ILLUSTRATION

Advertisements, editorial features or created media featuring action pictures (which show the product in operation and/or people benefiting from its use) have strong attention value. While these are mainly creative considerations, the quality of reproduction required directly affects media selection.

COLOUR

Colour is often used as an attention device. Printing in a second colour attracts attention (and highlights key parts of the message) while full colour can also

PREPARATION OF CAMPAIGN PROPOSALS – THE MESSAGE

show products and people in their natural colours. The creative need for colour to attract attention clearly influences promotional planning, particularly if creative requirements call for high quality colour reproduction (as might be the case, for example, for firms marketing office/hotel furniture and furnishings, workforce clothing/uniforms or industrial paints).

These last two attention devices are discussed in more detail later.

MOVEMENT

Movement or a video presentation on an exhibition stand, or a display unit which lights up from time to time, can attract attention through contrast with the static background.

Product demonstration can in itself attract attention, and not all media permit this. Once again, creative requirements influence media selection.

SOUND

The human voice can quickly attract attention and also convey a message, particularly when the right presenter is chosen to give the right tone of voice and authority to match the characteristics of the product. Music and other sound effects can similarly attract attention as well as influencing the listeners' mood. The need for sound to fulfill these functions again has media implications.

INTERACTION

Some media are more interactive than others – when participating in exhibitions or seminars, for example, it is possible to use several devices simultaneously: personal contact and demonstration can attract attention, as well as deliver promotional messages effectively. The television medium is becoming increasingly inter-active, and direct mail's facility for inclusion of reply-devices, informative booklets, or even samples for recipients to handle, can also serve to attract target market attention.

HEADLINES (AND BODY COPY)

Creating headlines which attract attention is the writer's speciality (as is producing interesting and compelling text for advertisements, house journals, product literature, news releases or feature articles). The headline device is examined later within the chapter.

There are thus various means to attract target market attention: whether or not this attention is retained depends on the promotional message's content.

MESSAGE CONTENT

Consumer advertising sells primarily by appeal to the emotions. Most business products are not so much sold, however, as *purchased* – by experienced professional or qualified specialists, accustomed to dealing with complicated issues. These executives look for relevant information and convincing argument (even the most rational individuals are, however, influenced by instinctive and emotional factors such as design, aesthetics and colour).

When planning promotional campaigns, many inexperienced executives make the understandable mistake of concentrating on what they want to say, rather than what their target markets wish to hear. The starting point for communications planning should be the purchasing patterns discussed earlier — who takes the decision whether or not to buy a product, what motivates them, what factors influence decisions, and at what phase are they in the buying process?

Furthermore, different market segments may call for different sales arguments according to the campaign objective — for one segment the aim might be to convert new users to the product, another campaign suggests new uses to existing purchasers, whilst in a third segment the objective is to retain customers who may be won over by competitors. Chapter 20 on objectives gave a matrix of six routes to increased sales, each calling for different promotional messages. Other campaigns might seek alternative objectives, or be targeted at distributors rather than ultimate purchasers.

The next step is to take these distinct campaign objectives and convert them into *communication* objectives — what must promotion actually *say*, and how is it best to say it? To resolve this problem, it is necessary to consider the communication process as such.

THE MARKETING COMMUNICATION PROCESS

Just as there are various models of buyer behaviour, so there are alternative models of how the communication process works. Again, there is no question of one model being right and all others wrong, but rather deciding which model applies to a particular situation.

Different models might in turn seek different categories of response, depending on campaign objectives. The type of response sought by the communication process can be classified as:

- *Cognitive* (imparting knowledge) — which seek to influence a prospect's awareness or comprehension of product data and other facts;
- *Affective* (changing attitudes) — which seek to influence a prospect's mental disposition, covering convictions, evaluations, interest, feelings, or preferences;
- *Conative* (influencing behaviour) — which seek to affect a prospect's actions, intentions, or actual purchases.

Promotion could for example seek to influence the prospect's general product awareness, his perception of an overall product group, or actual purchase of a particular supplier's brand. Alternatively, promotion might seek to influence perceived values such as price/quality, and could thus effect the price buyers are prepared to pay.

One well-known model of the communication process follows the A-I-D-A formula, the promotional task being to attract *A*ttention, awaken *I*nterest, convert this into *D*esire, and finally lead to *A*ction.

At any one time only a few companies may be actually interested in what an organization has to offer. There are always potential customers, but the problem facing the sales force is to identify them, especially when the purchase initiator is often hidden deep inside the customer's organization, inaccessible to uninvited sales representatives.

PREPARATION OF CAMPAIGN PROPOSALS – THE MESSAGE

The task of business promotion under such circumstances is to get potential purchasers to identify themselves, and encourage them to invite sales staff to make a presentation. The promotional message should therefore provide prospects with sound reasons to take action. Their response will provide sales representatives with a list of prospect companies which have an immediate or imminent need for the company's product. Business promotion following the AIDA formula and suggesting a course of action to follow (eg, telephone, return the coupon/reply card enclosed) can increase salesforce productivity.

The market for a product can be considered as a pyramid. At the apex are those few who are aware of an immediate need for a product. Many more potential buyers are nearer the base of the pyramid. Some may need the product, but not yet – they have sufficient stocks, are satisfied with their present suppliers, have recently installed similar equipment, or have no immediate plans for expansion. Others *should be* in the pyramid, but are not yet aware of their need.

An alternative approach therefore suggests an A-C-C-A process, with a lengthier hierarchy of effects which takes prospects through four levels of understanding. Prospects must first be made *A*ware of their actual need for a product. This awareness must be followed by *C*omprehension of what the product can do to satisfy this need – a creative task which, for more technical products, is by no means as simple as it sounds. The next stage is *C*onviction – convincing prospects the product actually does what is claimed. Good text should anticipate possible sceptical reaction by providing creditable information. It is not until these first three stages have been satisfactorily completed that the organization can hope for *A*ction, and an actual purchase.

Other variations suggest different hierarchies of effect:

- Awareness – Interest – Liking – Preference – Action
- Awareness – Interest – Favourable Attitudes – Action
- Information – Learning – Evaluation – Action

All these models seek varying degrees of the cognitive, affective and conative responses discussed earlier, in that they seek to influence knowledge, mental disposition, and ultimately action.

There are numerous other models. One suggests the promotional message must be seen, read, believed, remembered, and then acted upon. Another model, related to the theory of cognitive dissonance discussed earlier, recognizes the importance of product trial and therefore follows an A-T-R hierarchy of:

- Awareness – Trial – Re-inforcement

Most business purchase decisions involve dissonance: any chosen alternative necessarily involves some unattractive features, whilst rejected products have some favourable attributes. Emphasis is therefore placed on the re-inforcement after trial stage. This is particularly important when, as discussed earlier, existing users are likely to have a marked influence on potential purchasers.

Yet another model analyses the different role of marketing communications at the various stages of a six-step selling process:

- Make contact – Arouse interest – Create preference – Quote a price – Close the deal – Keep the customer happy

All models have one thing in common: they recognize the need for promotional messages to attract attention, without which existing and potential purchasers will not become aware nor proceed to later stages of whichever hierarchy of effects is applicable.

ATTENTION AND MESSAGE CONTENT

Despite earlier comments about the problem of overcoming noise and clutter it is, surprisingly enough, *not* difficult to attract attention – think of the 'pin-up' advertisements for industrial products which appear from time to time in trade and technical publications. Subsequent research might reveal high attention ratings and very favourable recall – but only for the lovely lady in question! Most respondents would not remember the product advertised, nor its benefits, nor the name of the supplier. Many business publications, alas, feature upside-down advertisements or other such creative gimmicks.

The difficulty lies not so much in attracting attention as keeping it. The solution is, however, surprisingly simple – offer a benefit in the headline. Benefits can sometimes be expressed in reverse, by offering to eliminate negative factors. The true problem lies in selecting, out of many product benefits, which key feature should be promoted. The question underlying all promotion is 'The company will achieve its objective if existing or prospective target groups know, feel or believe . . . *what*?'

To reach this decision, two questions are important:

1) *What do people buy?*

and

2) *Why do people buy?*

Both questions clearly approach message content from the target market's standpoint.

WHAT DO PEOPLE BUY?

This is not necessarily what the organization thinks it is selling! A manufacturer of beauty products once commented (in rather chauvinistic fashion) 'In our factory we make cosmetics – in our advertising we sell hope!', while a leading photographic company increased sales by selling 'memories' rather than cameras and film. Similarly, rather than consider the product sold or service provided, the Promotion Manager must concentrate on what his target market is buying. Purchasers of industrial power drills, for example, buy holes (precision holes, low cost holes, easy holes, and swift holes – but still holes!). The following possibilities – by no means exhaustive – may help in determining the content of promotional messages.

For products, customers might be buying:

- Cost savings
- Improved performance
- Increased productivity
- Increased profitability
- Security/safety

PREPARATION OF CAMPAIGN PROPOSALS – THE MESSAGE

- Solution to problem
- Speed of operation.

For services, customers might be buying:

- Problem analysis, and diagnosis
- Resource support, to increase sales
- Information, that facilitates better decisions
- Expertise, which improves purchasers' skills
- Convenience, making it easier for customers to buy and use
- Reassurance, to reduce risks

In some business purchase decisions, both lists apply at the same time: many technical products are inseparable from the service element, being too complex for customers to buy without expert advice from sales staff.

These suggestions by no means cover every possibility – the important thing is to decide message content on the basis of what the target market buys, rather than products sold.

WHY DO PEOPLE BUY?

If prospects are convinced they need a product, this is insufficient to result in a sale: they can always buy from a competitor. The Promotion Manager must also persuade them that his company is a dependable supplier, with back-up resources. In business selling, confidence in the supplier is often as important as the actual product.

The next task is therefore to consider the basis on which prospects choose between one supplier and another. Here again, there are suggestions which look at things from the customers' perspective. They might select suppliers on the basis of:

- After-sales service
- Availability
- Brand name
- Competitive superiority
- Complete product line
- Continuity
- Cost savings
- Credibility
- Credit extension
- Durability
- Financial support
- Literature and manuals
- Price
- Product quality – reliability, specification or suitability
- Proof of value
- Reliability – of delivery, product, service
- Sales representatives' calibre
- Spares availability
- Speed – of delivery, operation or response
- Supplier relationship

- Supplier reputation
- Technical co-operation
- Technological advance
- Training support services

The chapter on Purchasing Patterns established three types of buyer: if customers are resellers or government departments rather than industrial users, they might select suppliers by other criteria.

Retailers, for example, might select on the basis of proposed consumer promotion, evidence of likely product acceptance, trade terms and profit margins, funds for co-operative advertising, merchandising support, and ultimately their rate of stockturn and sales per square foot of floor space.

For government departments, many of the listed criteria still apply but, as the Decision Making Unit is often formally constituted, it may involve different individuals with different requirements. Furthermore, there may be additional 'political' implications: government intentions to develop British rather than overseas industries, for example, or to boost employment in particular industrial areas.

SOME CREATIVE APPROACHES

The creative brief concerns 'what' you say to appeal to a defined target market, as distinct from 'how' you say it – there is no point in spending hours polishing the text of an advertisement or news release, if it is based on the incorrect message from the target market's standpoint.

There are numerous approaches to creative planning and, yet again, there is no question of one being right and all others wrong. As you would expect, most were developed by advertising agencies in respect of consumer products, but they can nevertheless readily adapt to the special needs of business-to-business.

In considering what to say, what is termed *FAB Analysis* is often helpful, distinguishing between Features, Advantages and Benefits.

- A *feature* of a machine tool might be that its setting-up time is shorter than competitors.
- The *advantage* is that users commence production more quickly.
- The *benefit* is increased production, which in turn leads to other benefits such as increased profit.

An alternative approach is the 'USP' or *Unique Selling Proposition* which suggests that:

'The consumer tends to remember just one thing from an advertisement – one strong claim or one strong concept. Each advertisement must make a proposition to the consumer. The proposition must be one that the competition either cannot or does not offer. The proposition must be so strong that it can . . . pull over new customers to your product.'

This indicates a 'hard sell' or rational 'reason-why' approach, which applies to the content of news releases or created media just as much as advertisements.

Another famous practitioner stressed brand image, pointing out that:

PREPARATION OF CAMPAIGN PROPOSALS – THE MESSAGE

'It is the total personality of a brand rather than any trivial product difference which decides its ultimate position in the market.'

Marketing communications does not operate in isolation, as prospects already have an image of a brand or product or service or organization, based on past experience (which includes past promotion).

The promotional task is to strengthen and improve this image. Planning must concentrate on making sure that all marketing communications present a coherent total personality for the brand, or company. This approach suggests non-verbal communications (including visual signals such as house style, non-product 'company' associations, and connotations of prestige and quality), which create a favourable image just as important as the message content itself, which backs up this image by a supporting rationalization.

Another approach, developed by a leading agency, is the *'Single-Minded Selling Proposition'*. This agency's philosophy also stresses that the proposition must be *'made to come alive in a compelling way'*. In short, a strong message is in itself not sufficient – if expressed in boring fashion, a promotional message (however powerful its basis) will not communicate to the target market. The agency philosophy thus concentrates on 'how you say it', just as much as 'what you say'. This agency's procedures also call for a firm decision on what to say *before* detailed consideration is given to how best to say it, thus emphasising the need for creative planning.

Development of possible creative approaches has not been restricted to advertising agencies, however: one leading consumer goods company developed 'Ten Principles of Good Brand Advertising', from which business-to-business companies can learn a great deal. Each principle was discussed in detail, but the main points established were:

1. It is consumer oriented.
2. It concentrates on one selling idea.
3. It concentrates on the most important and persuasive idea available.
4. It presents a unique and competitive benefit.
5. It involves the consumer.
6. It is credible, sincere and true.
7. It is simple, clear, complete.
8. It clearly associates the selling idea with the brand idea.
9. It takes full advantage of the medium.
10. It demands action that will lead to the sale.

BUSINESS-TO-BUSINESS APPLICATIONS

These various approaches, although developed primarily for consumer products and services, have equal application to industrial markets.

Taking the Ten Principles as example, business promotion should be based on target market needs, should not scatter its impact, should concentrate on the most important benefit from the buyers' standpoint and equally on why they should buy from one particular supplier rather than competitors.

Business promotion must involve target markets, just as much as that mounted for consumer products. Industrial campaigns appeal mostly to reason rather than emotions, but the buyer's feeling about an organization should never be ignored. Promotion should, wherever possible, document, demonstrate or otherwise prove its claim – and do so in the target market's own language, in a manner which is completely understandable. The campaign must register the brand name and link it with the selling idea – there is no point in increasing competitors' sales. Effective promotion should transform passive acceptance or interest into action. Promotion should equally make it *easy* for the target market to take action.

The need to take full advantage of the medium is a clear link with the next chapter, which considers selection of media to transmit the message: certain selling ideas are better fitted to one medium rather than another – and may indeed dictate choice of media. Effective promotion varies the chosen proposition's presentation to capitalize on the physical characteristics and audience mood provided by the medium.

BUSINESS-TO-BUSINESS MESSAGES

Whichever creative approach is adopted, certain techniques relating to 'How you say it' have proved particularly successful in promoting industrial products and services. These include:

- Case-histories, illustrating the benefits obtained from using the product;
- Testimonials, in which an actual user confirms these benefits;
- Problem/Solution explanations (and examples);
- Demonstrations of benefits;
- Before/After comparisons.

SOURCES OF MESSAGE CONTENT

Selection of the key attribute for promotional messages must depend on target market needs. Nevertheless, earlier *Research & Investigation* should provide a host of creative possibilities from which to choose.

Sources of creative ideas include the following:

- *Company characteristics* – contemporary, big, expertise, helpful, resources, service facilities;
- *Company heritage* – 'established in year XYZ', the qualities of tradition, years of experience on which to call;
- *Comparison with competitors* – product comparison, rather than 'knocking copy' – factual statements about why a product is better are more effective than statements which denigrate rivals;
- *Disadvantages of non-use* – resultant drawbacks, missed opportunities;
- *Newsworthiness* – new or improved, topical events, company anniversaries;
- *Product characteristics* – availability (or rarity), country of origin, disposable/refillable, performance in use;
- *How the product is made* – raw materials, method of manufacture, quality control systems;
- *Price characteristics* – credit terms and financial margins, lasts longer, money off, cheaper (or more expensive);
- *Surprising facts* – about the product, users or usage;
- *User characteristics* – experts use it, most firms use it;
- *Ways of using the product* – particularly for multi-use products.

PREPARATION OF CAMPAIGN PROPOSALS – THE MESSAGE

This list necessarily overlaps the sources for industrial news stories listed in Chapter 16.

PUBLIC RELATIONS MESSAGES

PR messages differ in purpose from other promotional messages, but must equally be approached from the target market's standpoint. The questions to which journalists want answers are 'Who, What, When, Where, and Why?'.

Equally important is Presentation of the PR message, and the Institute of Public Relations' guidelines are reproduced in Appendices 1–3.

MESSAGE PRESENTATION

Just as no book can make the reader a skilled writer, none can produce expert graphic designers, layout artists, typographers or visualisers. This chapter can, however, draw attention to certain basic principles.

As discussed earlier, the promotional message must be so presented that it wins the battle for target market attention. Depending on the medium, however, this battle for attention may be partly won already. It is important to consider, for example, if messages are intrusive or welcome in the medium.

When designing material to attract attention, it is equally important for the Promotion Manager not to lose his own battle – many created media and advertisements are cluttered, or have components which conflict.

THE ELEMENTS OF DESIGN

Elements of design include visual presentation of the message's written components – headline, sub-headings, captions, and main text, which may in turn include other elements to be featured visually: company symbol/logotype, coupon text, and company name and address.

The layout of material should, like the text, have a logical sequence and follow, for example, the AIDA format – attracting attention through a benefit featured in headline and illustration, followed by text which converts interest into desire, leading through to visual presentation of the 'action' line. Printed messages which follow this (or perhaps the ACCA or ATR) format are more effective than those which leave readers to find their own way through the maze.

The 'balance' of presentation can influence how the target market receives a promotional message, and two alternative approaches are possible – symmetric and asymmetric. In the former the message elements are presented with even balance, while in the latter selected elements receive more emphasis than others.

Another device is that of 'contrast' – too even a presentation can prove unattractive or even boring. Attention can be attracted and maintained by contrasts – use of different colours, of black and white areas, or of text and illustration.

'Repetition' can play its part in presentation, with repeating patterns of text (or illustrations) acting as attention devices, and contributing to both contrast and balance.

These different elements must, however, be united harmoniously; there should be focus and impact, rather than disjointed elements in conflict. White space is important here and the Promotion Manager must avoid the mistake made by inexperienced executives whose attitude is 'I've paid £X for this, so I'm not going to waste a single centimetre'. The outcome is an overcrowded layout, with no white space to place emphasis on headline and illustration, to balance the various components, and lead the eye logically through them.

ILLUSTRATIONS AND COLOUR

The saying 'One picture is worth a thousand words' applies to business-to-business just as much as other communications – an effective illustration can attract attention and also 'demonstrate' product benefits. There are various types of illustration – line drawings, photography and phototechniques, wash drawings, or combinations thereof.

Illustrations – as well as headlines and body copy – may be strengthened by use of colour and, once again, various approaches are possible. Rather than print in standard black and white, the extra expense of colour may be well worthwhile: perhaps to illustrate products (or people benefiting from their use) in natural colour. Although termed 'full' colour, it is in fact achieved by printing in only four standard colours. An intermediate stage between single and full colour is 'second colour': material is printed in two colours – black and one other, red for example, which is used both to attract attention and emphasise parts of the message.

If producing multi-language colour material, useful guidelines for keeping expenses to a minimum are given on page 191.

In some cases it may be possible, by special arrangement with media-owners or printers, to print in special colours. This technique proved most effective, for example, with an aluminium producer who printed his advertisements in silver. This approach was extended when advertisements printed on aluminium foil were bound into published copies. On occasion existing media can be used to distribute created media, when a catalogue or leaflet is reprinted within selected publications or included as loose inserts. This procedure has sometimes been reversed, by arranging for media-owners to reprint catalogues (or advertisements) printed in their publications, thereby avoiding duplicate typesetting and preparation charges. These examples show yet again the inseparability of creative, media and production aspects.

TYPOGRAPHY

The message text, to which so much effort is devoted, must be presented in an attractive manner. Typography can enhance – or destroy – message delivery. Appropriate typefaces can increase legibility and develop a distinct company image. Equally important is typographic layout – lines of excessive length are difficult to read, unless they are 'leaded' (with horizontal spacing between lines, which occupies valuable space, perhaps unnecessarily). An alternative approach is lines of shorter length, with text set in columns.

Sub-headings serve a double purpose – they can lighten a heavy layout and make it visually more attractive, at the same time as they emphasise key points of the message. Booklets or other printed material which present readers with unattractive 'walls of words' can be made more digestible by appropriate use of sub-heads.

CONSTRAINTS

Various constraints may limit both message content and presentation. These can take many forms.

- *Legal and Voluntary* – there are laws and codes, discussed elsewhere, which affect both the content and presentation of promotional messages.
- *Process imposed* – the media selected to distribute the message may impose restraints: the printing process, for example, may make it impossible to include high-quality illustrations.
- *Media imposed* – some media-owners impose their own restrictions on material they accept. When text is reversed, white-on-black, for example, or very large type used for headlines, they are understandably concerned about possible 'show through' (ink soaking through to the other side of the page) or 'set off' (when ink transfers to the facing page).
- *Size/length imposed* – the size of advertisement or proposed booklet clearly imposes limits on the number of words that can appear. If size remains the same, the more words to be included then the smaller the typeface necessary.
- *Reader/Viewer capability* – the smaller the typeface used, the greater the likelihood the target market will be unable to read it. The same applies to audio-visual media: it is always possible to include more words by speeding up rate of delivery, but few listeners can comprehend a gabbled message!

Ideally, such restraints will have been ascertained at *Research & Investigation* stage, and creative planning undertaken accordingly.

CONTINUITY

'House style' or corporate identity can enhance the value of each individual message, since target markets then recognize company communications, all of which help build a favourable brand image. Communications which, although individually sound, chop and change from one message to another and one style to another, miss a great potential. Similarly, when using a range of media, the Promotion Manager should strive for 'synergism' or transfer. When this is achieved, the impact on the target market is increased by this multiple approach – the stimulus delivered by press advertising and editorial comment is reinforced by a direct mail shot and an exhibition stand which, in their turn, reflect audio-visual media and printed material.

OTHER MEDIA

These comments on message content and presentation have been expressed mainly in terms of print, since this is the largest medium in terms of its many forms – not only thousands of newspapers and magazines, but also direct mail and created media such as house journals and product literature.

The points made nevertheless apply to other media, subject to being adapted as necessary. It is important, for example, to take full advantage of the creative qualities of audio-visual media. Equally, the various message components should complement rather than conflict with each other – imagine a company video in which the 'voice over' delivers the wrong message (with too many words for the time available), while the vision demonstrates a different sales point, at the same time as an on-screen caption (too small to be read easily, but large enough to obscure the demonstration) distracts attention with yet a third message. It is more than doubtful if viewers would receive any effective communication! When creating audio-visual or other media, the Promotion Manager must therefore adopt a practical approach.

THE NEXT STEP

Having decided the marketing communications messages, the next step is to devise a media plan which delivers them to target markets as effectively as possible.

CHAPTER TWENTY-FOUR

Preparation of Campaign Proposals – The Media

MEDIA IN CONTEXT

The last chapter discussed promotional messages' content. It also established that it is misleading to talk of campaign planning: it is more correct to talk of campaigns in the plural. Each campaign should comprise multiple promotional activities: the advertising and editorial columns of existing media, together with created media such as merchandising and sales promotion. Within each activity are two distinct but inter-related aspects: the messages to be delivered (as discussed in the last chapter), and media to deliver them. This chapter concentrates on media planning.

THE MEDIA BRIEF

Earlier chapters on *Research & Investigations* and on *Setting Specific Campaign Objectives* detailed much of the information needed to plan promotional media effectively. Parts of the full 'media brief' were not available at those stages, however – the budget had not been decided, nor had message requirements been established.

MESSAGE/MEDIA INTERACTION

Media and message staff must agree how best to reach the target market: perhaps by news releases to an agreed broad group of publications, and/or advertisements of a certain size within these same media. Media staff must feel this preliminary agreement permits effective planning, while creative staff must similarly accept that the preliminary plan gives sufficient scope to express the promotional message persuasively. For created media, the same agreement is equally vital.

Message and media interests then set about their separate tasks. Creative staff prepare news release text and photographs together with advertisement copy and design proposals, while the next step for media staff is to plan in detail how to spend the appropriation so as to get maximum value for money, within the broad media groups agreed.

The two aspects of promotion – choosing media and preparing messages – are complementary, and message considerations directly affect media proposals. If an advertising schedule, for example, proposes half-pages in two colours in certain publications, this implies a creative decision that detailed written messages, together with relevant illustrations, can be delivered through advertisements of half-page size in press media, with a second colour available to highlight key points. At the same time, it is equally a media decision to book a number of two-colour half-pages in selected publications on certain dates at a cost of £X. Creative and media decisions are therefore usually taken simultaneously, but the dominant aspect could be either message or media. Media selection may be determined, for example, by the creative need for personal contact, for opportunity to demonstrate a product, or to describe and illustrate it in fine detail. Alternatively, creative needs may be overshadowed by the marketing need to inform a clearly defined target group, which one medium covers more effectively than others, through both advertising and editorial columns.

Media decisions overlap creative in another way, when attracting potential purchasers' attention. As was made clear earlier, it is insufficient to create a strong message and then place it in a suitable medium: positive steps must be taken to attract target market attention.

If the creative message follows the AIDA formula, for example, there are immediate media implications. The use of media devices (such as size and position) to attract *Attention* clearly affects planning, and the same is true of many 'action' devices. If the campaign objective is customer action, this may demand selection of media which facilitate direct response. Examples such as coupons in press advertisements, reader reply cards in magazines, stamped addressed envelopes sent with direct mail shots, or reply services on television and radio, all clearly illustrate how the final *Action* checkpoint has media implications just as direct as the opening Attention factor. Even the other two checkpoints – *Interest* and *Desire* – influence media choice: some media deliver audiences mentally 'tuned in' to specialist business areas, and therefore more receptive to relevant promotional messages. The same principle applies to specific positions within media, which similarly deliver audiences who, by reading that page's editorial, demonstrate their *Interest*. These self-selected readers are more likely to progress to the *Desire* stage of the hierarchy of effects, and are thus prospects for *Action*: actual purchase.

MEDIA ALLOCATIONS

The first step in devising any promotional plan is to divide the overall budget into separate allocations for each communications medium on which the campaign will be based – so much for advertising, so much for public relations, so much for merchandising and sales promotion, so much for other created media, and so on. This is sometimes called the 'Inter-Media' decision or 'Media Split' stage. A number of factors influence this decision, including:

- *The Product* – with complex products, effective promotion may demand emphasis on printed material or other created media, which can deliver a detailed message. Other products may call for media which facilitate demonstration or 'hands on' experience;
- *Product Life Cycle* – a new product is *news* and so calls for public relations activity, just as much as for advertising and sales promotion activity to induce the crucial initial trial or enquiry. After the launch, news value is reduced and promotional effort may transfer to reminder advertising. Later

still, emphasis may shift to advertisements and news releases which suggest additional product uses. At decline stage, emphasis may return to Sales Promotion, with special incentive offers to stimulate falling sales;
- *The Market* – the nature of the market and its buying-decision process also affect the media split – much sales promotion aims, through offers of informative booklets, to satisfy the market's need for information. Seminars and conferences can similarly directly help buyers (and sellers);
- *Marketing Policy* – the number, size and relative value of sales areas directly influence both media selection and the allocation of expenditure. If selling direct, the media split can be determined by the need for media which result in sales leads. If selling through agents or distributors, the need to list names and addresses can influence both media choice and message content;
- *Competition* – competitive activity can similarly influence the media split – if competitors dominate a particular medium, the Promotion Manager may need to concentrate his limited funds in another, where he is not out-spent by rivals;
- *Previous Activity* – as already established, promotional planning should be a circular process: evaluation of the results of last year's media split should influence this year's media allocations.

These various factors clearly reinforce the importance of thorough analysis at the earlier *Research & Investigation* stage.

British Business Press's survey of 'How British Business Advertises' lists a number of factors influencing company budget allocations to promotional activity. These included, in order of importance:

1. This year's special needs/activities
2. Product/market developments
3. Performance evaluation of media used
4. Previous year's media proportion
5. Market research findings
6=Departmental requests
6=Creative requirements

Newly-appointed Promotion Managers are often surprised to learn – the hard way, alas – that the perfect campaign is rarely produced at first attempt. As there is no *one* right answer, planners consider many alternative ways of spending the budget, evaluating one possible plan against others, before reaching a decision. The plan finally selected may be the outcome of calculating and then assessing perhaps dozens of alternatives.

Should the appropriation be provisionally divided, for example, between advertising and public relations, then possible plans for these two media will be prepared and overall costings compared: if effective advertising coverage can be achieved well within the provisional allocation, but additional funding is required to mount a satisfactory public relations campaign (or *vice versa*) then the media split will be changed and inter-media allocations adjusted accordingly. In practice, budget divisions are usually far more complex, with further allocations for merchandising and sales promotion as well as other created media. However many media the plan features, alternative costings are prepared and assessed until a suitable balance is achieved. The same principle of constructing alternative possibilities, and consequent adjustment, applies within any one media group.

MARKET WEIGHTING

Whether planning advertising, merchandising, public relations, sales promotion, or other created media, the problem is not simply to decide the degree to which they should feature in the final plan. The underlying problem is how the appropriation should be spread over the year, how it should be divided between different marketing areas, and what weight of promotion should be directed to each product line or to different target groups.

This is frequently decided on a 'case rate' basis, by which expenditure is allocated in direct proportion to sales. Thus if Sales Area A accounts for 30 per cent of total purchases, it seems logical to devote 30 per cent of the budget to stimulating that area. The allocation of expenditure across the year may be decided in the same way, according to each month's sales figures: months when the market is strong in terms of actual purchases thus receive heavier promotion than those when sales figures indicate that buyers are not responsive. Similar arguments can be applied when allocating promotional effort to product lines, and to different market segments.

Case rate spending provides a logical basis for promotional planning but, as explained later, an organization may deliberately depart from this planning base for sound marketing reasons.

DETAILED PLANNING

Within any media group, the same process of constructing alternative plans and consequent adjustment applies, just as for deciding the media split. Whether planning advertising, public relations, sales promotion or merchandising, or creating media, no organization will have sufficient funds to undertake *all* the many activities it would wish. Promotional planning is thus a matter of establishing priorities as well as considering alternatives – which campaign requirements are essential, and which could receive less emphasis?

Taking into account the proposed length of campaign, the types of promotional activity required, the ideal frequency of stimulus, and the candidate media that initially appear most suitable within each media group, the first step is to cost out a preliminary plan. The likelihood of these calculations resulting in a sum which precisely matches the allocation is small, so alternative possibilities are costed. Should the preliminary arithmetic exceed the allocation then expenditure must be cut back, and the Promotion Manager must evaluate the best way to do this. At the most basic level, there are four ways in which the preliminary plan can be adjusted. These are:

1. PROMOTION UNIT

One way to balance the budget would be to reduce advertisement size – and the last chapter warned that *very* large sizes are sometimes counter-productive. Another solution might be to dispense with the use of colour, of special positions or of peak time. Public relations savings might be achieved by moving press receptions to less expensive venues, or by reducing the hospitality extended. Similarly, the tangible incentives offered in merchandising and sales promotion activities could also be reduced.

If essential creative or other requirements make these alternatives unacceptable, other possibilities must be considered.

2. FREQUENCY

Another solution might be to reduce frequency and have, for example, advertisements on alternate weeks rather than every week, or to publish the house journal on a monthly rather than weekly basis. Although frequency is a basic variable, little is known *in detail* about its effects. Is there a minimum frequency requirement for business markets, and does light or heavy usage of a product equate with light or heavy exposure to the campaign? The possible effects of high frequency should also be considered, together with the campaign's *creative* content. Over-exposure to promotion may perhaps be counter-productive, and call for frequent change of message presentation for sake of variety. Reduction in frequency could thus achieve a double saving: the link between media planning and creative and production costs is again apparent.

Marketing requirements may however mean frequency reduction is unacceptable, and other alternatives must therefore be considered.

3. DURATION

Another route to reducing expenditure is to curtail the campaign and, rather than maintain it for a full year, omit periods when sales are minimal. This is not just a matter of how long the campaign runs, but also of its effects on the target market. What is the 'life' of a campaign, and what happens when a company stops communicating? A natural decline is inherent in any market and those remaining need regular reminders but, should promotion cease, how fast would its effect decay and how swiftly would sales fall? How strong is consumer loyalty and what contribution does promotion make to maintaining this loyalty? Under this heading the Promotion Manager must again consider the campaign's creative content. How quickly will the current campaign 'wear out', and how swiftly should it be replaced with a new one? This will in turn be affected by the previous variable – the frequency with which the target market receives promotional messages.

Marketing demands may again mean that target groups cannot be left without stimulus. There is, therefore, a fourth possibility to consider.

4. MEDIA LIST

The budget could be made to balance by reducing the number of media included in the promotional campaign. This reduction might be achieved in two ways. One could be *inter-media* – perhaps there are insufficient funds to mount campaigns through the full range of marketing communications media: advertising and editorial columns, backed by merchandising and sales promotion and other created media. This means in fact returning to the media split stage.

Alternatively, the cut-back could be *intra-media*, by reducing the number of publications included in the advertising schedule, cutting the house journal print run, limiting the range of facility visits offered, or reducing the numbers sent news releases or invited to press conferences. This intra-media restriction makes it possible to maintain the necessary weight of promotion in the selected media retained.

The implications of inter-media and intra-media restrictions are examined later.

The possible permutations for making budgets balance are thus basically four: dominance (in terms of level of activity), campaign duration, continuity, and the media list. Each possibility must take into account *non-media* considerations such as creative requirements, the various market segments and how often buyers must be reminded, and the sales campaign's duration.

The problem of adjusting these four basic variables is complicated by the fact that initial costings are only indicative, and a starting point for hard bargaining at the later execution stage. Furthermore, there are other possibilities to be explored:

MARKET WEIGHTING RECONSIDERED

The need to balance budgets often leads to reconsidering case-rate spending. Expenditure proportionate to sales is perhaps a chicken and egg situation. Should 30 per cent of budget be spent to maintain 30 per cent of sales – or were 30 per cent of sales (in this area or month or from that product line or market segment) achieved simply because the Promotion Manager devoted to it 30 per cent of expenditure? Two alternative strategies – increased or decreased promotion – are both based on *potential* as distinct from actual sales.

A. *Increased Promotion*. The Promotion Manager may allocate more than the case-rate proportion, to boost a particular month or area or market segment, on the marketing assumption that a potential increase could be achieved by added stimulus. Hence the promotional decision to step up activities in the selected area, market segment or time of year. This heavier weight of campaign may be financed by the other alternative to case-rate spending which, rather than calling for additional expenditure, actually releases funds.

B. *Decreased Promotion*. The marketing assumption here is that demand, in economic terms, is inelastic. At certain times of year, for example, cash flow problems mean some organizations keep their spending to a minimum. No amount of heavy promotion can persuade them to buy more, since they just do not have the cash to do so. There is, however, a minimum they must buy – and would do so even without promotional stimulus. Conversely, one loyal market segment might need fewer reminders and thus require lower frequency of stimulus. Hence the decision to decrease the weight of promotion directed to a particular month or market, in the belief that sales will remain stable even when promotion is reduced.

Balancing the four basic variables (promotional unit, frequency, campaign duration and media list) and re-examining case-rate spending offer numerous planning possibilities but, if these do not meet the organization's needs, further permutations can be considered.

MULTIPLE-SIZE CAMPAIGNS

Many campaigns are based on a variety of promotional units rather than featuring one uniform size throughout, thus opening a new possibility in the media 'balancing act'. In advertising terms, for example, the campaign may open with a half-page advertisement, followed by quarter-page advertisements for the next three weeks, reverting to a half-page advertisement and more quarter-pages in a repeating pattern. Use of two sizes achieves both impact and repetition. When launching a new product a third and very dominant size, perhaps a full-page, is sometimes used, simply for its merchandising effect on dealers and to provide representatives with a powerful sales tool in persuading them to stock and promote the new product. The same multiple-size approach can be applied to other media: many successful television and radio campaigns comprise longer commercials supplemented by shorter 'edits'. Similarly, merchandising and sales promotion campaigns can alternate between major and minor incentives. The need for creative staff to work in full co-operation with media planners, in ensuring that the promotional message can be presented flexibility, is again apparent.

DRIP *VS* BURST

A variation on the increased/decreased promotion and multiple-size approaches is to plan campaigns on a 'burst' rather than 'drip' basis. The drip approach implies steady promotion over time, on the assumption that 'constant dripping wears away a stone'. The burst approach, however, concentrates resources into a limited number of weeks to achieve a heavier weight of promotion within that period. A burst campaign comprises periods of heavy promotion, followed by periods of inactivity, in an alternating pattern. This version of multiple-size planning incorporates the increase/decrease approach, in that one multiple size is 'zero', ie promotion is completely cut in some weeks in order to boost the others. The advantage of the burst approach is that it concentrates campaign impact. The drawback is that it can result in uneven demand and thus cause stock control or sales leads problems. There is also the problem of 'decay' – how quickly will market memory fade in the intervals between bursts?

MULTI-MEDIA CAMPAIGNS

Multi-media proposals are difficult, laborious and time-consuming, but few campaigns are based on a single promotional vehicle: most employ various media at the same time. The economists' law of diminishing returns can, however, apply to promotional planning just as much as to other types of expenditure. When one medium carries a sufficient weight of promotion, it may not merit additional expenditure. Alternative media are therefore considered for this very reason, and also because they can reach the same market but by another means, for variety of impact. The marginal budgeting method outlined earlier can be applied to media in combination – will the last £X,000 spent on the first medium be as productive as the same £X,000 spent in alternative media?

The term 'media in combination' raises again two considerations touched on earlier: inter-media and intra-media campaigns. One concerns the media split stage and refers to multi-media campaigns which cover, for example, press advertising, merchandising, public relations and sales promotion. The inter-media consideration concerns media within a group, eg, within press using publications X *and* Y (*or* Z?). Both aspects of the term present promotional planners with the problem of distinguishing duplication from net extra coverage. These considerations in turn affect other variables such as opportunities-to-see, cumulative coverage, and frequency distribution, discussed on page 271.

A. Duplication. Duplication means contacting the same market by alternative means. All media duplicate to some extent, since business executives read newspaper and magazine editorial and advertisements, visit exhibitions, receive direct mail, watch TV and so on. The effect of duplication on the media audience is to change one basic variable: frequency. If monthly contact with prospective buyers is required, then monthly appearances in two media whose coverage overlaps means those who see both media receive double the necessary frequency. Two alternatives then present themselves: to maintain monthly appearances in one medium and delete the other from the plan, or to use the two media in alternate months. The latter decision maintains regularity, but gives this market segment a monthly stimulus through alternative means.

Although the campaign delivers the same message, the target groups receive it through a new medium for fresh impact, often with a different environment – through editorial rather than advertising columns, or at home rather than at work. There are important creative considerations, as some media groups are more complementary than others when used in combination. The term 'synergism' (or transfer) describes, for example, the degree to which those who see a given TV commercial re-create the visual component when the soundtrack triggers their memories. TV *plus* radio is the obvious example, but the same principle of beneficial 'transfer' with one medium reinforcing the other, applies to other combinations.

When media are *not* directly synergistic – specialist press, direct mail and exhibitions, for example – the Promotion Manager should, through creative planning, ensure that different campaign components nevertheless re-inforce each other, thus achieving synergism.

B. Net Extra Coverage. If duplication (and thus undue repetition) is to be avoided, planners must seek media which reach new potential purchasers to whom no promotional message has yet been delivered. Two additional media might be candidates for inclusion in a promotional plan. One could have much higher readership than the other, and would initially seem a better proposition. However, if the majority of these readers are already covered by current media, this means an unnecessarily high frequency of contact with these executives. If, on the other hand, the smaller readership avoids duplication, then this medium reaches entirely new prospects who have to date received no promotional messages. Net extra coverage thus increases the campaign's overall penetration. A variation of the net extra coverage approach is to select media which rectify any weaknesses in the coverage of those media already on the schedule, or adjust the frequency distribution discussed on page 271.

PREPARATION OF CAMPAIGN PROPOSALS – THE MEDIA

Duplication and net extra coverage reflect contrasting marketing objectives. If the campaign aim is to reach as many prospective buyers as possible (even if with only a single message) then the plan should seek net extra coverage and thus maximum penetration. If, however, the promotional objective is to achieve maximum repetition, duplication of coverage is preferable. In practice, however, no organization is likely to want a campaign at either *extreme* end of this scale.

C. *Cumulative Coverage.* Coverage is the proportion of the target group with at least one opportunity to receive the promotional message. The average number of people reading a publication remains relatively constant, but the same people do not necessarily read every issue. Additional messages in a series can thus add new readers, thereby increasing cumulative coverage (as well as giving those already reached an additional 'opportunity-to-see'). Cumulative cover in this sense reflects the campaign's overall penetration.

D. *Opportunities-to-see.* How many promotional messages will the target market receive? The answer to this question is often termed the average 'OTS' or opportunities-to-see (or hear). This is defined as the number of potential exposures received by the average reader/viewer/listener. Average OTS or OTH figures must be treated with care, for they can conceal major differences in the number of opportunities open to different members of the target groups.

E. *Frequency Distribution.* This term gives a detailed breakdown of opportunities-to-see across target groups. Coverage is very often linked with the numbers of opportunities-to-see (2+, 3+, 4+ and so on, for example), quantifying the percentage of the audience likely to have that stated number of opportunities to see the campaign. Frequency distribution should reflect the market weightings discussed earlier. The vital need for a full promotional briefing is again apparent.

F. *Added Cost.* There are thus different ways of mounting multi-media campaigns: all change yet another variable – cost. In addition to the cost of media as such, there is the added expense – in terms of creative and production time and effort as well as money – of preparing material for them. Multi-media campaigns have cost implications which extend beyond media selection, and emphasize the vital need to establish a clear campaign objective.

RESOLVING THE INEVITABLE CONFLICT

Balancing these numerous variables necessarily involves some element of conflict. The Promotion Manager must avoid trying to meet *all* requirements, since it is unlikely there are sufficient funds to do so. Balancing the variables by merely reaching a compromise is likely to result in ineffective promotion. *All* promotional plans necessarily represent some degree of compromise, however – to satisfy the full requirements for one of the basic media variables probably means having to fall short on the others. It is important, therefore, to establish the relative importance of impact versus duration, coverage rather than repetition, and the priority of other factors. Trying to satisfy all requirements equally may lead to the appropriation being so widely spread that the promotional campaign ceases to have any impact.

To avoid a weak compromise, many practitioners advocate the well-established 'concentration-domination-repetition' principle. They plan campaigns that concentrate promotional effort within a limited range of media. Within those media, rather than place messages in the hope that people will see them, they dominate each medium by use of the attention devices discussed earlier. Finally, since existing customers need reminding and there are always new entrants to the market, messages are repeated regularly.

THE SHOTGUN PRINCIPLE

The very opposite approach to promotional planning is the 'shotgun' principle. This alternative approach is often followed by those organizations with fragmented markets which cannot be defined by conventional criteria. It may be impossible to 'concentrate' on clear but widely diffused markets (such as firms with cash flow or security problems, for example, or which need temporary buildings on a short-term basis) when there may be no medium, or group of media, giving specific coverage of these target groups. If concentration-domination-repetition is not possible, an alternative strategy is to pepper these diffused markets on the shotgun principle, often with a wide spread of small advertisements which, through their headlines, select potential purchasers from the total media audience reached. Many 'shotgun' schedules are then followed by individual campaigns aimed at any specific user categories which, by their response, indicate they are likely target markets. The shotgun approach has in such cases clearly served a market research function.

MEDIA PLANNING STAGES

There are thus two distinct stages to promotional planning. First comes the arithmetical chore of costing and balancing alternative plans. Second, and more important, is evaluating these possible plans to select the best. The second task involves just as much arithmetic as the first, in assessing factual data about coverage and costs. Many organizations now use computers to assist in these calculations. Assessing alternative plans also involves, however, value judgements about qualitative factors such as the means by which the message is communicated, and the prospective purchasers' state of mind when they receive it through editorial or advertising columns, or through one medium rather than another.

THE NEXT STEP

With campaign plans prepared – the message proposals reviewed in the last chapter, and the media proposals just discussed – the Promotion Manager's next step is to evaluate them carefully, to ensure they will achieve the company's chosen objectives.

CHAPTER TWENTY-FIVE

Approval of Promotional Proposals

Approving campaign proposals is more complex a matter than it would first appear. Time is needed to review proposals overall, to check the text of proposed advertisements and PR material, to consider the media schedule and press circulation lists, to assess proposals for merchandising, sales promotion or other created media, and to ensure all component parts of the campaign interlock. When the campaign plan is a complex one, this task may take some weeks. Sometimes campaign approval is an on-going procedure rather than a single task but, even with relatively simple proposals, it is rarely possible to give an instant OK since approval has repercussions which extend far beyond promotion alone.

Before campaign proposals can be approved, they must be checked from several different standpoints. The assessment process has both interesting and routine aspects: where many executives slip up is that eagerness to consider the more glamourous creative aspects means they sometimes overlook checking the duller internal and external background on which the campaign is based. In consequence, basic errors can easily pass unnoticed. While there is no single perfect solution to any company's marketing problem, there can be many imperfect ones! My practice is to check the two duller aspects before the interesting: others may prefer to reverse the order but, either way, it is essential to evaluate proposals from both standpoints.

It is important to scrutinise proposals meticulously before giving approval: it is equally important to do so as swiftly as possible. Early approval gives more time for execution, thus preventing the mistakes which so often occur with rush jobs. Delay in approving PR proposals, quite apart from increasing the possibility of error, can result in missed deadlines and thus missed opportunities. Swift approval can also lead to cost savings: undue delay – particularly on the advertising side – can result in the Promotion Manager finding all the best positions already booked by competitors, and having to bid at high rates for the few remaining spaces! Buying created media at the last minute can similarly prove very expensive.

INTERNAL ASPECTS

The first step before planning any promotion was investigations into firm and product, market and marketing policy, previous promotional activity, restraints and competition. Preparation of proposals took time, however, and it is therefore essential to check whether things have changed in the interim.

If *major* changes had occurred, promotional planning should of course have returned to the initial *Research & Investigation* stage, since the changes are of such importance that they affect the entire planning base.

This chapter, however, is concerned with changes of relatively minor importance. If proposals are not amended accordingly, however, these changes could weaken (and in extreme cases completely undermine) campaign effectiveness.

Numerous minor changes may have taken place since the original investigations. For example, the original marketing plan might have been to launch a product in a number of sizes. If subsequent production problems necessitate a minor reduction in the range, then message proposals must clearly be amended – there is no point in stimulating demand for a size which will not be available. Such promotion would result in disappointed buyers and perhaps an increase in sales of competitors' products.

Similarly, if proposals list addresses and telephone numbers (of sales offices, dealers or agents) it is vital to check if the list has altered in the meantime: many promotion executives have been embarrassed through insufficient attention to such details when colleagues complain about the 'old address' appearing in promotional material! Much the same can be said about price listings. Message content can easily be amended to take account of such minor changes.

The Promotion Manager must also ensure that media timings dovetail with marketing activities. To assist representatives in their selling task, the campaign could include press advertisements phased over time to obtain a steady flow of sales leads, and direct mail (phased in with individual journey cycles) to herald the call. Campaign timing is vital, and promotional proposals must interlock with marketing activities. Equally, it is usually unwise to stimulate the market before products are ready for prospects to buy. If for some reason operations are not proceeding precisely to plan, then either the company must take action to remedy the breakdown, or alternatively promotional proposals must be amended to take account of the changes.

Promotional proposals seek to solve a particular problem, but the problem itself may change: the Promotion Manager must therefore check such eventualities before approving any campaign proposals. Clearly, approval cannot always be immediate, for it may necessitate consultations with production, sales or transport managers, and many others.

EXTERNAL ASPECTS

Before considering the campaign's creative aspects, it is necessary to check proposals from another less interesting but nevertheless vital aspect: that of background constraints. There are numerous legal and voluntary controls which affect promotion.

All executives involved in promotion should certainly obtain a copy of the *British Code of Advertising Practice*, published by the CAP Committee, Brook House, Torrington Place, London WC1. Under the general supervision of the Advertising Standards Authority, the Code has the support of the industry organizations representing advertisers, agencies and media-owners, whose representatives constitute the CAP Committee. As the Code itself points out, its rules are not the only ones relevant to advertising. There are many provisions, both in the common law and in statutes, which concern the form or the content of advertisements.

APPROVAL OF PROMOTIONAL PROPOSALS

High on the list must come the new Control of Misleading Advertisements Regulations which came into effect in June 1988. The Trade Descriptions Act of 1968 is enforced by the Trading Standards Department of Local Authorities, while the Office of Fair Trading has a Misleading Advertising Section. Investment-related advertising is regulated by the Financial Services Act of 1986.

The Code of Advertising Practice does not replace the law: its rules, and the machinery through which they are enforced, are designed to complement legal controls.

This Code does not apply to independent television and radio commercials which are subject to a separate, closely related *Code of Advertising Standards and Practice*, administered by the Independent Broadcasting Authority (IBA) of 70 Brompton Road, London SW3 1EY. There is also a supplementary *Code for Teletext Transmissions*, covering Oracle advertisements.

It has become almost universal practice to forward scripts of proposed TV advertisements for clearance in advance of production. The IBA's Advertising Control Division and a specialist advertising copy clearance group set up by the programme companies work in close co-operation: scripts are considered in relation to the Code to ensure that the commercials in their final form are likely to comply with the Code. In due course specialist staff of the Authority and programmes companies join in closed-circuit viewing of finished commercials before they are finally approved for broadcasting, to ensure that they conform to the agreed script and there is nothing unacceptable about the tone and style of presentation, or other aspects of the subject treatment.

Control of radio advertisements is equally thorough: all advertisements for independent local radio must comply with the IBA Code which, originally drawn up for television, was amended to take into account the special requirements of radio.

Other individual media may have their own Codes, and there is also *The British Code of Sales Promotion Practice*. In addition, various professional membership organizations have their own codes of conduct.

The earlier R & I chapter stressed, under 'Constraints', the need to be aware of such legal and voluntary controls. These controls are not static, however: like products or the marketing situation they too may have changed since the initial briefing, so campaign approval necessitates re-checking, as a necessary safety measure. Quite apart from being desirable in its own right, such double-checking can avoid the consequences of failure to comply – consider those unfortunate organizations which find themselves deprived of promotional support through lack of acceptable material (quite apart from having wasted considerable funds in producing these unacceptable items).

In this respect, The Promotion Manager should recognize that many of the central bodies have an advisory as well as a policing function. In addition to their external supervisory and public function as recipients of complaints, they also serve an internal industry function and can be most helpful in giving practical advice in cases of doubt. Advance checking can save time as well as money, quite apart from preventing errors.

With background aspects duly checked, the Promotion Manager can now tackle the more interesting task: evaluating proposals from the communications standpoint.

PROMOTIONAL ASPECTS

Checking campaign proposals is something *everybody* thinks they can do – show an advertisement to a layman and he can always suggest improvements! Much the same comment can be made of merchandising, public relations, sales promotion or proposals for created media.

Even experienced marketing executives often make the understandable mistake of commenting that they like (or do not like) certain proposals. Whether or not *they* like proposals is irrelevant: proposals must be evaluated from the standpoint of the target market at which they are aimed, rather than self-reference criteria. Too many executives look only at the pieces of paper in front of them without 'reasoning back' to check if the proposals integrate with the marketing objective underlying the entire campaign. Before considering any media or message proposals, the Promotion Manager should remind himself of the answers to two vital questions:

WHAT IS THE SPECIFIC CAMPAIGN OBJECTIVE?

As was made clear earlier, it is pointless hoping that proposals will 'increase sales' (or 'improve our image'). How are these increased sales to be achieved – increased purchases by existing users, conversion of new users, or supplier-switch by buyers of rival products? These and other possible objectives discussed earlier affect media selection as well as message content. Good promotional material (whether advertising, merchandising or sales promotion) gives a clear indication of the company's marketing objective and whether increased sales are to be achieved by a source switch from competition, by bringing new users into the market, or by persuading existing purchasers to use more. The objectives for an 'image' campaign should be equally apparent.

WHAT FUNDAMENTAL PROPOSITION WAS SELECTED, TO MAKE THE TARGET GROUP RESPOND?

Crucial to message proposals is analysis of *why* the target group should switch supply sources, use a product more frequently, or buy it for the first time. Of the many appeals that could be made to potential buyers, which is the correct message platform which will trigger them into action? Low cost? Better performance? Effectiveness? Reliability? Value for money? If promotion features the wrong product benefit, out of the many, clearly the campaign will fail to achieve its objective.

Good proposals give a clear portrait of the target purchasers, and their motivation in buying products: studying the material should enable the Promotion Manager to deduce (*without* his prior R & I knowledge) that the target market is analytical chemists, for example, who are motivated by their need for precision measurement facilities.

Only once the answers to these two questions are clearly established can attention be paid to the campaign proposals themselves, and a third vital question be asked.

HOW EFFECTIVELY WILL THIS PROPOSITION BE CONVEYED TO THE SELECTED TARGET GROUP?

This evaluation in turn breaks down into two separate checking operations – media and messages. Procedures will vary according to the medium under review, but the underlying question remains the same.

a) Existing Media – the Advertising Route. When considering advertising proposals, could the creative work be improved? Does the headline convey the selected product benefit effectively, and is this backed up by equally persuasive copy? After preparing creative work, it is advisable to leave it overnight – what the Promotion Manager thought wonderful when he wrote it may later seem poorly structured, long-winded or just badly worded. He should also ask himself some basic questions – is the message benefit-oriented? Believable? Compelling? Complete? Enthusiastic? Informative? Justified? Does it lead to Action? Does the illustration convey the selected proposition to maximum advantage as regards printing quality or transmission, as well as content?

Good creative work is vital for effective promotion, but it is a mistake to seek creativity for its own sake. The campaign must relate to marketing strategy and, when approving campaigns, the Promotion Manager should beware of proposals which sell creative gimmicks rather than products.

It is equally important to check proposals from the media standpoint, to ensure the schedule is as effective as possible in media selection and in use of the selected media. Chapter 24 on the preparation of media proposals outlined the two-stage process – construction of numerous alternative schedules, followed by evaluation to select the best, so this aspect of campaign approval was discussed earlier. It is necessary, however, to set this checking operation in the context of the two preliminary questions – what is the specific objective, and what promotional appeal was selected to appeal to the target group? Only after the answers to these two questions are clearly established is it worth checking the efficiency of the media schedule – there is little point in aiming with great accuracy the wrong missile at the wrong target!

b) Existing Media – the Editorial Route. Approval of PR proposals should be equally thorough, to ensure the old journalistic standby questions of *Who, What, Why, Where, When* and *How* are satisfied, that this information is presented correctly as recommended by the IPR Practice Paper, and that the company does not commit any of the 'Top Ten Errors' listed in Chapter 16.

c) Created Media: Merchandising and Sales Promotion. The same criteria should be adopted when some tangible incentive is offered to push products towards people, or to pull people towards products. It is easy to generate response, by means of a particularly generous offer, but it may be the wrong response from the wrong people for the wrong reason! Hence the importance of subjecting proposals to the same scrutiny.

Other Created Media. Much the same checking procedure should be applied to created media, but two additional questions should be asked – how is the organization to create the necessary audience, and how will the created medium be delivered to it? As Chapter 18 pointed out, audio-visual and printed materials serve no purpose sitting on storeroom shelves.

Having evaluated individual components of the promotional plan, it is essential to ask a fourth fundamental question.

ARE THE PROPOSALS COMPREHENSIVE AND COHESIVE?

a) Comprehensive: The Promotion Manager must ensure that his company is making maximum use of *all* means of marketing communications. Pressure of work can sometimes lead to certain media being overlooked: it is useful, therefore, to return to the concept of message sources to ensure that promotional plans do in fact cover every possible means by which target markets receive messages about the company and its products or services.

b) Cohesive: Approval of proposals must also ensure that the various campaign components interlock. The work-load involved may necessitate looking separately at each campaign component, but an overview must also be taken. Marketing communications effort can be wasted if advertising delivers one promotional message while public relations adopts a different theme, and merchandising and sales promotion activities follow separate paths. Under such circumstances, the target marked would soon become very confused.

Rather than such fragmented effort, the Promotion Manager should strive for a synergistic approach whereby each component reinforces the others, thereby multiplying the media effect.

Similarly, proposals should be cohesive over time, so that all new marketing communications build on and benefit from earlier campaigns.

THE NEXT STEP

Once the Promotion Manager has approved campaign proposals from these standpoints – internal and external background, and promotional aspects – and has checked that they are both comprehensive and cohesive – he is then in a position to confirm that the proposals in their final form should make maximum contribution to achieving company objectives. The next step is to put these proposals into effect.

CHAPTER TWENTY-SIX

Execution of Promotional Proposals

The Promotion Manager's next step is to put the approved proposals into effect: this is more difficult than would first appear, as some campaigns include numerous messages intended for the advertising and editorial columns include a wide range of existing media, as well as merchandising and sales promotion activities, and production of other created media.

The task of executing proposals, like that of preparing them, can be undertaken in different ways. The promotion department may do the work in-house, it may employ an advertising agency or public relations consultancy, or tasks may be shared with these and other external services. Some smaller firms rely on media-owners to implement proposals as well as for help in preparing them.

Whether undertaken in-house or via external services, execution of proposals involves four tasks. One concerns routine implementation and the second the more positive aspect of continuing improvement. The third task involves adjustments following evaluation of results, while the fourth concerns unexpected events.

IMPLEMENTATION OF PROPOSALS

The task of converting proposals into action divides into two broad areas: media and messages. The need for accuracy in both respects is emphasized by media-owners' deadlines, which allow little or no opportunity to correct errors. If a media-owner's press date is 1 September, material is needed by that date if it is to appear on time. For public relations purposes, timing may be even more precise, and is measured by hours (or even minutes) rather than dates. Media-owners' deadlines are difficult if not impossible to postpone.

IMPLEMENTING THE MESSAGES

The text of news releases must be presented in a format acceptable to the Editors to whom it will be sent. Advice on currect presentation is given in the Institute of Public Relations' *Recommended Practice Paper* reproduced in Appendices 1–3.

Advertisement text, and that for created media, must be marked-up for typesetting, and proofs checked. Any necessary artwork or photography must similarly be commissioned, printing plates made, and further proofs checked. Advice on these aspects was given in Chapter 23.

Other promotional media included in proposals must similarly be meticulously implemented and checked.

IMPLEMENTING THE MEDIA

Converting promotional proposals – which are only plans on paper – into firm orders placed with media-owners, or news releases despatched to selected editors, is more than a simple routine operation, although these two operations are in themselves major administrative tasks.

Carelessness can result in many problems. News releases or advertisement orders have sometimes been sent to the wrong publications: this is not as improbable as it would seem, as many similar titles can easily be confused. When booking advertising space, such an error could lead to financial difficulties, since an order placed for unauthorised space may necessitate cancelling some much-needed bookings, to recoup the mispent money. There is no such financial penalty for a misdirected news release, but harm may still be done: the Editor who would have used the release did not receive important information to pass to his readers and, if his was the only publication not to carry the news, considerable ill will could result. The Editor who received the misdirected release will probably not use it, and may be unreceptive in future when the Promotion Manager *does* have something of interest to his readers.

Carelessness could lead to further problems, particularly when simple typing errors occur. If a launch advertisement is scheduled for the 13th, but the space-order is incorrectly marked for the 31st, the company will be deprived of promotional support at a vital time. When the error is discovered (on Friday 13th!), it may be too late to cancel the unwanted booking for the 31st, for which the company is legally liable to pay. Typing errors could cause further financial problems if the true cost of an advertisement is £5,200 but the amount which the Board approved is in fact only £2,500. Should such errors be made by external services rather than in-house, the client is of course under no obligation to pay for unauthorised expenditure.

This administrative chore of converting a single promotional plan into individual orders or news releases should not be under-estimated. Promotional proposals might include advertising and public relations messages for a large number of media: more complex campaigns could cover dozens of different publications – national and local newspapers, specialist and general magazines, as well as television and radio stations, and exhibitions or other media. These proposals must now be converted into individual orders or news releases for each medium concerned, which may possibly total a hundred or more. Each individual order must be accurate as to name of medium, sizes and positions and dates, as well as costs and discounts and other vital items of information. Needless to say, news releases must be accurate as to factual content, as well as presented in an acceptable form. Accuracy in implementation is equally important with other aspects of the plan.

Administrative work is not at an end, however, even after individual advertisement orders have been typed, checked and posted. Reference copies must be filed and careful checks made that all orders are acknowledged by media-owners. Posting an order does not ensure appearance, for the order may perhaps go astray. Such mishaps are infrequent but the consequent absence of promotional support could have damaging effects. To facilitate checking procedures, many order forms incorporate tear-off acknowledgement slips for media-owners' use. Some media-owners return these slips, while others prefer their own 'Acknowledgement of Order' forms: either way, responsibility for checking that orders are duly acknowledged still rests with the advertiser or his agency. Similar follow-up action often follows public relations activity, to check if journalists received news material, or perhaps require further information.

IMPROVING THE PROPOSALS

There are two ways in which promotional plans can be made more effective – by efficient execution, and by continual improvement.

PLANNING *VS* BUYING

Implementing promotional plans is more than simply an administrative task, and the difference between planning and buying is an important one. The extreme case is television advertising, where media proposals might show a series of commercials to be transmitted in various time segments on various future dates. When the plan was prepared, however, it was not known what programmes would be transmitted (and might attract AB business audiences, for example) or what viewing figures would be achieved many months ahead. Accordingly, TV time-buying requires skilled negotiations with TV contractors, to ensure commercials are scheduled for times when they will be seen by the largest number of people in the correct target groups. Similar detailed negotiations are necessary with owners of press and other media.

Buying differs markedly from planning: it demands a highly competitive approach which some practitioners find more stimulating than the earlier planning stage which, in contrast, seems a rather abstract arithmetical exercise. The extreme view was expressed by the cynic who commented that 'The greatest work of fiction of the 20th century was a media-owner's rate card!' Some practitioners argue that the intellectual qualities called for in planning and buying are so diverse that few individuals can do both jobs properly.

Buying created media calls for similar knowledge of the media marketplace, and equally for negotiating skills.

PROPOSAL IMPROVEMENT

Few promotional plans are ever executed exactly as originally planned. Proposals should be kept under constant review and improvements made whenever possible.

Marketing communications media change ceaselessly: new media constantly appear and existing media adapt to new circumstances. This means that if proposals are implemented *exactly* as originally planned, it is more than probable that someone is asleep on the job! The publication of new circulation figures, readership data or the issue of a new rate card should lead to re-examination of advertising proposals, as should the launch of new titles or new information about forthcoming editorial in existing media. Such new information presents fresh opportunities for public relations activity just as much as advertising.

A later chapter examines evaluation of results, but this task should not be left until *after* the campaign has appeared. Performance should be monitored throughout, and improvements can be as important as the original plan. A marginal increase of, say, ten per cent in editorial or advertising coverage is equivalent to a ten per cent budget increase, and so proposals should be kept under constant review and adjusted in the light of subsequent information.

FLEXIBLE EXECUTION

This paragraph could appear in any of three chapters – Preparation or Execution of Proposals, or Evaluation of Results – in recognition that some promotional plans are prepared on a flexible evaluate-as-we-go basis. When launching new products or services to diverse and unknown horizontal markets, with no previous data on which to build, and when the research to provide market information would be unduly expensive, campaigns are often planned on an open-ended basis. Rather than book a series of 12 advertisements (which would secure a series discount saving, but commit expenditure to a medium or market segment of yet unknown value) the initial space order is for a few insertions only, often in horizontal media, with the bulk of expenditure deliberately held in reserve. Response to these advertisements is then evaluated: those media giving value for money remain on the schedule, while those with poor response are removed. Chapter 24 on Media Planning described the 'shotgun' approach in which peppering the market is followed by specific targeting to those market groups which, through their response, revealed themselves as likely purchasers. In such circumstances the four stages of R & I, planning, execution and evaluation are inseparably linked, with promotion also serving a market research function.

In addition, further changes may call for proposal adjustment.

OTHER CHANGES

In addition to normal adjustments, other changes may become necessary from time to time, arising from the inevitable set-backs – and unexpected opportunities – which occur in normal business practice. These changes can be either minor or major.

MINOR CHANGES

Most promotional planners complain that they never have sufficient money at their disposal, but very few budget to spend *all* the appropriation. In preparing proposals, the Promotion Manager should similarly keep part of the appropriation in reserve, recognizing that no amount of forward planning can predict every possible future event. Unforeseen eventualities are bound to occur, and fall into two categories – set-backs and opportunities.

On the negative side, unexpected costs may be incurred if, for example, a photographic session does not go as planned, if media rates increase, or if some other campaign aspects demand unforeseen expenditure. On the positive side, attractive offers may be made by media-owners, and there may be unexpected public relations opportunities.

A contingency reserve allows for both positive and negative eventualities, but deciding the level of contingency reserve means trying to predict the unpredictable! This is a difficult decision for, if the Promotion Manager underestimates and contingencies call for more expenditure than the amount set aside, something must be cancelled to provide the necessary money, and the carefully planned campaign is undermined. If, on the other hand, contingencies are overestimated, it is tempting to fritter away the unspent balance at the end of the year, rather than face criticism from financial staff when seeking future budget increases. A highly volatile market may call for a considerable reserve, while for a stable market a nominal sum might be quite sufficient: the correct amount is often determined by trial and error over time. In some cases, however, the unexpected may be of such magnitude that it is beyond the scope of the contingency reserve.

MAJOR CHANGES

The great effort spent on meticulous promotional planning is sometimes, alas, wasted, because of unexpected events. The analysis was correct when proposals were put forward and approved, but unexpected changes mean the campaign is no longer valid for the new situation. Such circumstances may follow unexpected changes to the entire market, arising from major P-E-S-T developments, or perhaps a new competitor entering the arena.

Under such circumstances, the promotional task is to prepare new proposals in the shortest possible time, to deal effectively with the new situation. The ability to 'bounce back' is as important as handling the new situation with a clear head. Hopefully, however, no major upheavals will occur and contingency reserves will be sufficient to cope with any minor unexpected changes.

In order circumstances, however, major changes may make no call on contingency reserves, but force a cutback in promotion. A fire, explosion or strike which halt the production line all illustrate this possibility, for the Promotion Manager might then halt campaigns which stimulate demand his company cannot satisfy. At worst, the company might face a crisis management situation, as discussed on page 175. At best, after announcing the circumstances, the company might cancel all promotion other than 'progress' news releases or occasional reminder advertisements, until such time as production recommences.

FURTHER ROUTINE ADMINISTRATION

Even after a promotional plan has been booked and acknowledged, various changes are usually necessary as a result of on-going review and improvements, or because of major or minor changes. It may become necessary to transfer a booking from one date to another, for example, or to cancel some planned activity. Often there are special forms for these purposes and 'Amendment Orders' – frequently printed in red for immediate attention – may be issued to effect changes within a series of insertions. Similarly, when cancellations are called for, special 'Stop Orders' are used. As before, Amendment or Stop orders must be meticulously checked, and care taken to see that they are duly acknowledged.

The final comment, before leaving this administrative aspect of promotion, is that a great deal of routine is being taken over by the new technologies.

Computer services can undertake much of the book-keeping work, thus freeing promotion staff for more constructive activities.

THE NEXT STEP

With the campaign now running, the Promotion Manager's next major task is to evaluate its results to see what lessons can be learned for the future. Before proceeding to this final stage, however, a safety precaution is to double check follow-through arrangements, as described in the next chapter.

CHAPTER TWENTY-SEVEN

Follow Through

This chapter is brief – and ideally should be superfluous! If a company invests time, effort and money on promotion to stimulate the market, it is self-evident that it should be ready to cope swiftly with response generated by that promotion.

In practice, however, marketing communications is alas not always fully integrated with other activities. There are many cases where promotion staff, having taken 'follow through' for granted, learned later that unacceptable delays occurred before action was taken. In one extreme case, there were even complaints that an advertisement had caused so much work in answering enquiry letters!

Whilst the Promotion Manager may not be *directly* involved with efficient follow-through, this does not mean he is without responsibility: internal marketing communications should ensure that all concerned are fully briefed in advance, and are ready to take whatever action is necessary (whether this be handling telephone enquiries, despatching literature, or following up sales leads), thus averting wasteful dissipation of effort.

If necessary, workload problems can be contracted out to specialist organizations which undertake the administrative chores involved. There are a number of external services which can handle telephone enquiries, for example. Alternatively, if a campaign features the sales promotion offer of an informative booklet (publicised through both advertising and editorial columns), the Royal Mail's *Admail* service – by which incoming post is re-routed – can be most useful. The organization can cite a local or prestigious Head Office address (subject to Post Office agreement), and yet have purchasers' requests redirected to another office or to a 'fulfilment house' (a service organization which holds booklet or other stocks and posts them on the company's behalf). This can encourage response at the same time as it reduces administrative costs by cutting out internal re-routing of customer enquiries; it also saves valuable time, thus reducing delays in responding to these requests. A word of warning is necessary here – are such costs to be charged against the promotion budget?

THE NEXT STEP

With the campaign now running, the Promotion Manager's next task is to evaluate its results, to see what lessons can be learned for the future.

CHAPTER TWENTY-EIGHT

Evaluation of Results

Evaluating results is an important task for the Promotion Manager. This final stage of promotional planning comprises three inter-related components – checking back, allowing for other influences, and looking ahead.

CHECKING BACK

A first stage in evaluation is the relatively routine task of ensuring that the company got value for money. Did advertisements appear as booked: in the specified positions on the relevant pages on the correct dates? If bookings were run-of-paper, where did media-owners place the advertisements, and how did their position compare with competitors? Was the illustration reproduced to maximum effect as regards printing quality? For industrial clothing or paints, for example, colour variations could detract considerably from an advertisement's effectiveness. Has the publisher, in fact, inserted the correct advertisement? It is not unknown for a media-owner to repeat an advertisement instead of replacing it with a new one as instructed. What about adjacent editorial? A chemical supplies firm would rightly be dissatisfied to find its advertisement on a page featuring an article on chemical pollution (whereas an advertiser whose service is the *prevention* of such possibilities would, of course, be delighted). If advertisements feature coupons, do they back upon others on the reverse of the page? Should this occur, neither advertiser can obtain maximum results. There may be few occasions when the Promotion Manager need take up such matter with media-owners, but mistakes do occur from time to time, and it is essential therefore to examine every voucher copy.

It is equally important to carry out similar checks with all other forms of promotion: created media, direct mail, exhibitions, merchandising, radio and TV commercials, and sales promotion.

Monitoring should similarly check if news releases were carried by the media to which they were sent: public relations results may, however, have been influenced by other events.

ALLOWING FOR OTHER INFLUENCES

When evaluating the results of his company's activities, the Promotion Manager should keep a formal record of those circumstances which, unless allowed for, would give a false impression of campaign effectiveness. Such events should be categorized under four inter-related headings – favourable or unfavourable, one-off or repeat.

On the negative side, if a news release was not carried, perhaps this was due to a major event of far greater news value. If this were a one-off happening, the organization has alas been unfortunate – but it, for example, this more newsworthy item is an annual event, the Promotion Manager would be well advised to re-time releases in future years. The same comment applies to news conferences.

Similar records should be kept of other events which influence promotional effectiveness: a cold spell or heat-wave, for example, will push up enquiries for industrial heating or air-conditioning and, whilst promotion can help channel demand towards the company, it would clearly be incorrect to conclude that it *caused* increased sales. Many events can influence results, favourably or unfavourably: these include strikes, fuel crises and so on.

A detailed record is invaluable in assessing past performance and also serves as a practical guide for future planning, indicating desirable strategies or avoiding action to incorporate within next year's campaigns. Annual events can enhance sales of some products at the same time as they depress others and, if any market is regularly affected in this way, future promotion should be adjusted accordingly.

LOOKING AHEAD

Checking value for money is important, but future improvements represent a far more significant aspect of evaluation.

In order to look forward, however, it is first necessary to look back and ask: did the organization achieve its promotional objective? This question in turn leads straight back to the second stage of promotional planning. First was R & I, gathering information on which to base the plans. Second came setting specific objectives. The final planning stage should complete the circle, with evaluation of this year's results providing additional information on which to base next year's planning.

The direct connection between results and objectives is clearly demonstrated by the DAGMAR concept. This acronym stands for 'Determining Advertising Goals for Measured Advertising Results', an approach developed by R. Colley. The same link should apply to merchandising, public relations or sales promotion planning but, while it is easy to say DAGMAR, the same facility does not apply to DMGMMR, DPRGMPRR or DSPGMSPR! At its most basic, the DAGMAR approach stresses the vital need for a specific objective, and then asks if the company achieved it.

If the objective was achieved, the Promotion Manager should not become complacent – could the campaign have done better? Failure to achieve the objective, on the other hand, could be for various reasons – the objective might have been over-ambitious, or perhaps the promotional campaign was at fault. Alternatively, circumstances may have changed during the year, or perhaps evaluation was insufficiently accurate. But, whatever the reason – wrong objective, wrong campaign, wrong evaluation or change of circumstances – the DAGMAR approach leads to re-examining the inter-relationship between promotional plans and marketing objectives. If the company did not achieve its objective, it is not necessarily promotion that was at fault. Hence the need to analyse results meticulously. Much depends on whether there is a direct response to promotion, or alternatively if results are evaluated indirectly by research.

DIRECT RESPONSE

The improvements to which evaluation can lead are best demonstrated by those organizations with promotional activities which result in response they can measure: organizations selling direct or through their own (or agents') showrooms, those whose advertisements feature coupons or invite enquiries, and firms using direct mail reply cards or offering tangible merchandising or sales promotion incentives. Direct response can also arise through media-owners' reply service facilities. The proportion of business-to-business firms coming within these categories is likely to be far higher than that for consumer products or services.

Such direct response can be 'keyed' so that respondents indicate which direct mail shot or merchandising or sales promotion incentive motivated them, or which advertisement they saw in which publication and on what date. Inclusion of a 'key number' such as 'FT7' would indicate that a coupon came from an advertisement in the *Financial Times* on the 7th. Even when advertisements contain no coupon, they can be keyed by asking readers to write to (or telephone) a particular department or to address their reply to a certain individual, to Desk Number X or Room Y. Direct mail reply cards can of course be keyed directly.

A great deal can be learned from analysis of keyed response. Take as example a promotional campaign which includes merchandising and sales promotion incentives, direct mail shots with reply cards, and regular advertisements featuring coupons, appearing in numerous different publications. Analysis of returns could suggest many improvements for the future.

Some response criteria have marketing as well as promotional implications: they indicate new potential markets or likely sales areas, or touch on other aspects of marketing. Other criteria have media or message planning implications.

- *Product offer* The product (or service) promoted is the core element of any promotional campaign. Through direct response campaigns, organizations learn market reaction to different product versions, accessories and prices. Differences in presentation could result in a ten or 15 per cent fluctuation in response, but a good product offer badly presented will still bring response. A ten–15 per cent fluctuation, according to how the offer is presented, puts promotion into perspective, but nevertheless represents a significant contribution to profitability, or even the difference between profit and loss. Factors which could account for this fluctuation include the following:

- *The medium* – the response achieved by one medium can be compared with numbers produced by others. Media can be ranked in response order and those with poor returns eliminated. Production as well as media costs are relevant in this respect: the more media used, then the higher are production costs. There may thus be a double saving when uneconomic media are deleted, and the money can be spent to better advantage elsewhere;
- *Coverage area* – one medium may bring large numbers of enquiries, but those from outside the company's service area are of little value. Regional variations can be equally important for those with national distribution: if one area responds more than others, this local interest could call for additional emphasis on local media. Alternatively, poor returns in one area

would lead the Promotion Manager to investigate the cause. If he discovers intense local competition, then competitive strategy in that area clearly needs re-consideration. Another possible reason is that even so-called 'national' media vary in intensity of coverage in different parts of the country: low penetration in particular areas might call for reinforcement promotion in local media (strong local media may in fact be the very reason for poor penetration by the nationals);

- *Type of response* – analysis of types of response can yield valuable information. If enquiries come mostly from one category of executive rather than another, or if some industries show more interest than others, this could indicate target groups ripe for special sales drives. Promotion in such cases clearly serves a market research function;
- *Cost per reply* – large numbers of enquiries are insufficient in themselves: response must be from prospective customers and at an economic rate. Enquiries (from respondents of the right type, within the sales area) can be evaluated in terms of value for money, and cost per reply calculated. Media can then be placed in cost-rank order, and publications with uneconomic returns eliminated. The budgeting chapter (22) outlined the marginal method of fixing the appropriation, based on such immediate evaluation of results;
- *Conversions* – where customer response provides leads for sales representatives, the Promotion Manager can calculate how many enquiries convert to actual sales. One medium might have a low response rate, but if every enquiry leads to a sale it clearly merits retention on the promotional plan. Conversely, publications with uneconomic conversion rates would be discontinued;
- *Promotional unit* – large advertisements cost more than small ones and special positions or colour also increase costs. Comparison of response rates can indicate whether the added expense was worthwhile. Response to different levels of merchandising or sales promotion incentives can be evaluated in the same way;
- *Frequency* – high frequency costs more than less regular market stimulus: evaluation of results can indicate if the additional cost was worthwhile. Research can also cross-check if heavy or light exposure to promotion matches the profile of heavy and light product usage;
- *Timing* – response analysis can indicate the most suitable day of the week for promotional effort, or when the buying season starts. Timing can be a matter of seasons, weeks or days;
- *Message theme* – the chapter on approval criteria (25) asked 'What fundamental proposition was selected to make the target group respond?' The results of alternative message themes can be contrasted to show which is the more effective;
- *Message expression* – the approval chapter also asked 'How effectively will this proposition be conveyed to the selected target group?' Any creative theme can be expressed in limitless ways: the fundamental proposition remains constant throughout, but is conveyed by different headlines, illustrations, text and typefaces. Analysis of which version pulled best has clear implications for message planning;

EVALUATION OF RESULTS

- *Message life* – an effective promotion may not last indefinitely – evaluation of response rates might reveal that it had 'died' and the time had come to stimulate the market in a different way. This may link with frequency, in that the more often the target market receive a promotional message, the more quickly it may wear out. For this reason, many campaigns feature a series of linked messages, which appear on a rotating basis for change of impact. Other organizations, particularly those who concentrate on new entrants to their markets, find the same promotions continue to pull year after year;
- *Incentives* – to stimulate response, many campaigns feature merchandising or sales promotion incentives. The effectiveness of alternative offers can be evaluated, but the earlier *conversions* criterion calls for a warning. As already established, it is *easy* to get response, but it may be of the wrong kind – from people who want something free, rather than to make a purchase. It is important, therefore, to choose an incentive which, by its nature, appeals mainly to the selected target group;
- *Reply devices* – the aim of direct response is customer *action*, and some response devices may prove more productive than others. Different ways of inviting customer response include:
    1. *Post this coupon* – with or without *Freepost*, and with one or more addresses. Variations are advertisements or created media designed as reply-paid folders, or inclusion of business-paid reply cards and envelopes with direct mail shots;
    2. *Call at showroom* – this overlaps with the first category in that many respondents, rather than post a coupon, will call at the company's showrooms, or those of distributors. Other promotions suggest a call directly;
    3. *Telephone this number* – this can be the advertiser's own number, the Post Office's operator-connected *Freephone* service (whereby the company or brand name can be used as the 'number'), or the *Linkline* (0800 prefix numbers) service. As the *Follow-through* chapter (27) stressed, it is essential to ensure the company is geared up to handle the response generated. If necessary, the workload can always be contracted out: there are various commercial facilities for answering incoming calls, with services ranging from 'live' answering to recorded messages;
    4. *Action signals* – under this heading, rather than creative expression, it is relevant to mention visual triggers such as small scissors on coupons, or 'post today' stickers on direct mail shots.

    These reply devices are not exclusive – some campaigns feature two or more.

- *Cross comparisons* – these various comparison criteria frequently overlap. Industries or executives in one area, for example, may be attracted by one promotion rather than another, *and* respond more in certain months. These regional and other differences should be fed back into subsequent media and message planning, and lead to appropriately different promotional patterns. The logical extension of such response evaluation is of course database marketing, discussed earlier.

Checking keyed responses involves considerable labour, and much valuable information is alas thrown away for lack of staff – yet the savings which evaluation could achieve would more than pay the staff costs involved, and even make a major profit contribution!

INDIRECT RESPONSE

Even when promotion does not result in direct response, the Promotion Manager must nevertheless attempt to evaluate results: this might be by sales audits or customer surveys.

SALES AUDITS

Suppliers without their own outlets often evaluate results by analysing orderbooks to check seasonal or geographical variations in relation to promotional effort. 'Sales in' to agents, distributors or reseller markets are not always followed by 'sales out' however, and this directly influences possible re-orders. Factory sales are an insufficient measure of success, since products might sit on showroom shelves with no sales resulting. Many companies therefore measure results by sales audits: if stocks held at outlets at the start of a sales period are known and deliveries during that period are taken into account, the difference between this figure and the total remaining at the end indicates the quantity sold. If the promotional objective was to extend distribution or to stimulate current outlets, a sales audit will tell whether or not the company achieved success. A number of market research companies offer a variety of auditing services on a commercial basis. A good audit gives additional valuable information – where are products sited in the showroom, and how many are actually on display? Equally important it can give similar information about competitors, to indicate who is winning the battle for display at place of purchase.

CUSTOMER SURVEYS

Rather than such indirect evaluation of results, many firms directly research *purchases* rather than sales. A sales audit may reveal an increase, but does not tell *how* this was achieved. For effective promotional planning, it is important to know in which way this came about – increased purchases by existing users, conversion of new users, or buyers of rival products switching supply sources? Direct customer research can give valuable information which no sales audit can reveal.

Some organizations, rather than measure customers' actions, seek to measure changes in, for example, their product awareness. If the organizational objective is to change potential purchasers' attitudes, the Promotion Manager may commission research to ascertain viewpoints before and after the campaign. Even here, however, it is essential to have a *specific* purpose, since 'attitude' is an all-embracing term. What precisely should the organization seek to change – its image, the degree to which prospects believe product claims, their liking for the firm, or the likelihood of them buying its products?

TEST CAMPAIGNS

Test marketing, a technique pioneered with consumer products, can on occasion be applied to business-to-business markets. A full product launch, however carefully planned, is both expensive and risky. Many firms therefore try to reproduce in advance, on a smaller scale, the conditions they will encounter on a national basis. The test campaign must recreate in miniature the proportionate weight of promotion to be mounted nationally, and the same applies to sales effort – it is pointless to force success artificially by mounting a level of activity which cannot be sustained on a full campaign basis.

Test marketing can reveal operational weaknesses, and provide the opportunity to adjust the promotional plan accordingly. In other cases, two different test campaigns are mounted in parallel, to evaluate the effect of different product formulae or prices, to select the most acceptable to the market. Different weights of promotional expenditure, different media plans (or alternative messages) can be tested in the same way.

FUTURE ACTION

The purpose of evaluating results is *action*, and this can be of two kinds:

FOLLOW UP LEADS

Evaluation of results can lead to positive action such as addressing a target group not covered by the original market definition but which, by its response, proves its interest in the product. Evaluation thus leads to changes in marketing activity, rather than promotion alone. Alternatively, the target market remains unchanged but, through evaluation of results, the campaign's productivity is improved by getting better results for the same money.

ELIMINATE FLAWS

A variation of 'better results for the same money' is 'same results for less money'. Money saved by correcting weaknesses can be used for what could not be afforded before – and no budget is ever sufficient to undertake *all* desirable promotional activities!

IN DEFENCE OF UNPRODUCTIVE PROMOTION

A promotional activity which does achieve the desired result is not *necessarily* a waste of money: it can also be regarded as investment. The 'investment' comes from finding out – the hard way – that it did not work, and this prevents further waste in the future. Much promotional expenditure is alas wasted by those who make *no* effort to evaluate results, in the mistaken belief that it is impossible to do so. In consequence, their campaigns continue repeating unproductive messages year after year through unproductive media: this is very different to investing to prevent waste.

COMPLETING THE CIRCLE

Proposal improvement is as important as the original plan, and monitoring performance throughout a campaign is as important as subsequent assessment.

Promotional planning must be a closed loop: this chapter completes the circle since what is learned from evaluating results provides the basis for future planning. Completing the circle also raises again the important matter of relationships between in-house promotion departments and external service organizations. Many advertising agencies and PR consultancies complain of minimal feedback from clients about the results of campaigns mounted on their behalf. Without such information, how can they improve future promotional effectiveness?

A salutary thought on which to conclude is that if the Promotion Manager tells his external advisers that the brief is 'the same as last year', then either he or the external service should perhaps be fired, since 'no change' means that all the time, effort and money spent on promotion over the past year apparently has had no effect whatsoever!

THE NEXT STEP

The Promotion Manager should now return to the *Research & Investigation* stage, as he now has new data on which to base future promotional planning.

Appendix 1

Institute of Public Relations Recommended Practice
Paper No. 1

THE NEWS RELEASE

INTRODUCTION

The purpose of a news release is to provide news or information to the media that you would like to be published, and which is worthy of publication.

Your news will be in competition with information from many other sources, so correct presentation of your news release is essential if it is to be noticed and used.

This practice paper provides a guide to the preparation and presentation of news releases, to assist members of the Institute, their colleagues and staff, to follow accepted practice.

CONTENTS OF NEWS RELEASES

- Be brief and factual
- Separate technical data from the main news items
- Always include the following:
- *A title for the story (not a headline)*
- *The date, preferably in the recommended style of Oxford Dictionary of Printing, for example August 12, 1982*
- *A reference number, to make the release quickly identifiable*
- *The name and address of the organization issuing the release*
- *The name and telephone number (both during working hours and after hours) of a person from whom further information can be obtained.*

LAY-OUT

Paper size. The Recommended size is International A4: 297 × 210 mm ($11\frac{3}{4} \times 8\frac{1}{2}$ ins). White paper is considered most suitable.

Headings. The news release should be clearly identifiable as such, to distinguish it from ordinary correspondence. Include the term **'News Release'**, or **'Press Release'** or similar, boldly, in the heading. Other descriptive phrases such as **'Press Information'** are acceptable.

The heading should not be more than 60 to 75 mm ($2\frac{1}{2}$ to 3 ins) deep.

Space between heading and title. Leave a space of 40 mm ($1\frac{1}{2}$ ins) between the heading and the title. This space is used by the News Editor or copy taster to indicate how and where the story is to be used in the newspaper.

Title. Type the title in capitals. Any second title, sidehead or crosshead should be typed in upper and lower case.

Underlining. Do not underline any part of the News Release. (*Underlining is a printers mark meaning* **'Set in italics'**). Emphasis should be obtained by the relevance, content and position of sideheads and crossheads.

Margins. Leave a margin of at least 40 mm (1½ ins) at each edge of the paper. This allows the sub editors to write instructions to compositors and make-up departments on the release.

Spacing. Always use double spacing, with extra space between paragraphs. This extra space enables the chief compositor to cut up the news release and hand it out section by section to the compositors.

Sub-headings. In a lengthy story use side heads. They help break up the story, and add to the visual appearance of the type-written material.

Do not use a sidehead within three lines of the bottom of the page.

Carry over copy. Do not run over copy to the next page if it breaks up the sentence or paragraph.

Type the word **'More'** at the end of each page to show that the story is continued on the next page. At the end, type the word **'End'**.

Continuation pages. Number each page. Repeat the title at the top left of each continuation page.

Names of people. Begin with first names. If not known, use initials. Include titles, such as **Mr, Mrs, Sir, Dr**, etc. Make sure you use correct abbreviations. Always use capital letters for proper names.

Institute members. Always include the appropriate suffix (**FIPR, MIPR** etc.) when members of the Institute are mentioned.

EMBARGO

An '*embargo*' requests the recipient of a News release to withhold publication until a stated date and time. Embargoes should be avoided, if possible. Their use is a matter of convention, and they are not binding on the media. If an embargo is essential, then the reason for it should be made clear in the release. The word **'Embargo'**, and the date and time for publication, should appear above the title of the release. A recommended form of words is as follows.

> **EMBARGO.** This information is sent to you in advance for your convenience (*give reason for embargo*). It is not for publication, broadcast, or use on club tapes before (*time, GMT or BST*) on (*date*).

TIMING

Remember copy deadlines when issuing a release. A morning release may appear in evening papers the same day, and 'kill' the story for the following morning dailies. Weekly papers may have deadlines three days in advance of publication date.

GENERAL

Ask yourself, '*Have I included* **"Who", "What", "Why", "Where"**, and **"When"**.' See also **Practice papers Nos. 2** (*Photographs accompanying News releases*) and **3** (*Press kits*).

Appendix 2

Institute of Public Relations Recommended Practice
Paper No. 2

PHOTOGRAPHS ACCOMPANYING NEWS RELEASES

INTRODUCTION

A photograph can add considerably to the value of a news release. Pictures of a new machine may remove the need for hundreds of descriptive words. A photograph of a speaker or celebrity in action may achieve publication where mere words may not. A photograph, with a fully explanatory caption, may suffice to put your story across. Good pictures can only enhance a good story.

Picture size. For black and white prints, the recommended size is ten inches by eight inches. Print on resin-coated paper.

Captions. Every photograph or illustration *must* be fully captioned.

Tital of caption. A caption needs a title to give an immediate indication of its subject matter. If the photograph accompanies a news release, the caption should be the same as, or a shortened version of, the news release title.

Caption lead. The lead of the caption must state the relation between the photograph and any accompanying news release. It should be in the same, or very similar, words as the opening paragraph of the news release. The caption should be typed in double spacing, and should point up the meaning of the photograph.

People. Where people are shown in the photograph, name them correctly, in order, left to right.

Source and date. The caption should give the name, address and telephone number of the issuing organization. State the date (*month and year*) of issue.

Negative number. Quote the negative number, or other reference number, on the caption.

Affixing captions to photographs. Affix the caption to the back of the photograph so that it can be read with the photograph also in view. If the caption is typed on the lower part of a sheet of paper, the top part can be affixed to the back of the photograph, with the typed portion showing below the edge of the photo, facing forward. For transmission by post, the typed portion can be folded over the face of the picture. In affixing captions, do not use glue as, should editorial staff wish to separate words and picture, damage to one or the other is inevitable. A small piece of clear tape holding the caption to the reverse of the picture will suffice.

Posting pictures. Always use a stiff-backed envelope, or one that has been

stiffened by a sheet of light paste board. When posting photographs write on the outside **'Photographs** – *Please do not bend'*.
Copyright. Any copyright conditions should be clearly stated on the back of the photograph. For example: *'Copyright by* **J. Smith, 1 Great James Street, London WC1N 3DA.** *No fee required for reproduction.'*

See also **Practice papers Nos. 1** (*The News Release*) and **3** (*Press Kits*).

Published by: The Institute of Public Relations – Member Services

Appendix 3

Institute of Public Relations Recommended Practice
Paper No. 3

PRESS KITS

INTRODUCTION

A Press kit usually consists of a wallet or folder, sometimes bearing the company's name or logo, which contains a number of papers, photographs, brochures and so on, which are intended to give the recipient a considerable amount of information about the event to which the Press kit relates. Considerable controversy surrounds the use of Press kits, largely because they tend to contain information (*such as advertising material, sales literature, price lists*) that the newspaper correspondent does not need or want. Properly used, a Press kit can provide a journalist with all the news and background information that he needs to make a good story without burdening him with irrelevant facts.

When to use a Press kit. A Press kit is best used in connection with a special event to which journalists have been invited or may be expected to attend. Suitable events include exhibitions, facility visits, opening of new premises, Press conferences or briefings, launching of major new products.

Form of Press kit. All material should fit into an A4 folder or wallet. This may be printed specially for the occasion, and bears the title of the event. Alternatively, a simple transparent plastic folder may suffice.

Contents. The Press pack should contain only relevant material. This will include a news release, possibly photographs, data on personalities involved, drawings and diagrams, location maps etc., as circumstances dictate. The pack should also contain a list of contents so that the journalist can ascertain that he has missed nothing.

Issuing organization. The name, address, and phone number of the organization responsible for compiling and issuing the Press kit should be clearly indicated.

Distribution. It is good practice to distribute Press kits by post or hand on the day of the event to those journalists invited but unable to attend.

See also **Practice papers Nos. 1** (*The News Release*) and **2** (*Photographs accompanying Press releases*).

Published by: The Institute of Public Relations – Member Services

Index

Advance 177
Advertisers Annual 85
Advertisers, Incorporated Society of British 28, 132, 139, 197, 211
Advertising:
  advantages of 83
  cost of 84
  disadvantages of 84
  general 5
  general databases 83
  information sources 85, 95
  media, miscellaneous 165
  media, range of 84
  on tube trains 144
  outdoor 141
  overview 83
  timing of 84
Advertising, Institute of Practitioners in 211

Benn's Direct Marketing Services Directory 137
Benn's Media Directory 177
BRAD Directories and Annuals 85
BRAD National Guide to Media Selection 85
British Business Press 104
British Council 178
British Overseas Trade Board 179
British Rate and Data (BRAD) 75
British Rate and Data's advertiser and Agency List 44
Broadcasters' Audience Research Board 150
Broadcasting, Blue Book of British 177
Broadcasting legislation, Government proposals for 156
Broadcast Marketing Services 160
British Advertising Agencies, Association of 43
Budgeting:
  'chairman's rules' 240
  competitive parity 243
  composite 245
  divisions 247
  'guesstimates' 240
  long-term planning 247
  marginal 244
  methods 241
  no budget 240
  percentage of anticipated sales 242
  percentage of last year's sales 241
  promotion as investment 238
  promotional share 243
  promotion in context 237
  rewards of promotional expenditure 237
  target sum 245
  unit percentage 242
Business Sponsorship of the Arts, Association for 197

Cable Audience Research, Joint Industry Committee for 155
Campaign objectives:
  action matrix 229
  advertising 219
  aids to buying 224
  analysis of 216
  business environment 218
  by-products 224
  changing market 221
  communicating information 217
  company reputation 218
  competitors' customers 227, 228
  customer base 217
  declining sales 225
  demonstration 219
  direct sales leads 216
  distribution 222, 223
  existing users 219
  increased sales 226, 227
  mailing lists 223
  market decline 220
  market research 223
  new customers 221, 227, 228
  other lines 222
  previous purchasers 220
  product 218, 219
  product awareness 218
  product launches 218
  production 221
  promotion 225
  resistance 221
  sales force 217
  service 218, 219
  supplier 224
  target audience 217
Campaign proposals:
  approval 273
  attention devices 250
  body copy 251
  colour 250, 260
  constraints 261

INDEX

continuity 261
creative approaches 256
design 259
external aspects 274
headlines 251
illustration 250, 260
interaction 251
market weighting 266
media allocations 264
media briefs 263
media interaction 263
media planning stages 272
message content 251
movement 251
objectives 276
planning 266
position 250
'shotgun principle' 272
size 250
sound 251
sources of message 258
staff conflicts 271
target group 276, 277
typography 260
what people buy 254
why people buy 255
Capital Radio Sales 160
Central Office of Information 179
Cinema:
   information sources 164
   overview 163
Cinema Advertising Association 164
Cinema and Video Industry Audience Research Committee 165
Circulations, Audit Bureau of 100, 130
Communications media – an overview 5
Conferences and Exhibitions Diary 131
Consultants 31, *see also* External services
CPT (cost per thousand) 78
Created media:
   advisory bureaux 185
   annual reports 186
   audio-visual devices 186
   awards 187
   competitions 187
   conferences 187
   corporate identity 187
   demonstrations 187
   design 187
   exhibitions 188
   facility visits 188
   films 188
   gifts 188
   house journals 189
   incentives 188
   merchandising 189
   planning 185
   point-of-sale material 190
   printed material 191
   prizes 187
   provision of equipment 191
   range of 185
   sales force 192
   sales promotion 193
   samples 191
   speakers panels 194
   sponsorship 194
   telemarketing 195
   telephone 196
   training 196

Database marketing 135
'Decision Making Unit' 233
Demonstrations 129, *See also* Exhibitions
Direct mail:
   advantages 133
   disadvantages 135
   information sources 137
Direct Mail Producers Association 138
Direct Mail Sales Bureau 138
Direct Mail Services Standards Board 139
Direct marketing 135, *See also* Direct mail
Direct Marketing Association, British 138
Directors, Institute of 44, 139
Division of work 26

Editorial:
   advertisement department 52
   advertisement manager, role of 52, 53
   advertisement reps:
      supervision of 55
      training of 53–4
   advertising:
      direction of 55, 56
      follow-up 59
      publication 58
      vouchers 58
   circulation 49, 50
   division of work 53
   invoicing 58
   make-up 57
   marketing 52
   merchandising 52
   order confirmation 56
   production 49, 57
   promotion 50
   proofs 57
   research 51
   subscriptions 50
   see also Press
Exhibitions:
   advantages of 127
   audience research 129
   disadvantages of 128
   information sources 130
   types of 127
   venues 132
Exhibition and Conference Factfinder 131
Exhibitions Bulletin 131
Exhibition Industry Federation 131

INDEX

Existing media 5
Export, Institute of 179
External influences 20
External people 22
External services:
  account planning by 39
  buying power of 32
  campaign planning by 38
  control, department of 42
  cost of 32, 34, 36
  experience of 32, 35
  general 26, 28, 31
  inertia of 34
  location of 43
  mergers 42
  operating arrangements of 36
  organization of 36
  proposals by 40, 41
  quality of staff 35
  quality of work 35
  range of services 35
  research, department of 39
  selection of 34
  size of client account 36
  specialists 42
  terms of contract 36
  time taken by 33
  viewpoint of 32
  vouchers 42

Follow through 285
Free Newspapers, Association of 109

Hollis Press and Public Relations Annual 178

Independent Radio Contractors, Association of 162
Independent Radio Sales Ltd 160
Industrial Marketing Research Association 213
In-house services 28

List Brokers Association, British 138
London Enterprise Agency 211

Magazines, *see* Press
Marketing and Promotion Association 45
Marketing communications department, structure of 25
Marketing communications, four P's of 8, 21
Marketing, Chartered Institute of 28–9
Marketing mix 20
Marketing policy:
  consumer 14, 15
  industrial 14, 15
Market Research Companies, Association of British 212
Market Research Society 213
Markets, business *vs* consumer 12
Media:
  attention factor 68
  audience 73

availability of advertising in 71
competitive activity in 72
complexity of 70
control of 72
constraints of 71
convenience of 70
cost 76
criteria for comparison 65–6
environment 68
evaluation of 67
facilities of 72
flexibility of 70
frequency of message 69
indirect influence of 71
overall comparison 79
penetration *vs* profile 75
qualitative criteria 67
quantitative criteria 73
range of 65–6
speed of operation 69
timing 69
wastage 76
see also under individual headings – eg editorial, television
Media Expenditure Analysis Ltd 86
Media Independents, Association of 44
Media Monitoring Services 89
Media-owners:
  financial circle 47
  role of 47
  structure 47
Media Register, The 89
Media reports 91, 94
Mediascope 91
Mediatel 92
Merchandising 6, 7
Message sources 9

Packaging 12
Periodicals, *see* magazines, under Press
Periodical Publishers Association 106
PIMS London PLC 179
Planning 19, 22
PNA Media Guide 180
'Portfolio' services 45
Positioning 22
Poster advertising:
  advantages of 141
  buying 142
  disadvantages of 142
  general 90
  marketing 143
  research 142
Poster Audience Research, Joint Industry Committee for 143
Post Office, the 139
Promotion department 27
Practitioners in Advertising, Institute of 45
Press:
  expenditure 89

INDEX

circulation:
  controlled 101
  free 103
  free research 102
  hybrid 103
  directories 103
  free publications 108, 109
  magazines:
    free 193
    general 97
    research 104
    special interest 98
  newspapers 97, 106, 107
  product cards 103
  readership surveys 105–25
  research data 100, 104, 107, 109
Price 12
Product 11
Promotion department 27
Product demand 12
Production classifications 90
Production costs 79
Promotion 8
Promotional units 77–8
Promotion Manager, role of 26
PR Planner UK 180
Promotional proposals:
  administration 283
  changes 282
  execution of 279, 282
  implementation of 279
  improving 281
  messages 279
  planning *vs* buying 281
PR Tel 132, 181
Public relations:
  errors made by PROs 173
  feature articles 173
  international 178
  issue of news material 171
  media 170
  monitoring 179
  organizations 175
  photographs 171
  press kits 172
  reference sources 177
  rules of 174
  source of news stories 172
  targeting of opinion-formers 169
  what to publicise 173
  where to send news releases 173
Public Relations Consultants Association 45
Public Relations Year Book 46
Purchasing patterns:
  buy-classes 232
  buy-motives 234
  buy-phases 234
  buy-roles 232
  buy-stages 235
  buy-types 232

how decisions are made 231
promotional planning 235
time-lag 235

Radio:
  advertising 159, 161
  audience research 161
  independent local 159
  structure 159
Radio Audience Research, Joint Industry Committee for 161
Radio Marketing Bureau 162
Research and investigation:
  background 209
  competition 208
  constraints 207
  knowledge of organization 201
  market classifications 202
  marketing policy 206
  market segmentation 203, 204
  P-E-S-T 209
  previous promotion 207
  product 201
  psychographic analysis 203
  relevant organizations 212
  research 211
  service 201
  target groups 205
  target market 202
Results evaluation:
  checking back 287
  customer surveys 292
  direct response 289
  future action 288, 293
  indirect response 292
  other influences 287
  product offer 289
  sales audits 292
  test campaigns 293
  unproductive promotion 293

Sales force 7
Sales promotion 6, 7
Scottish and Irish Radio Sales 160
Service 11
Sound Advertising Sales 160
Sponsorship: information sources 197
Sports Sponsorship Advisory Service 197
Staff 23–4
Supplier organizations, role of 19

Target Group Index 93
Target market motivation 13
Technical Journalism, Who's Who in 182
Television:
  advertising 146, 154
  advertising sales structure 148
  audience research 153
  breakfast 148
  business services 152

INDEX

cable 151, 153, 154, 155
Channel 4 147
expenditure 89
increased programme provision,
 consequences of 157
independent 145, 150
programme content 146
research 150
TV-AM 149
videotext 149
viewer services 151

Tourist Authority, British 131
Trade and Industry, Department of 44, 130, 210
Tube Research Audience Classification 144

Universal News Service 181

Verified Free Distributors Ltd 109

Willings Press Guide 182
Workload 31